The Strange Case of Israel Lipski

A Story of London's East End in 1887

The Strange Case of Israel Lipski

A Story of London's East End in 1887

BOB BIDERMAN

Originally published in Great Britain by Black Apollo Press under the title *Eight Weeks in the Summer of Victoria's Jubilee*, 2012

Revised and re-titled as *The Strange Case of Israel Lipski, 2017*

Copyright © Bob Biderman 2012, 2017

ISBN: 9781900355926

For information about this and other titles, please go to our website: www.blackapollo.com

CONTENTS

INTRODUCTION

THE OLD MAN with mutton-chop whiskers whose job it was to meticulously log the hourly readings in a stiff-backed journal marked "Greenwich Meteorological Bureau" almost had a heart attack. Rubbing his eyes in disbelief, he stared at the precision built Negretti & Rossi thermometer as if it had gone truly mad. Suddenly, in the past hour, the mercury had risen to a remarkable 139 degrees. Of course the thermometer had been basking outside in the ferocious sun - but 139? This was England, after all. Not India.

Jubilee Summer, the summer of 1887, was hot and dry. A few rainy mornings in early June had given way to cloudless skies, scorching days - the thermometer had gone crazy on the 14th of the month - and a terrible drought. But the cracks which erupted in the water-starved soil was the farmers' problem. In the City the brilliant sunshine, the most ever recorded for a single month in the island's history, was looked upon as a celestial sign, a further indication, if one was needed, that God looked down with favour on the bountiful half century presided over by Her Majesty, Queen Victoria.

And a glorious fifty years it had been. Not only was Victoria the mistress of both land and sea throughout a good part of the world, but, from the signing of the Treaty of Paris in 1856, England had begun an unrivalled epoch of peace and prosperity. As the Council of the Society of Arts had said on awarding her the Albert Medal, "In no similar period during the world's history has there been any such progress in the practical arts and science which have had so beneficial an effect on the material comfort and happiness of the human race."

When she had come to the throne, the first London railway was still unfinished, the telegraph had been a crude and doubtful experiment, no vessel had yet steamed across the Atlantic, the powers of electricity were barely known, the first Daguerreotype portrait had yet to have been taken, and people were just beginning to light cigarettes with a match. Yet, by the time of her Golden Jubilee, the wealthier homes in London had been electrified, several telephone companies were competing to send voices instantaneously from one office to another across town, the petrol engine was just moments from factory production, 'Type Writers' were perched heavily on stenographers' desks, and the hand-held camera using light sensitive film was being offered up as the device which would change the way we viewed the world.

A glimpse of this economic miracle can be captured in a rather amazing statistic: for the year 1887, of the top ten world ports, measured by gross tonnage received, Britain had four. London was number one, Liverpool came third, right behind New York City, Cardiff was sixth and seventh was Tyne. In that year over 361 million tons of raw materials such as cotton fibre, metal ore, raw wood and hides were heaped onto British docks to be brought by goliath steam engines north, toward the towering smoke stacks and brick towns blackened with soot. There in the hungry factories of Manchester, Birmingham, Sheffield and Leeds, the raw stuff from African mines and American plantations was churned into the goods that made Britain the envy of the world. Reconstituted by the manufacturing processes which England had conceived in the century before, the matter which had so recently arrived was now packed neatly into crates, sent back to the ports and shipped again to Europe, Asia, the Americas - wherever the crow could fly or the eagle soar - 221 million tons of machinery, hardware, books, cloth

8

and pottery, bound for the boutiques of Paris or the last haberdashery at the edge of the world.

As the seat of Empire, London of 1887 was the most populous city on earth. When Victoria had started her reign fifty years before it had little over one and a quarter million inhabitants. By the time of the Jubilee the population had nearly tripled to four and a quarter million. In fifty years the city had been transformed from an isolated capital of an island stronghold to a cosmopolitan metropolis. One by one the old gabled shops had fallen along with the quaint inns and galleries, court-yards which had defined life in Elizabethan days, to be replaced by the grander, more pretentious edifices of imperial commerce. Old ecclesiastic landmarks, many designed by the likes of Wren, had been swept away to make room for imposing structures built of limestone and plate-glass.

Great new avenues opened up that year, like Charing Cross Road which linked Trafalgar Square to Oxford Street. Wide thoroughfares had been constructed to accommodate the ever increasing traffic and to give the city a more European feel - the numerous horse drawn tram lines, public carriages and omnibuses layering the new boulevards with steady deposits of manure which lent the Victorian city its distinctive redolence. London, however, proudly laid claim to the brilliant solution for getting its new army of bureaucrats from the rapidly expanding suburbs into the centre without contributing to the already monumental piles of horse droppings by constructing the world's first underground railway.

It was a time of dynamic energy and change. The defeat of Liberals in 1886 had opened the door to rampant economic buccaneering. The temperance movement, which had set their hopes on one more victory for Gladstone's moral crusaders, suffered a great setback with the resurgence of the Tories. Beholden to the breweries for providing them with their enormous campaign chest, Salisbury and company unleashed their prime benefactors who began knocking down what remained of old London to build a new kind of drinking establishment. Rich with polished mahogany and logos ornately etched in smoky glass, these new pubs were at the forefront of a massive speculation in property which, more than the Dickensian reform movement, was responsible for the tearing down of the worst of London's slums.

In every conceivable way, London was getting wired. Dozens of tiny, competing electrical companies were frantically stringing lines from noisy generators placed, willy-nilly, in the most unlikely parts of town, to those offices and homes that saw themselves as the vanguard of a new age, the first to suffer the harsh glare of the light bulb. Side by side, telephone lines were being draped, often dangerously close to the generator wires, causing massive distortion in the precocious phone transformers. ('If you have trouble hearing, try jiggling the receiver,' read one company's instructions to the unitiated subscriber.)

The age of consumerism had begun. New product ideas hit the papers with each edition: everything from baby bottles with built in thermometers to sugar substitutes - like saccharine to help the buxom lady trim her pounds. Suddenly a new career had sprung up - the sales consultant - and London found itself with hardly a square foot of brick wall bereft of advertising slogans which, in contemporary serial fashion, repeated their phrases over and over again, ad nauseam.

But even though the coffers of the rich were stuffed to overflowing, all was not sweetness and light. Impressive as Britain's mercantile figures looked, trade had actually contracted from the proceeding year which itself had been a year of recession. "Perhaps no one cause in particular can be assigned for the continued depression of British commerce," wrote a contemporary economist, "but the falling off is so great that there must be some cause for it. The amount is now becoming very serious and it is affecting all classes of the community..."

Some more than others, he might have said. Another financial correspondent wrote: "The depression in our agricultural industry is causing great distress among the labouring community who, finding themselves unable to subsist in the country, are crowding into towns and in consequence, the complaints and absence of employment have been loud and bitter."

The boom-bust cycle of capitalist economies had yet to be thoroughly analysed for economics was still a gentleman's art. In fact, by 1887 Marx had only just been translated into English and John Maynard Keynes was trying on his first pair of trousers. But the realities of an unfettered marketplace based on an increasingly competitive trade with a newly industrialized Europe didn't need much probing to see what was staring them baldly in the face.

Like all recessions it had hit the farmlands first. Thousands of agricultural labourers were leaving the countryside every year in search of work. Most of them took the opportunity of subsidised emigration programs, enduring the agonised weeks of steerage in order to settle in the far corners of the dominion: Australia, New Zealand and British North America. In 1887, some two hundred and fifty thousand British workers left for a chance to remake their lives in the "classless" societies of the new worlds. In the same year over eighty thousand former emigrants came home again, disgruntled with the hardships of colonial life or having

11

given in to the nostalgic reminiscence of England's "green and verdant shores."

For those farm labourers who put down their spade and hoe and remained in Britain, the vast majority - over 40,000 a year - made their way to London where they found themselves competing for accommodation and jobs with the other immigrant force which, for the last decade, had surged in ever swelling waves onto the quays of Britain's great harbours. This "foreign element" - mostly Eastern European Jews who had been impoverished by Czarist dictates limiting their occupations and rights of abode - had been swept up in the great economic tide to be deposited, like flotsam, in places as diverse as Cape Town, Buenos Aires and New York. Some tens of thousands ended up climbing, stiffly, from the holds of cross-channel ships, into water taxis that left them hungry and homeless on the East End Docks of London.

The East End was quite a different London than the one illuminated brightly for the Jubilee. Bleak and dour, to the outsider at least, it was considered by the professional and artistic elites - who never stepped foot beyond Aldgate if they could help it - to be nothing short of a "human dustbin overflowing with the dregs of society." A series of dull, squalid narrow streets and alleys branching off the main business arteries of Whitechapel and Commercial Roads and running south to the docklands of Wapping, it was looked upon with a mixture of fascination, fear and loathing by the middle classes whose visions of the area were influenced by the lurid and somewhat grotesque journalistic sketches of Mayhew and the mawkish paintings by Gustave Dore.

In reality, the East End was a vital economic appendage of the other London and just as much a product, participator and shaper of the times. Certainly one of the most densely populated areas in Europe, these streets were anything but the great receptacle of rogues, knaves, wastrels and tramps that the received wisdom of the "better classes" tried to make out. Contrary to the image of dereliction and disease, the communities of the East End were a multitude of small beehive industries which competed successfully with the sluggish factory shops still closely tied to the patronage system. Largely populated by an "alien element" which put its own cultural identity before the "English" notions of order and cleanliness (articulated in intricately demanding rules of social conduct), the belief persisted that life in the East End was barely civilized.

What made the East End "alien" territory wasn't so much the dirt but the Jews. By 1887 they had taken over a number of the streets completely. Cramming as many as twenty people into a small, three-room house, an estimated 50,000 refugees from the Czarist pale squeezed into an area no larger than a village. But while this ghetto was certainly no more or less a world apart than many that had existed throughout Europe over the centuries, what was so extraordinary is that it seemed to have sprung up overnight.

In fact, a small, stable Jewish community had been in London for hundreds of years, though the difference between the new immigrants and their religious brethren was as great as the distance they had travelled to get there. Steeped in the culture of Spain before the inquisition, these early Jews had come to England by a different route. Well educated and proud as any high-strung aristocrat, they had for the most part arrived from their refuge in Amsterdam soon after Cromwell's desperate invitation to the independent financiers of Europe, giving them rights of abode and certain privileges if not complete and equal freedom. These Sephardic Jews, who soon assimilated into the higher strata of British life had little in common with the new immigrants

13

except, perhaps, a shared history of persecution and aspects of an ancient religion.

Hard on their heals came a scattering of German and Eastern European Jewish merchants, aware of the new opportunities that had opened for them in this northern outpost of capitalist enterprise and tired of the anti-Semitic hostilities which swung according to the cycles of economic growth and contraction like the hand of a pendulum - one day giving them honours, taking them away the next.

By 1887 these older Jewish settlements had become the basis of the established Anglo-Jewish community: well-settled and affluent - though, like most communities of Jews, slightly apprehensive at what the future might hold for them. This deep seated and basic insecurity echoed through the pages of the Jewish Chronicle, the leading voice of their community, which stated in its editorial celebrating the Queen's Jubilee, "Happily we have shown that we are not unworthy of the liberties which we have claimed as our right." Few other Englishmen felt the need to prove themselves worthy of liberty as did the Anglicised Jew.

Yet, by Jubilee Summer, the list of their successes was endless. Besides Disraeli, a lapsed Jew but well aware of his heritage, there was Sir Moses Montefiore, who represented the Queen in the mid-east, Michael Josephs, well respected in the halls of science, David Solomons, the first Jewish Sheriff of Middlesex; as well as the famous names in finance - the Rothchilds, the Goldsmids, the Mocattas. "The future Jewish historian," wrote the Chronicle, "will have to describe the Victorian age as the most marvellous era in Anglo-Jewish annals. For it is impossible to imagine another space of fifty years working a revolution equally vast in the condition of the Jews of this country, and more truly causing a people that walked in darkness to see a great light."

It was left to the Jewish Board of Guardians to make sure that light continued to shine. For dark clouds were hovering over the eastern horizon; smoke from the Russian crucible brought to the boil and now spilling over the borders of the pale. Five million poverty stricken co-religionists compressed in an area which was fast becoming an economic wasteland, looked anxiously to the west for salvation. The Ashkenazi, throwing what little they had into muslin sacks by ones and twos, by the hundreds, by the thousands, were on the move. One of the greatest mass migrations in human history had begun.

The image of this great wave of destitute refugees sweeping across Britain was received by those aware of the situation with dire foreboding, if not barely restrained panic. For those governmental advisors who had long feared a workers' rising - the kind that had shaken the halls of class and privilege on the continent - the thought of a new army of impoverished gypsies helping to sew the seeds of revolution and anarchy in the fertile soil of England's working classes by taking jobs from the already hard-pressed native labouring men was enough for them to start questioning the historic policy of free and open refuge to all. For the Jewish Board of Guardians, the question was posed differently. Could England, which had paved the way toward full economic, social and political assimilation afford to take the chance of unleashing the genie of anti-Semitism and the threat of dreaded pogroms which were then spreading through Europe like a syphilitic plague?

The Guardians, who were elected from the various Jewish synagogues and organizations, set to work on a strategy of stemming the tide. The first line of defence consisted of spreading the word as best they could through whatever established networks reached inside the Russian Pale. This consisted mainly of a letter-writing campaign, where the correspondent would confirm what was probably known - that British streets were not paved with gold, and occasional advertisements in the local Jewish press trying to explain the serious unemployment situation. The second, and more costly, plan was to help refugees continue their journey by subsidising their passage to other locations, such as North America, Argentina and South Africa, where economic opportunities, they argued, were far more optimistic for them.

Such efforts, as King Canute had proved centuries before, were doomed from the start. Tides, whether from the sea or from the land, can never be stopped. Given the choice, nearly all of the immigrants would have gone to America. But, for most, it was a matter of funds. If they had the money to pay the fare, they could choose where they wanted to go. If they only had a few gold coins, they piled into the steerage section of the vessels bound for England.

For the poorest of the poor Polish and Russian Jews, it was often necessary for families to send their most likely breadwinner – usually the father or the eldest son – on that perilous crossing to some strange and lonely shore (a destination sometimes unknown to them). The hope being, if he were lucky, he might, by scrimping and saving every penny earned, quickly send for the rest. Carrying a change of clothes a loaf of black bread, a few precious coins, a scribbled address of a distant relative or a friend of a friend, crudely forged documents or some money set aside to bribe the Russian border guards, the hapless family emissary made his way as best he could to one of the North Sea ports - usually Hamburg.

There, if he wasn't robbed bedding down for the night in a park or, if the weather was inclement, on a hard wooden bench in the railway terminus, he would be approached by an agent perhaps representing a steamship company, or maybe one of the many sharks who made their living feeding on the innocent fish who swam their way. Purchasing a ticket, however, was no guarantee the refugee would get to where he wanted to go. Often illiterate and knowing only the limited world of the Eastern European ghetto, they were always at the mercy of those whose business it was to prey on the homeless and the weak. Many a voyager stepped on shore at London, Liverpool or Glasgow thinking he had made it to the streets of New York.

Describing a typical scene at the London docks, Beatrice Potter wrote, "There are a few relations and friends awaiting the arrival of the small boats filled with immigrants: but the crowd gathered in and about the gin-shop overlooking the narrow entrance of the landing-stage are dock loungers of the lowest type and professional 'runners.' These latter individuals, usually of the Hebrew race, are among the most repulsive of East London parasites; boat after boat touches the landing stage, they push forward, seize hold of the bundles or baskets of the new-comers, offer bogus tickets to those who wish to travel forward to America, promise guidance and free lodging to those who hold in their hands addresses of acquaintances in Whitechapel, or who are absolutely friendless. A little man with an official badge (Hebrew Ladies' Protective Society) fights vainly in their midst for the conduit of unprotected females, and shouts or whispers to the others to go to the Poor Jews' Temporary Shelter in Lemen Street. For a few moments it is a scene of indescribable confusion: cries and counter cries; the hoarse laughter of the dock loungers at the strange garb and broken accent of the poverty-stricken foreigners; the rough swearing of the boatmen at passengers unable to pay the fee

17

for landing. In another ten minutes eighty of the hundred new-comers are dispersed in the back slums of Whitechapel; in another few days, the majority of these, robbed of the little they possess, are turned out of the 'free lodgings' destitute and friendless."

Of those who did arrive with little more than a farthing to their name, a few of the more fortunate were approached by "legitimate" agents who ventured to place them - for a commission - with a man who needed a "greener" for his trade and a family that needed another lodger to pay the rent. This informal network of poverty-stricken immigrants and struggling entrepreneurs who depended on a pool of dirt-cheap labour to produce saleable goods at the lowest possible price was the basis of the East End sweat shop system. It was a system of employment both dehumanising in its slavish demands and grotesque in the brutality of its do-or-die approach to life. But for the huddled masses of refugees who had few skills, it was often the only chance they had to survive.

1887 was the year Charles Booth published the first part of his monumental work on the inhabitants of the East End. Summing up his section on the Jewish immigrants, he wrote: "These foreign Jews are straight from the pressure of grinding despotism; some may add nihilism and the bitterest kind of socialistic theories to very filthy habits; but the meek and patient endurance with which they live their hard lives, and their ready obedience to the law, do not suggest any immediate fear of violent revolutionary activity on their part. They seem capable of improvement, and so far have improved. It may take them 'several years to get washed,' but if we compare the new comers with those of the same race who have been settled here some time, the change is very marked. The streets in which the former herd on arrival

18

become more foul than ever before, but those occupied by the latter are quiet and orderly."

This kind of naive paternalism from the liberal reformers was considered quite tolerant for its day. The notion that it was the duty of those more privileged and educated to teach the less fortunate the error of their ways so they could live a proper, clean and wholesome life was part and parcel of the imperial mentality which saw England as the guardian of morality for half the earth.

Booth's functional sociology at least showed that poverty wasn't a disease or a chromosomal defect of laggards and layabouts but a structural fault of the economic system. He had no analysis, but his massive tables of statistical information spoke for itself. The fact that dockers were paid 4 pence an hour, when they could get work, or that a seamstress slaving through a twelve hour day might make two shillings if she were lucky, made for figures that didn't add up - especially if medical care, school fees and rates were taken into account.

The recession had pushed the British workers further up against the wall making their desperate situation even more untenable. And into this morass had dropped the Jew, creating their own survival economy based on minimal profit and maximum self-exploitation. It was a situation rife with danger, like a powder keg placed in the middle of Hell's Kitchen.

Everyone knew it could blow up. And that was something nobody wanted. Certainly not the Jewish Board of Guardians. Certainly not the Queen or the rest of her establishment. And they all knew that it would only take a spark. Then, one day, it happened. Just four days after London's great Jubilee celebration for Queen Victoria. In the heart of the East End an Angel had been killed. And a Jew, they said, had murdered her. The summer had been hot. It was to grow hotter.

19

The Crime

June 27, 1887

BATTY STREET. The name had a touch of the peculiar, leading one to suspect there was something uniquely deranged about it. But that was far from the case. It was, in fact, one of many dreary little streets with an uncertain water supply that ran south off Commercial Road; a street of tired row houses facing a similar row of dark facades without the hint of a smile – in defiance, perhaps, of its slightly wacky name.

Number 16 had already been awake for a good five hours by the time Leah Lipski and her upstairs lodger, Mrs. Levy, came home after a quick shopping trip to Petticoat Lane. Outside, in the passageway, an elderly woman – Mrs. Rubenstein – was seated in her chair, making the most of the morning sun as she tended her little grandchild, the youngest of Leah Lipski's brood of five. So focused was she on her duties, looking out for the child, and, perhaps, dreaming of life back in the Polish shtetl, that she didn't notice her daughter approach with Mrs. Levy – the widow who shared the upstairs room with her. Besides, at that hour (nearly 11 AM) there was quite a bit of competition for her attention; the street life, even on a narrow road like this had all the appearances of an ongoing beggar's carnival with a constant stream of characters passing in review – from organ grinders, with their flea-bitten monkeys, prying another farthing out of the penniless neighbourhood, to the barrow merchants pushing their little carts, selling anything from Lucifer matches to rancid meat thinly disguised as 'cat food'.

Going inside the bleak entrance of the three story house, Leah Lipski walked through the narrow hallway, past the door on the left which led to the room in which most of her family squeezed together and continued along to the kitchen with its bare oak table and skinny larder and bunk beds tucked into a little cranny where two of her children slept. Stopping to put down her provisions she noticed the metal pot was still filled to the brim with the coffee she had fetched from a nearby shop earlier that morning when one of her lodgers – a young man named Israel – had asked her for his breakfast at around half past eight. She had thought it curious the coffee was still there since he had seemed so anxious when she saw him earlier that day. But he was in such a state – perhaps he had forgotten.

When she pictured this young man with lipid blue eyes, she recalled the time some eighteen months before when Katz, the umbrella maker, had sent the 'greener' around to her former house, just a few streets away, to ask for room and board. Standing awkwardly, pale and wane in his rumpled clothes, he had the same look of dream-like disorientation that she knew so well from others straight off the boat who had waited before her door. What made him different was his manner; boyishly shy, there was a sense of quiet dignity about him confirming her carefully nurtured instincts that this was someone she could trust to pay the rent on time, and, as importantly, to keep the delicate balance which was necessary in maintaining such a densely populated household. She quickly sized him up as one of those determined young men, without financial resources or physical prowess, who still had a naïve certainty that through sacrifice and hard work they could succeed where their fathers had failed, and carve out a

22

business from nothing but sweat and grizzle.

Her own husband, Philip, had once looked that way to her. Five children later he was still doing piece-work for a tailor. They survived like all the others, by pooling their resources and treating a penny like a pound. Subletting their Batty Street house from someone who had sublet it from someone else and he, again, from another, they paid the lease by taking in lodgers. In total there were fourteen people stuffed into three rooms. Fifteen into four if you counted the young man in the attic.

Even so, after all this time, what did she know about him? Not much, really. Israel Lobulsk from Warsaw. That was his name before he had changed it to Lipski – to Anglicise it, he had said. The landlady took it as a compliment; it made him part of the family and when they moved to Batty Street from Batty Gardens, Israel came along with them.

As for his apprenticeship in the umbrella trade, he had been a keen and ready student, quickly becoming a skilled stick-finisher. Certainly, Katz had no complaints. In fact, it wasn't long before a match had been arranged between the young man and Katz's niece, Kate Lyons. It was one of those formal arrangements, quite business-like, and clearly a sign of faith in this young man's future prospects.

Yet who could have foretold the extraordinary weather conditions – those weeks upon weeks of blue sky and brilliant sun, the parched earth, the lack of rain that had thrown the umbrella trade into such a terrible state? What could a man like Katz have done but lay off his employees, at least till the weather got worse – or better, depending on one's perspective.

That was the problem, she had told him. To sell your labour for tuppence was one thing if you had a job and were learning a trade. To find yourself out of a job and your trade suddenly worthless was quite another. For what good was an umbrella-stick finisher during a drought? What could he do? Make walking sticks, perhaps. Except for that, he'd have to go into business for himself.

She knew he would prefer to have waited till he saved up a nest egg, but now there was no alternative. He took what he had, which wasn't much, and pawned it, getting enough to rent the Batty Street attic and buy a few tools. He had got up the courage to ask Anna Lyons, Kate's mother, for a small loan – which he promised to repay promptly with a good rate of interest. She pawned her pearl-handled hairbrush and gave him the proceeds – one gold sovereign.

Katz, he told her, had given him a few business contacts. Israel tracked them down, showed them a few samples, mentioned a price. They told him what they would pay. It was a thoroughly ruthless amount, little more than the cost of the materials and wages. He did some quick sums in his head and agreed. He would be working for nothing. They knew that and so did he. But he would be working.

That was the week before. The last few days he had quickly set up shop with the help of the lad, Pitman, who had also worked for Katz, running back and forth, getting last minute supplies and seeing if he could drum up future business. Yet everything was more expensive and took more time. Wasn't it always like that?

Leah, the landlady, had been aware of his dilemma. A small artisan with no business experience had an infinite number of problems to solve before he could ever hope to turn a profit. She had seen him, stiff and anxious, struggling to get it all together by the time his new employees, two men he had found milling around the hardware shop, came to work – one to shellac the finished sticks, the other to fix on the metal tips. What could he tell them if there was nothing to do? And worse, what would he tell his customers if he couldn't deliver?

Then, this morning, when she saw him in the kitchen, he had summoned up all his courage – or so it seemed to her – and finally asked for a small loan, just a few shillings extra to purchase another vice for the workshop. Unhappily, she turned him down. She had nothing that month, nothing at all. Especially since the new woman in the upper front room had asked her to wait a week on the rent, pleading that she and her husband had spent the last of their money on doctor bills as she was having such a difficult pregnancy.

His smile had been wafer thin and stoic, like someone who had managed to find a tiny bit of irony in a wave of bad luck. He had asked for his coffee and she left to fetch it for him. That was two and a half hours ago. Now it was still sitting there in the metal pot. She touched the side. It was as cold as a gravestone.

The landlady's thoughts were suddenly disrupted by Mrs. Levy who had just entered the kitchen followed by an elderly woman whom she, unfortunately, recognised. Dinah Angel was the mother of the front room tenant on the second floor – the one with the pregnant wife. When Leah Lipski considered this woman who boldly swept into her house as if it were her own, always making demands, always critical though pretending not to criticise, she thought how ridiculous it was that someone like her should be named after a messenger from God. Her own mother, Mrs. Rubenstein, who lived in the house, might have been stone deaf and might drift easily into a world of quiet fantasy, but she was a real angel compared to the one who just came in. That one, the mother of the peasant upstairs – there was nothing quiet about her. So even though her instincts had told her that the couple above were going to be trouble when she first rented

25

them the room, the landlady couldn't help but hold a touch of sympathy for that harassed young woman whose mother-in-law expected her punctually for breakfast every morning at 9:30 AM.

On the other hand, knowing she was a *kvetch*, a complainer of the worst sort, the landlady was still willing to admit that life for Dinah Angel was hard. She was a woman alone and that in itself was difficult. Some people, she thought, could be in Heaven, itself, and find things to complain about. So what if she were in a strange country where she didn't ask to be taken? God sent people on journeys that only He understood. And unlike some, Dinah Angel had her children, her sons, and that was more than enough to be thankful for, she thought.

In the end, the landlady did have a touch of sympathy for the old hag. For she understood that even with all her *kvetching*, what motivated Dinah Angel was fear. She was afraid as they all were afraid. She was afraid of the bleakness, the foulness, the drunks on the stinking streets who found a moment of raw pleasure in throwing stones at Jews. She was afraid of the endless void of poverty and hunger which always threatened to swallow them up – for even if they had enough to eat today who could be sure about tomorrow? And her defence – and everyone had their defence, didn't they? – her defence was to lash out at everything, especially those that she loved. So when she spoke about her daughter-in-law so disparagingly – 'She sleeps – that she is good at! She eats and sleeps! What will she do when the child comes?' – what she really meant was, 'How will she cope? How will they survive?' That she couldn't say, not in those words. What she said instead was: 'So where is she now? Almost noon and where is she? You see if I'm right! I'll tell you where she is, that lazy good for nothing! She's in bed!'

When Dinah Angel had finished relieving herself of her bile which, it seemed, helped lighten her chest, she shuffled her arthritic body back down the hallway toward the short flight of stairs which led toward her daughter-in-law's room. Mrs. Levy, who had busied herself unpacking the supplies from their shopping trip – salt, some onions, black tea, fresh bread – placing them on their appropriate shelves, now turned toward the landlady, pursed her lips and shook her head as if to say she wouldn't want to be in that poor young woman's shoes, not for anything. It was bad enough to be pregnant and penniless. And then they both looked up at the cracked plaster ceiling, imagining the scene above.

What they heard was the clumping of Dinah Angel's heavy feet going up the stairway: thump, thump – and then a pause to catch her breath. Thump, thump - pause. Thump, thump – pause. The cycle repeated itself nine times over. Then the shuffling of feet on the plank floor, the rattle of a door and her grotesque voice entreating Miriam to open up. A minute of silence. The door rattled and in a firmer tone, she called out to her daughter-in-law again.

Mrs. Levy glanced at the landlady who returned her questioning look with one of her own. Miriam Angel, like her mother-in-law, was a creature of habit. Besides, it wasn't like her not to answer the door. Mrs. Levy was about to say that the poor woman must be ill, but she hadn't time to speak the words. They heard a sound - a very terrible sound. They didn't know what it was, but they understood it was bad. And as they rushed up the stairs, not really knowing what to expect, they were certain that whatever it was, Mrs. Angel left to her own devices would only make it worse so they had better get there fast.

They saw her in the half-light of the upstairs hall, bent at the waist, as if trying to peer in through the keyhole. She

27

straightened up as the two women came toward her. The look on her face was one of profound confusion, as if she could hardly make sense of what she saw. Mrs. Levy leaned down and looked through the gap in the door where a replacement lock had been clumsily fitted. It was a difficult perspective with which to get a proper view, but she thought she could see Miriam lying on the bed.

While Mrs. Levy began pounding on the door, calling out the young woman's name, the landlady walked over to the stairway which led to the attic. Half way up there was a small window that looked into Miriam Angel's room. The glass was clouded and covered on the inside with a thin gauze curtain. Putting her face to the glass, the landlady could see the ghostly shape of Miriam Angel on her bed, her chemise drawn up to her thighs. Her legs were bare. Her body was completely motionless.

'The future Jewish historian will have to describe the Victorian Age as the most marvellous era in Anglo-Jewish annals. For it is impossible to imagine another space of fifty years working a revolution equally vast in the condition of the Jews of this country, and more truly causing a people that walked in darkness to see a great light.'

The Jewish Chronicle on the Queen's Jubilee

PART I

Weeks 1-4: The Inquiry

CHAPTER 1

THE OFFICE OF the Jewish Record was small and cramped. A large Georgian window would have overlooked the road below had not the view been hampered by years of accumulated grime. As well as the stale light, a lingering odour of rancid grease from the workers café below wafted through the floorboards. However, neither the dankness nor the sour smell fazed Israel Zangwill in the least as he sat upright at his desk, hidden behind a wall of inky papers heaped in disordered piles – each stack belonging to one of a number of scribes who came to this cloistered room on occasion with the intention of completing an article or picking up a new assignment, while coveting a few square inches of precious desk space for his own.

Mordecai, the managing editor (who was also the publisher of the Record) was puffing on his pipe stuffed with tobacco fresh from one of those newfangled air-tight tins which had just been introduced earlier that year, letting the billows of acrid smoke overcome the smell from downstairs while perusing a copy of the Pall Mall Gazette. Zangwill (known simply as 'Z') was hard at work, scribbling out the completion of his weekly column. He couldn't help but note that the

31

portly proprietor, though reading silently, would on occasion send forth signals through his pipe that he had come across something which either disturbed, amused or angered him. One could learn to read those signs, Z suspected, like smoke puffs used to telegraph messages of great or (in Mordecai's case) minor importance. Dipping his stylus into the adjacent inkwell, he let that notion percolate even as he scratched out another series of well-crafted phrases which seemed to roll effortlessly from the nib of his pen. As the idea began to take shape in his head, he found himself staring at Mordecai's pipe, which up till then had been quietly issuing gentle curls of pale blue and had suddenly started to blaze with sparks of incandescent red.

This growing obsession with Mordecai's smoke signals caused Z to feel some annoyance because he knew that his carefully nurtured train of thought was about to be decisively broken. At the same time, it pleased him that another interesting character trait had been effectively made part of his literary palette for use in dressing up a minor figure in one of his vignettes sometime later. But what had made Mordecai's pipe so fiery hot? Could it have really been the paper that he gripped in his thick, stubby fingers (the tips of which were stained indelibly black from too many years of fondling smudgy newsprint). It piqued Z's curiosity. The Pall Mall Gazette was written to outrage, he thought, but someone like Mordecai had been inured to its strident tone, the bull-horn of its drum-beating crusader, W. T. Stead - a man with wild eyes and biblical beard who had fascinated him for so long. How different these two newsmen were! Stead thumped and shouted whereas Mordecai held his hat in his flabby hand and did nothing more than whisper. How Z wished he, too, were able to shout and thump and thrust his verbal sword so finely honed. Oh, well – that would come later. But still he wondered what there possibly was in the Gazette that could merit such a visceral eruption.

Suddenly Mordecai stood up from his chair and turned, so that his short, rounded body with its undulating folds of untrammelled flab directed itself forward toward Z's desk. It was not a pleasing sight - so unappealing, in fact, that even though Z could feel his editor's presence in the small of his back, he steadfastly refused to look at him. But, in the end, there was nothing to be done. The man was upon him. Z could pretend not to notice for only so long before it became impossible. How could he not notice a pipe-smoking ape wearing a ridiculous toupee whose ponderous bulk waggled audaciously beside him?

Had he read the afternoon paper? Mordecai hovered over him waiting for a response. Z sighed. No, he hadn't. Mordecai shook the broadsheet directly in Z's face. Page 3, that's where it was. Page 3, that's where he should read. And Mordecai pointed out the article with the stem of his pipe. Z must read it, he said. With a sigh, Z reached out his hand. But Mordecai pulled it back. Having changed his mind, he decided to read it aloud, himself:

Mysterious Occurrence in the East End
Two Persons Poisoned

A mysterious affair has occurred in Batty Street, Commercial Road, Whitechapel, resulting in the death of a Polish Jewess and such injuries to a young man as are expected to result in death. At No 16, Batty Street, leading out of the Commercial Road, resided several Polish Jews. Among them was a man named Isaac Angel, a boot riveter, who, with his wife, Rachael, occupied the two rooms of the first floor. On the top floor were also two rooms, one of which was rented by a single young man named Israel Lipski, aged twenty-two, and a walking-stick maker. About half-past six o'clock yesterday morning, Angel got up and left home, as usual, to go to his employment, leaving his wife in bed. At that time, Mrs Angel, who was only twenty-two years of age, appeared to be fast asleep. About half past eleven Mrs Levy, another lodger, not seeing or hearing anything of Mrs Angel, became alarmed, went up to the bedroom, and burst open the door. A shocking sight presented itself. Mrs Angel was lying on the bed, apparently dead. She was terribly burned, evidently with some acid, about the head, face, neck and breast. Dr J. Kay, of Commercial Road, was sent for. The medical man found that Mrs Angel was dead, the cause of death being in his opinion, poisoning by nitric acid. Dr. Kay then noticed a man lying under the bed on his back, apparently dying. This proved to be Lipski, and his clothing was much burned by the acid. Dr Kay ordered the man's removal to London Hospital. Today it is reported that Lipski is progressing favourably. He vehemently denies having murdered Mrs Angel.

Mordecai stopped reading and gazed at Z to ferret his reaction. Z looked back at him, blandly, without emotion - which caused his editor to wrinkle his narrow brow in wonder at Z's apparent equanimity. And then, asking him what he made of it, Z replied that it wasn't a particularly good piece of journalism – at least by the standards of the Pall Mall Gazette because, first of all, they had the poor woman's name wrong – it was Miriam Angel, not Rachael – and, secondly, at the beginning they made it sound as if the man, Lipski, found poisoned with her was about to die, whereas four or five sentences on he's progressing favourably. He wasn't sure what to make of that.

There was little left in life to surprise the cholesterol-charged editor of the Record, but somehow Z always did. How did he know about the name? He had been to Petticoat Lane that morning, Z responded. There was nothing but

34

chatter regarding the murder that took place the day before. Even the beggars were talking about it.

A low moan seemed to emanate from Mordecai's belly bringing with it the distinct smell of pickled herring as it emerged from the dark reaches of his intestines. It was a moan that Z had often heard before and it seemed to turn the hapless creature standing before him into a more sympathetic being, one of his brethren, for it was not really his own moan that emerged – not one of personal pain – but rather a lingering, ghostly collective moan that spoke of miseries over thousands of years.

It was never good for a Jew to be accused of murder, Mordecai told him, but to be accused of killing an Angel is very bad, indeed. To which Z pointed out that in this case the Angel was, herself, a Jew. But Mordecai shook his head, accidentally scattering burning ash from his pipe onto one of Z's stacks of paper and watched in despair as if that itself was a message from God while Z quickly brushed aside the smouldering ember. To Z it might have been yet another act of editorial clumsiness but to Mordecai it was a visual metaphor writ large having to do with sparks upon dry tinder.

Only last week he had written of the need to quell the massive wave of immigrants from the villages and towns of Russia and Poland before the East End was totally inundated with those who only brought with them more poverty and disease. Yes, they were his brethren. Yes, it was the community's duty to protect them. But wasn't their first obligation to those who were here already? And weren't enough mischief-makers writing about the East End as if it were nothing but a breeding ground for crime and pestilence – escalating their call on Parliament to act? So it was up to them, he had argued, to show that their people were moral, clean, upright, hardworking and loyal – a great bounty to the country in this glorious Jubilee Year. It was up to them to do this before the horrors of Europe were upon them and that dreaded word they dared not speak fall deadly from their lips yet again. *Judenhass!* Yes, they need only look at Prussia and the remnants of the Austrian Empire. It happened there and it could happen here!

Z listened with patience to Mordecai's tirade and then when smoke had started to abate and the chimney had cooled down, he asked whether Mordecai would like him to follow this story of the Whitechapel murder. An article, he said, from the Jewish perspective might be appropriate.

And what would an article from the Jewish perspective entail? Why should they publicise a story of a Jew who killed an Angel – even if the Angel was another Jew? What could they gain besides trouble?

But the story was already out, Z reminded him, and it was bound to get bigger as gruesome murders always do even without the added interest of the Angel killing Jew. Mordecai, he argued, owed it to his readership to present a calm and factual analysis to counter the scandal sheets that would dig up any gory detail and print it if they felt it would sell more papers. They didn't have the same obligation to set the record straight as he did. After all, this was his community and his people.

Mordecai bit down on the stem of his highly coveted Meerschaum pipe and contemplated Z as he often would when he felt it difficult to respond – either because he didn't know what to say or did, but hadn't found the words to say it. Silence in Mordecai's case did not always mean consent. This Z knew from experience. But in the past, when Mordecai listened mutely to Z's proposals, it usually meant that the decision to publish would be made after Z had written it. So writing it or not, was up to Z. Whether the words he

36

eventually wrote would find a home on the pages of the Jewish Record, however, was up to Mordecai and if he was feeling overly bilious that day.

CHAPTER 2

LIKE DICKENS, WHOM he both feared and admired, Z had a great suspicion of facts. Even though *Hard Times* had been published some thirty years before, the ideas in the book still rang true for him as did the metaphor of Coketown where fact, fact, fact, was everywhere in the material aspect of the place and fact, fact, fact, was everywhere in the immaterial. This, after all, was the heyday of the statistician - those grey, robotic men who sat at neat and tidy desks in bleakly lit offices transforming all life into numbers at a stroke of their pen. He hated them, not for who they were but for what they had done – squeezing out all emotion and history from ideas and events so they could more easily be quantified – which had the effect for him of turning people into unthinking machines (probably what the statisticians were after, he suspected).

Of course he did understand there was a functional purpose to gaining certain information – if only for a preliminary understanding of what had happened and when it had occurred (leaving aside for a moment the very important 'why and wherefore'). Except there were no simple questions, not for someone like Z, at least. For as life itself was complex, existing on many different levels and myriads of planes, so were questions. And answers – well, they were even more complicated. Answers depended on who was giving them and where the respondents were in their head at the time they were asked. In fact, if pressed, Z would have probably admitted what for any journalist (or their editors, at least) is absolute anathema – that there were no real answers that could bring forth that state of blessed assuredness craved by the many who needed certainty as their bromide so they could sleep easily at night.

And yet like all men whose career lay before them, Z had a practical side which fortunately allowed him to dispense with those notions set out above – at least long enough to accomplish certain journalistic tasks necessary to construct a coherent story. So journeying to several sites and speaking to some key people, he was quickly able to gather important information regarding the events that happened after the body of Miriam Angel was discovered and the young man, Lipski, was taken away to hospital. Z made extensive notes based on questions he asked of those he chose to interview, some of whom were more forthcoming than others - which is often the case when people are confronted by a member of the press but even more so with Z who didn't look or act like a typical reporter.

Toward evening, Z finds himself walking through the passages of some of his old haunts, places he knew long ago before he left the East End. Even as night falls, the pavement of Wentworth Street is teeming with children. The road is dark and gloomy, but life abounds. Like a greedy voyeur, nothing escapes his eye. The contrast between the West End and the East, thought Z, was denoted by the brightness of one and the obscurity of the other. There was a push among reformers to illuminate the ghetto streets and just the other day he had read in one of the papers a commentary that stated in its usual authoritarian tones, 'Homes would become more cheerful and attractive; life would become healthier and the plague of crime would die out like toadstools under the sun, if the dire streets of the East End were finally electrified.'

Was it any wonder that the people of the area, which the press had termed 'The Wicked Quarter Mile', were attracted to the brightly lit world of the public houses? Back on the great highway, with its cheapjacks and shooting galleries, its roar and rattle, its hawkers and quacks expounding the miracle of some new patent medicine, it was all lit up in blazing naphtha. At the newsstand posters shouted out the gruesome headlines in huge black text. But the images described therein were flat, like paper cutouts. When Z walked those same mean streets he viewed them with more dimension. The houses all had people and the people all had lives. He knew something about the lives they led because he had once lived there himself; so he could see them sympathetically, not just as representatives of the grotesque.

For Z, as a writer, the streets of Whitechapel were peopled with actors in the horrifically grand, magnificently ironic carnival of life. And his job, like a Jewish Balzac, was to record a chapter in the universal human comedy – but one that related to his people. As he walked, he observed and tried to capture the visual rhythms and melodies:

Two young men, one with a bundle of papers and the other a bootblack, share half a cigar that has been dropped, smouldering on the pavement by a gentleman who has hurriedly jumped into a Hansom cab. Nearby a boy without legs sits upon his ragged jacket before an empty metal cup. Next to him a blind man ekes out a tune on a homemade dulcimer. But they are merely backdrops to the ongoing drama of the street – a crowd surrounds a buggy which has been loaded with the body of a woman, drunk and very nearly dead, while, simultaneously, another throng is drawn, compellingly, to a street hawker whose mesmerizing patter casts a spell over his bedazzled audience.

All these characters – the newsy and the bootblack, the legless boy, the blind man, the drunken woman, the charismatic hawker – will later be fleshed out and bestowed with humanity to become more than objects of pity or scorn;

40

they will come to possess hopes and fears, joys and sorrows, tragedy and humour. For now, however, they will remain quick sketches.

Z pockets his notebook and then looks around for someplace to quench his thirst. He enters a pub called the White Hart set on the northern side of the High Street before which the kaleidoscopic music of an organ grinder is bringing some much needed cheer to the road. There he sees a man sitting at the bar and recognises him as someone he knows, someone who worked as a stringer for the East London Observer. Z joins him for a drink. Almost at once the name of Lipski comes up. Everyone on the paper, the stringer tells him, is vying to get some kind of handle on the story. And winking – the man clearly had a few before Z came in – he says, in confidence, of course, that he has just been to London Hospital and, in fact, has seen Lipski, himself. Later Z tries to record what the man in the pub had narrated to him:

> *He entered the long corridor leading to the open ward where the ordinary patients were treated. Normally, Lipski would have been placed in the separate Jewish ward, but it was full at the moment. At the nurse's bay he found a sister who was preparing some fresh bandages for her patients. He asked her how Lipski was doing. She said he was doing as well as could be expected and that he'd been visited by Dr Calvert and Dr Down and both agreed that the injuries were not very serious. The membrane of the throat was all that had been injured by the nitric acid – which, it appeared he had administered to himself.*
>
> *How could she be sure?*
>
> *That was the doctor's opinion.*
>
> *How was he feeling now?*
>
> *He has not passed a comfortable night, poor fellow, she*

41

responded – he's been tossing and turning with only an occasional fitful doze. She said that with sympathy, without displaying any sign of repugnance for the man.

Where was he now?

She pointed to a bed half way down the long ward, on the right hand side. Walking toward it, he saw the patient lying there with his eyes fully open. He appeared to be staring vacantly at the ceiling while his hand clutched convulsively at the coverlet. His throat was bound up with bandages. His dark hair was tangled and unkempt. His face was pale and sallow - beardless with just the hint of side-whiskers.

Sitting opposite him was an interpreter who was also serving as a police guard. He was there, he said, to take down any statement Lipski needed to make. Only one visitor had called on the patient so far, he claimed – a young Jewess who came and sat by his bed for over an hour on Tuesday night. The greeting between her and the patient was most affectionate and the girl expressed her firm belief in his innocence and in the truth of the rambling story he told her about two men coming into the house at Batty Street asking him for work and subsequently pouring some liquid down his throat and that of the woman Angel – a story which the facts of the woman's door being locked on the inside and his being found beneath the bed almost entirely disprove.

But we shall see, for tomorrow is the inquest…

CHAPTER 3

THE CROWD BEGAN forming around Vestry Hall in Cable Street hours before the coroner arrived to start the proceedings, hoping to catch sight of the featured players – the stars of the grotesque which outdid even the oddities on display at the hideous waxwork museums and storefront freak shows scattered along Whitechapel. Because no matter how good a rendition a waxwork might be, no matter how contorted the likes of the Elephant Man, they couldn't hold a candle to the drama taking place on Cable Street that day – here the horror and the blood were all too real and the performance didn't cost them a farthing.

For this was an event even more extraordinary than the Jubilee parade just weeks before when the Queen rolled past in her golden coach on her way down Mile End to the token of her munificence – the rapidly constructed, bare to the bone, Palace of the People. Three cheers: a tiny nod of the regal head, a peremptory wave of the imperial hand and she was gone, never to be seen by them again. But this – this was an event of their own. It happened of them, by them, to them and, what's more, it was still fresh in their consciousness. For it was only the day before yesterday that the body of that hapless young woman was carted out of Batty Street, her mouth stained yellow from the nitric acid forced down her throat, her half naked body mercifully covered so the prurience was left to the feral imagination of those who crushed up against the phalanx of police straining to block their way, saving the last shred of dignity for this wretched corpse on its way to the autopsy table where a six month foetus would be ripped from her lifeless womb and her vagina scrapped and inspected for any traces of sexual molestation (as if there was anything left to molest). And all this – except, of course, the final, degrading humiliation on the cold stone of the autopsy table – all this was done by one of their own.

Who would have done such a terrible deed? Not that terrible deeds weren't enacted each and every day in that cauldron of Hell's kitchen. But this went beyond the mundane horrors of poverty and prostitution, this verged on pure, unvarnished evil. And yet, perhaps, that was part of its fascination. For monstrosity itself created a profane celebrity of sorts. The greater the monstrosity, the more infamous the villain – and in the minds of those native born denizens of the doss house who tenuously shared their turf with the deluge of the Diaspora, the villain in question smacked of the Wandering Jew who needed blood to bake his matzos.

The inquest into the death of Miriam Angel was held Wednesday evening, June 29th, in one of the smaller rooms of Vestry Hall by Mr Wynne Baxter, the coroner, accompanied by his deputy, Mr Collier. The body of the woman was lying at the mortuary a little distance away, where the jury had already been to view it. By the time the proceedings started, the little room was packed to overflow while in the corridor and the street outside a large crowd waited anxiously, eager for any report or rumour.

Isaac Angel, the husband of the deceased woman, was the first witness called. He was short and stocky, with coarse, black hair plastered over his brow; his face a yellow, sickly hue. The fact that he hadn't shaved for several days gave him an unkempt appearance, which his shabby clothes, punctuated by a dirty red cravat, only intensified. His brief residence in London hadn't yet given him much fluency in English so he addressed the court in Yiddish, his native tongue - a language

44

that was barely understood by the interpreter who supposed like many of his sort that it was simply bastard German.

In the early part of the evidence one of the jurymen, who understood the nuances of that unique verbal formulation which allowed Eastern European Jewry to communicate with one another no matter what linguistic region they happened to have found themselves in, protested against the 'inefficient' manner in which the interpreter was performing his duties and went so far as to suggest that the questions were neither properly put to the witness nor were the answers accurately given. The coroner replied that the interpreter had been appointed by the police, and therefore he must take it that the gentleman was properly qualified to interpret the evidence. The juryman was still unsatisfied and brought forward a man named Harris who was standing at the back of the Court who, he suggested, would do the job better. The official interpreter strongly objected to this blatant attempt to take away his business. Ultimately a compromise was worked out at the suggestion of the coroner who intimated amid applause that it was only fair that a poor foreigner should be as fairly treated as an Englishman. The man Harris was therefore allowed to stand by while the evidence was being given and to correct any mistakes made by the official interpreter in the translations.

The result of this arrangement was that when corrected in his translations by Harris, the official interpreter became quite livid, even though another juryman – also familiar with the tongue - ventured to express his belief that this man had absolutely no idea what was being said by the witness. That was too much for the dignity of the official, who rose with folded arms, and uttered a long drawn, 'I beg your pardon, sir,' and stared at the offending juryman for some five minutes until the coroner, looking at him severely, requested him to sit down – a command which he speedily complied with.

When, finally, the court was brought to order, Isaac Angel briefly stated that he and his wife came from the Province of Warsaw and that on the morning of the tragedy he left home at a little after six o'clock for his work at George Street where he was employed as a boot riveter. His wife was still in bed at the time of his leaving but was awake and saw him saying his prayers. Just before he left she asked him what he required to eat when he came home. At this point in the evidence, the coroner said it was most important that he should ask the witness whether he had any intercourse with his wife on the night of Monday or on the morning of Tuesday. After considerable difficulty in interpreting the question and some hesitation on the part of the witness, he answered point blank that he had not. In further examination, he stated that he had never seen any intimacy between Lipski and his wife, admitted that she was six months pregnant, and swore, with tears in his eyes, that they had always lived on most affectionate terms.

Philip Lipski, the husband of Leah Lipski and the tenant of the house where the tragedy took place, said the accused (who was no relation) was about 22 years of age and unmarried, haling from Warsaw and that at about half past six or seven in the morning of Tuesday he was in the yard at the back of the house when he saw the young man and asked him what he was doing. The accused had replied that he was looking for a piece of piping. In response to a question by the coroner, he said he had never seen any sign of the remotest intimacy existing between the accused and the deceased.

The last witness of the evening was Dr Kay who affirmed to having been called in to 16 Batty Street on Tuesday and finding the woman dead and subsequently, after seeing Lipski beneath the bed, to finding a bottle between the bedclothes bearing the label of Bell and Co, Chemists, 6 Commercial Road containing a small portion of nitric acid, which he had no doubt was the liquid administered to the deceased and to the accused. Speaking of the results of the post-mortem which he had made on the body that afternoon, he said he found it to be that of a well-nourished woman with all the organs in a very healthy condition but the heart being empty proved that the immediate cause of death had been suffocation. The corrosive liquid or nitric acid, the stains of which he had seen on the body, had made its way down the wind pipe and had charred the bronchial tubes and lungs and also into the stomach while the fact that the deepest mark of the liquid was on the portion of the stomach which proved that the woman was lying on her back when the liquid was administered. He had taken from the body a six moths foetus. There was an appearance of recent intercourse having been had with the woman, but he could not assert it positively without a microscopical examination. There were no marks of violence on the private parts of the woman or on her thighs. At the suggestion of the coroner, the doctor promised to make a more minute examination of the vagina and for the purpose of receiving his evidence on the subject, the inquiry was adjourned until Friday morning.

When the inquest was reconvened it was in the larger and more spacious Vestry Hall where many more of those eager to partake in this gruesome drama could be seated. Mr Baxter and Mr Collier, his deputy, utilized the quarter of an hour before the commencement of the inquiry scrutinizing an elaborate plan of the ill-fated premises submitted him by Inspector Final, who was in charge of the investigation of the case.

The first witness of the second day was Mr Charles

Moore, a young man living at 96 Blackchurch lane, where he managed an oil shop. After a little preliminary tiff with the coroner, he said that on Tuesday the 28th of June about nine o'clock in the morning a man came into his shop and asked for a pennyworth of aqua fortis, producing at the same time the bottle which had been shown at the last sitting of the Court and was now lying on the coroner's table. The bottle was a two ounce container which was therefore about half filled – a pennyworth being equivalent to an ounce. In reply to the query as to what the purchaser required the liquid for, he said he used it in his trade. The man who came into his shop was about 22 years of age and evidently a foreigner by his speech. The witness had gone with Inspector Final that morning to the London Hospital and was shown a man in bed who he believed to be the same man to whom he supplied the aqua fortis.

Mrs. Lipski, the wife of the tenant of the home, stated that Israel Lipski – the accused – who rented the upper room in her house, had formerly worked outside of Batty Street, but on Monday this week he commenced carrying on his business there with the assistance of a boy named Pitman. On Tuesday last she was asleep on the ground floor – where there were only two rooms - when her husband left. Therefore anyone coming downstairs would have to pass the door of her bedroom to get out into the street although admission was obtained to the yard without going through the kitchen. At 8:30 on Tuesday morning she got up, went to the kitchen and saw Israel Lipski there. He asked the witness for some coffee, but, finding that she had none in the house, she asked him to wait there while she proceeded to Blackchurch lane to purchase some. She was absent for about twenty minutes and when she returned 'Israel' – as she called him – had gone. However, she prepared the coffee and called upstairs,

'Israel, come down, the coffee is ready!' to which the boy Pitman upstairs replied that he was not there. She did not see Lipski again until she met him in custody at the Leman Street Police Station. At ten o'clock she left the house and proceeded to Petticoat Lane to purchase some meat. She was therefore in the house for about an hour and ten minutes – between ten minutes to nine and ten o'clock – during which time she was positive that no one could have gone upstairs, her mother, Rachel Rubenstein and Leah Levy being also in the kitchen. On her return from the Lane, she met her mother and Mrs. Angel, the mother of the deceased woman. Mrs Angel went upstairs and when she had no success in rousing her daughter-in law, called down to Mrs Lipski for help. Dropping the things she had in her hands, Mrs Lipski ran upstairs and asked Mrs Levy to look through the keyhole to see whether the key was inside. She did so and called out that the key was, indeed, inside upon which Mrs Lipski proceeded partly up the next flight of stairs where there was a little glass window built into the wall that looked into the Angels bedroom. Peering through the window she just managed to make out the shape of the deceased lying in the bed. She then rushed out to find Dr. Kay, the neighbourhood physician. Upon her return, the room was then broken into and the witness saw Miriam Angel lying sideways on the bed. Mrs Lipski noticed that the legs of the deceased were covered, that her chemise was buttoned and that no part of her body was exposed.

Recalled to give further evidence, Dr Kay stated that since the last sitting he had examined the vagina of the deceased and had put it under the microscope. He produced a glass bottle with some of the matter taken from the vagina, but he was still unable to say with any degree of certainty from his examination whether it pointed conclusively to recent intercourse. It might, however, be submitted to a further chemical examination. Questioned by the coroner, he said that when he first saw the body of the deceased it was not exposed but on turning the bed down to see if any violence had been offered her, he found that the legs, thighs, and genitals together with the lower part of the abdomen were exposed and the position of the woman was very suggestive.

Richard Pitman, the lad employed by the accused, said that he had started work that prior Wednesday and had worked there till Monday night. He came again at eight o'clock on Tuesday morning – the day of the murder - but left at 9:30 to have his breakfast, returning an hour later. The front door was shut when he went out and he shut it after him. It was at eleven o'clock that he heard of the tragedy. He saw Lipski at half past ten when the accused gave him some instructions. At the time, Lipski also said that he had been out to buy a sponge and a vice and that he was going out again. He then left the room but Pitman could not say if he had actually left the house. He affirmed that to his knowledge stick makers used methylated spirit in their trade, but he could not say if acid was used. He also stated that when he saw Lipski, the accused had on his black coat (produced) but there were no stains on it then.

The coroner having summed up, the jury returned a verdict of 'Wilful Murder' against Lipski, who was committed for trial on the coroner's warrant.

CHAPTER 4

IT'S EARLY SATURDAY evening. The pungent smell of manure hangs thick in the air. Margaret Harkness (known to her friends as 'Maggie') is walking along Whitechapel Road fascinated by the exotic mix of peoples swept up in the kaleidoscopic, sepia-tinted madness. Taking out her little moleskin journal, she scribbles down some notes about the rich diversity that surrounds her (or as she believes it to be): 'An Algerian merchant walks arm-in-arm with a native of Calcutta. A little Italian plays pitch-and-toss with a small Russian. A Polish Jew enjoys sauerkraut with a German...' – though her guess as to the origin of these people has to do with her own peculiar fantasies. And then her eye fixes upon the down-and–outs, the lingerers soused in gin, who, themselves are observing this parade of humanity, but with narrow eyes and barely restrained hostility. Of them she writes: 'The East End loafer, monarch of all he surveys, lord of the premises. It is amusing to see his British air of superiority. His hands are deep down in the pockets of his fustian trousers, round his neck is a bit of coloured rag or flannel, on his head is a tattered cap. His is looked upon as scum by his own nation but he feels himself to be an Englishman and able to kick the foreigner back to his native land if only the government would believe in England for the Englishman...'

The people who flock to Whitechapel Road on Saturday nights are like moths attracted by the flaring gas torches set before the stalls of vendors shrilly crying out their wares: 'Buy! Buy! Buy!' That one word, repeated thrice, sums up for her the crazed desperation of the hawkers frantic to survive in this cutthroat artery of impoverishment. As she walks, as she observes, she is slowly transformed into her other self, through whose mind she can enter her most beloved character – the gentle Captain in the Army of Salvation. She tries once more to imagine what he would have made of all this and then she sees an old woman selling pig's feet, her wrinkled head wrapped in a shawl, who just the other day she came upon dead drunk. Instead of letting her lie there on the ground, as she had done, he would have escorted her home to that dark and dingy cellar she shared with three other crones – three fearful hags who frightened her but not the good Captain. He would have treated them with the respect they hardly deserved because, to him, they weren't hags at all, but simply the innocent children of God.

She stops before an arcade, a storefront freak-show – one of many on the road. Outside the door stand two men dressed as Ottoman warriors brandishing swords. A crowd of children flock around them, begging for coins so they can gain entrance to see the main attraction – The Boy With The Skeleton Arm. Passing the doorkeepers she enters the low-ceilinged room used for the penny entertainments. Inside the walls are plastered with old circus and carnival posters of lion-tamers, bare-back riders, high-wire acrobats and clowns which in this musty space seem odd and even a bit creepy as the colours, once bright and cheery have, in the dampness, become muted and anaemic.

The entertainment – or what passed for such in this chamber of curiosities – had already begun (though it never really ceases) and consists of a youth, half naked and quite normal looking except for a limb that was severely atrophied. What makes this lad – known on the street as 'Skeleton Arm' – unique is his ability to use his withered appendage for deeds of prowess such as throwing knives and lifting heavy iron bars. And the audience who had paid their penny to see this queer mix of ordinary and bizarre, pushed forward to get a better view, tramping over nutshells and other bits of detritus dropped on the earthen floor.

Maggie has come here several times before and is lured back not by the grotesque performers themselves but by the reaction of the audience who seem to find immense pleasure in witnessing pathetic creatures even more miserable than themselves – at least this is what she feels.

About 300 people crushed inside to see Skeleton Arm, dressed up as Buffalo Bill, and his colleague, a sullen midget masquerading as Napoleon. There were all types - mothers carrying market baskets, old men, youths, and children who stood gawking at these human disfigurements while a girl turned the handle of an organ filling the room with deafening sounds, loud and discordant. And as Maggie made ready to leave – for she could only bear to stay for several minutes - she heard a woman say, 'How could God Almighty make anything so ugly?'

It was a beautiful night and on reaching the open air Maggie looked up at the stars with a sense of relief; they seemed so far away, so still, so restful. Then glancing at a sign plastered on a newsstand screaming the words, 'Shocking Murder in Whitechapel!' her thoughts turned back to that terrible day on Batty Street again.

The day of the murder, that hot and sultry morning of 28 June, she had been at the market picking up the few meagre necessities her budget would allow. Suddenly she had felt something strange in the air, something she had experienced only once before, when she was living in the country as a child and had noticed that the animals in the fields had started acting very odd, doing things she had never seen them do, as if possessed, and it had frightened her because it seemed

53

that the world was being turned askew and she and all the animals were being tilted into another dimension despite themselves. It was a similar feeling that day. No one knew what it was, but it reminded her of those animals. People had begun to quiver and pale and then they had started to move around restlessly. There was a feeling of unease and apprehension. Everyone knew something was wrong but no one seemed to know what it was. And then a procession, like the movement of ants, was drawn magnetically, to Batty Street. Why? No one understood. The crowd grew ever larger, people kept coming, endlessly, taking over the narrow street until the police arrived and pushed them back so they could establish a cordon sanitaire. Then a body was carried out of number 16 wrapped up in cloth and a cry rose from the crowd. A short while later a man was brought out, weak, pale, barely alive if alive he was, and another cry arose, but this one frightening and the crowd of mourners now became a mob.

Even though Maggie, herself, had been caught up in that bizarre frenzy she still had managed to keep her journalistic head and continued to ask questions, observing and taking notes. And she remained as the crowd, having finally satisfied its morbid fascination, began to drift away.

'The only things in which East End people take much interest are murders and funerals,' she wrote. 'Their lives are so dull; nothing else gets their sluggish blood into motion. But a murder is like giving them a dose of smelling salts. Was the person poisoned or was her throat cut? Did the corpse turn black or did it keep until the nails were put into the coffin? The thing that strikes me most about East End life is its soddenness...'

It was then she had seen a young woman, standing outside the Batty Street house. A man dressed in soiled worker's clothes stood over her, threateningly, shaking an accusing finger as his body quivered, his grotesque countenance flushed red in uncontrollable anger till it seemed about to explode. But instead of rupturing into violence, the misshapen face had suddenly transformed into pitiful sobs and tearful supplications to God in a language Maggie scarcely understood.

The young woman suffered this abuse without flinching. Her features were wooden, her disposition inert. If he had struck her, Maggie felt she would have accepted it as fitting punishment. For what? The question was irrelevant. It was as if life had bestowed nothing but misery upon that poor woman and, for reasons that would remain forever elusive, she was convinced the blame was hers alone.

The man, now weeping uncontrollably, was led away into the Batty Street house, leaving the young woman standing outside by herself. It was then Maggie had caught her eye and felt that mysterious link to another soul that happens rarely in one's life when two opposites connect by chance and sense the fascination of what might have been if they were born into a different world. But she also felt the depth of despair in the obscure figure standing alone across the road, the painful emptiness of solitude. At least she thought she did. For Maggie, as many writers, was keen to fill a vacuum with thoughts and emotions that would have been hers had she been placed in some other role.

Several months before this episode on Batty Street she had been on a march for Simon Tweed, a boot finisher from Whitechapel who had died, according to his comrades, owing to the results of overwork. Tweed had sweated 18 hours a day throughout the year at 10s per week. One day his body just gave out. He was taken to hospital but died soon after - at the tender age of twenty-four.

When the procession reached the West Ham Jewish cemetery where Tweed's body lay in state awaiting burial, the marchers boldly broke through the gates and entered the chapel where a nervous Rabbi was holding service for the grieving relatives. Chanting and waving their banners, the marchers commandeered the coffin and carried it out to the freshly dug grave in order to hold a service of their own. They were soon confronted by a force of 100 policemen who barricaded the chapel doors and made free use of their batons. Fighting ensued and a number of people were trampled in the struggle.

This incident caused Maggie much anxiety when she thought about the event sometime afterward. She saw Tweed as a martyr to the barbaric labour practices that broke so many lives, their youth and vitality slowly squeezed away like drayage mules driven mercilessly night and day until time came to hobble them off to the glue yard. But, she also questioned the motives of those who tried to steal the coffin from the family of mourners. For the leaders of that manifestation, she thought, Simon Tweed was little more than a symbol, dipped in red, used to goad the troops and fan the flames of revolution – a revolution that, in her mind, would only lead to more torment and bloodshed.

Slowly she found her allegiance shift from those leaders, brazen and proud, who wrote and spoke grand phrases, whipping up passions but rarely waiting around to pick up the pieces that lay shattered on the pavement. Instead she became attracted to the lonely settlement workers who volunteered their time to care for the needy, enduring the filth and privation to do God's work – for their calling could only be supported by God since the State had long since abandoned them.

And so she chose a career as a writer. Her mission was to

capture on paper, with pen and ink, the lives and labours of the people who existed in such vile conditions in the very heart of the greatest Empire the world had ever known. Done with care, understanding and passion she felt that her words would, some day, cut like a rapier through the mental lethargy of those privileged and pampered who refused to see the hell that existed right around the corner from their beloved Stock Exchange – or, if they did, could hardly identify with the tragedies which played themselves out on a daily basis. The day when she could accurately mirror that world was still some years away. But in the meanwhile she continued to pursue her research by living in a squalid room and observing, methodically, all the misery that surrounded her. The streets had become her canvass; the people, her subject and the dire poverty of their lives, her rationale.

Maggie takes the potatoes she purchased from the hawker, who once was a sailor, back to her room. It's a small, box shaped space with just a bed, a flimsy wardrobe and a desk which was simply a pinewood writing table into which some former tenant had carved, all in German, the word '*Liebe*' and then, next to that, the word '*Hass*' and perpendicular to both the word '*Angst.*' Even though the furrows made it difficult to keep her writing singularly clean and flowing (for she took great pride in her penmanship) she made no attempt to even the surface of the wood because, in a curious way, these words embossed by that unknown hand seemed to represent to her the holy trinity of life in the East End – Love and Hate connected by Fear.

The world she had entered was one that was filled with smells of the unknown – the food, the dirt, the very air she breathed all had the sense of the unfamiliar. Yet there was something distinctly exotic here, in the faces of the people, dark, pallid, pained and yet so expressive and so unlike the rough and ruddy faces of her younger years in the countryside. But it was the smells, the raw, filthy odours, which had first hypnotised her far more than the visual as these effluvia entered her body and lingered there mingling with her bodily chemistry until she, herself, was part of them. It horrified her, these smells that invaded her propriety. And yet once she had allowed it to happen, they took her over and, far more than the visual images which formed the matter of her work, they soon became part of her inner ambiance – so much so that when she left this world to re-enter her own little England, it was the scent of rosewater and cologne that seemed to her strange.

When she sat at her little desk, pencil in hand, the words came out but not in the same manner as with Z. There wasn't that easy flow as if tapping into an inner stream and running with the current. For her words were more tortured as she was writing to expose the evils of poverty and misfortune and thus needed to find the phrases that described the imagery which related to those concepts. If her eye was to be a camera, her pencil was a stylus of light that she indelibly imposed onto her canvas. But her camera was focused on subjects she, herself, had positioned, so her eye could only see what her brain allowed.

Today, however, her writing took a different turn. The pencil in her hand seemed to override her censorious biology which had been so effective up till now keeping it in line. And she wrote of a woman, maybe her age, maybe a little older or a little younger. The actual age didn't matter for it wasn't the years that accounted for the pallid face and sunken eyes of this character. It was something else, not the phases of the moon nor the elliptical motion of the earth around the sun, that gave this woman's face its mystery. As she put down her pencil and stared at the jagged carvings in the wood, Maggie realised she could describe the face in minute detail. She could even write about a mole curiously located under the woman's nose that became a hypnotic focal point for anyone who looked at it. But she couldn't get any deeper than that even though she was aware what lay beyond the crust was far more interesting. She could make this character walk and she could dress it in believability, if believability existed in simply three dimensions, but she couldn't get underneath the skin - the fourth dimension where the heart and soul resided. And that is exactly where she wished to be – someplace on the other side of the looking glass. Though, once there, she wasn't absolutely sure she could find her way back out again.

CHAPTER 5

IT WAS A strange and curious meeting. She knew him slightly; he didn't know her at all – at least he didn't think he did. But that didn't matter as they had been fated to connect – or at least it seemed that way when they thought about it some time later.

Mordecai was the one who made the match, unwittingly, of course. It was he who said it would be good for their dealings with the Jewish Board of Guardians. And, really, it was a simple request. A journalist wished to write an article on the arrival of refugees at the London docks and needed the services of an interpreter. The journalist had contacted the Board and the Board had contacted him. There would be no payment involved – it was one of those gestures deemed necessary in maintaining good relations with the news media which the Guardians understood to be vital to their continued success in keeping the lid on the boiling cauldron of what had come to be known as 'the immigrant question.'

For his part, Z had no real objection as long as he had the time. He was astute enough to realise that journalistic careers were built around the currency of the 'quid pro quo.' But what he didn't know, because Mordecai hadn't told him (since Mordecai, himself, didn't know), was that the journalist he was slated to escort was a woman. And that was all because of a splotchy ink job which blurred the 'iss' in 'Miss' and made it gender free – just an 'M' and a blotch. Z, however, wasn't the sort to take offence at a female member of the writing class. Indeed, he had no objection to women doing anything and in later life found himself in the front ranks of those brave men who campaigned forcefully for gender equality. But that didn't mean he wasn't surprised to see a womanly figure awaiting him at the appointed spot, notebook and pencil in hand, wearing a very determined expression.

They waited some hours for a boat to arrive. Boats came and went according to the tide and the weather conditions at sea where the currents and winds and the waters' swell played havoc with any pretence of accurate landing times. You could never tell exactly when one would dock. For those who waited at the jetty there was always a strange silence of expectation – that curious calm before a tumultuous event. The few friends and relatives, dressed in their second-hand finery, stood poised to greet the lucky ones, helping to ease their entry into the rough and tumble East End birth canal, braving the harbour chill and shuffling their feet to keep their near-to-ragged bodies warm while up above, at the gin depot, the loungers, the roughs, the casuals who drank away their earnings as soon as a penny hit their calloused hand, pointed their battered fingers and laughed a drink-soddened cackle at the thought of more destitute 'greeners' emerging, hungry and bemused, from their watery tomb and climbing, legless, onto shore, looking as ridiculous as so many others had before them.

There was another group Z pointed out to her, a nasty lot, waiting like wolves for their prey to be delivered. They were, he said, the most repulsive of East London parasites – but, like all God's creatures, parasites or not, they needed sustenance; for it was fear of starvation that brought them to this sorry state where they would feed on their brethren like shipwrecked sailors on a windswept isle who eat their mates out of desperation, because they're too frightened or hungry or stupid to realise that the sea, itself, is full of nourishment if they only knew how to harvest it.

61

Nearby a squat little man with a sweaty brow wearing a badge that Z told her identified him as the representative of the Hebrew Ladies' Protective Society, looked nervously at the wolves already starting to lick their chops in anticipation of fresh meat soon on its way. But he was slow and clumsy, while they were quick and lean. Perhaps he would rescue a young woman that day before she was swept up by a smarmy landsman who knew her language and even the town she came from and would help her find her way through the treacherous London jungle which was no place for a young woman like her to be travelling through alone. What happened then? Perhaps she would be bundled off in his carriage and taken back to Tilbury, bound for the promised land – or so she was told. And that would be the last anyone would see of her until she reached the brothels of Argentina. If the squat little man wearing the badge of the Protective Society got to her first, he might save her from that particular misery. But, then again, who knew what adventures lay along the mysterious path of life? From a single bleak and dismal moment in time one would be hard put to predict the next. The hapless woman bound for the Argentine brothel might end up marrying a displaced Sephardic aristocrat who had carved out a cattle empire in the Pampas while the young girl saved by the squat little man could find herself making match boxes at six pennies a gross and living in a dingy cellar with twenty starving children. Life, said Z, held out infinite possibilities and we, as mere mortals, could only sit back and occasionally wonder at the many and multifarious facets of the unknowable universe.

Maggie was truly horrified to hear him speak like that. Suffering was a sin and a terrible crime against humanity. It was up to the knowledgeable people of the world, those of strong, abiding moral fibre, to stop this abomination. How

62

would this be done? Through exposure, education and organisation, of course: exposure though the written word which could win the hearts and minds of those who hold the reins of power; education of all about the evils that persist and organisation of resources to put an end to crime and suffering.

And what, asked Z, if it were in the interests of people who hold the reins of power that suffering exists? For is it not true that power is built on wealth and wealth is built on the suffering of others?

If that be the case, Maggie responded, then the reins must be removed from those unworthy hands and placed in the grip of others who have accepted the moral obligation to uphold natural justice.

And Z said to himself – for he didn't dare say it to her – 'If it were only that simple…' But a moment later his thought burst like a bubble pricked by the arrow of time as the first boat of the afternoon arrived through the narrow entrance of the landing stage, disgorging the voyagers from another planet, those glassy-eyed refugees from the firestorm in the East which scattered them like terrified animals escaping the annihilation of their ancestral forest, destitute (40% came with less than 10 shillings in their pocket) and homeless. As they emerged, tired, hungry but aching to breathe freedom's pure and wholesome air, they were besieged by the parasites who pushed forward seizing hold of the bundles and baskets of those hapless newcomers who had no one on shore to meet, and carting them off to parts unknown with promises of work and lodging and something hot to put in their shrunken stomachs. The diminutive man from the Hebrew Ladies' Protective Society struggled through the crowd looking for unescorted females and handing out cards to others instructing them how to find the Poor Jew's

Temporary Shelter in Leman Street. But it was a hopeless task with all the shouts and cries, the chaos and confusion of the emerging masses, accompanied by the callous laughter of the unemployed dockers who watched in coarse amusement, happy to see these miserable unfortunates who were even worse off than themselves and happier still to shout in a language the others could scarcely understand that they should get back on the boat and leave because nobody in England wanted them.

Maggie watched in horror and tried to write up the scene even though she felt it indescribable. It happened in a blink of an eye and was over in an instant as some were carted off by the touts and the rest melted away into the teeming roads right behind the docks that led into the slums of Whitechapel - all except for one slight girl, not more than sixteen years of age, with mousy hair and a look of sublime wonder who was led away by the squat little man who wore an official badge on his jacket.

Afterward, she questioned Z more about those people, those phantoms from another world who passed like docile cattle from boat to shore and then disappearing into the East End abattoir. He told her that most immigrants travelled across Germany by train for the ports of Bremen, Hamburg or Rotterdam. There was a fierce competition between the shipping companies for the refugee traffic, since ships which made the eastward journey across the Atlantic found them the easiest and most economic cargo for their holds, as they were self loading and the profit per pound was better than that for a sack of potatoes. The British lines competed with the continental companies – it was cheaper to travel from Europe to England and then from Liverpool to America than from Europe direct to the United States – where most of them really wanted to go. Fares to England were low – Hamburg to London was as little as 15s – kept cheap by agents who leased part of a ship's hold and then sold individual tickets to migrants, filling up the allotted space as far as it would go (and often further), and, in the process, netting themselves a tidy profit. There were at least four steamers a week from Hamburg, three from Rotterdam and three from Bremen.

Most of the refugees arrived with little or no money, Z said. Some of them – linguistically confused and misdirected by unscrupulous agents - didn't even know where they were headed. Was it London, Liverpool, Belfast, Glasgow or some port in America? It wasn't till they actually disembarked that they found out where it was they had landed. Until then they sat in the hold or crushed up on deck, looking bewildered, dressed in their unkempt Eastern European clothes, and praying to their God to lead them somewhere safer than the place they had so sorrowfully left: that place they had loved as their homeland, not the nation but the village or the shtetl where they were born as were their parents and their grandparents - reaching back into the hollowness of time, some many hundreds of years ago when the Jews were first invited to settle in what was then the Polish Kingdom.

At first, Z told her, the immigrants who arrived without resources of their own were left to starve or, at the most, given a stipend to travel on, hoping that this harsh treatment would serve as a warning to others who might have also thought of entering this unwelcome land that somehow persisted in myth as having streets paved with gold. But nothing could quell the human tide which had no time for logic or for reason and when, in 1884, the realisation finally hit home that little could be done to stop the endless flow, a baker, himself a former refugee, set up the Jews' Temporary Shelter - much against the wishes of the all powerful Guardians.

It was only later, horrified by stories of young Jewesses

being forced into prostitution, that the wealthy daughter of Sir Anthony de Rothschild, aided by Claude Montefiore, founded a Jewish Ladies Society for Protection and Rescue Work. And it was this organisation that employed an agent to wait at the docks for boats likely to be carrying single girls without friends or family to meet them. But even so, for every one approached and 'saved,' ten others disappeared into the teeming crowds, many of whom were then lost to the parasites who knew how valuable a commodity young womanhood was, regardless of class, race or the dire state of their wardrobe.

CHAPTER 6

THEY STROLLED BACK together from the mouldering docks, following the well-trod route into Whitechapel oblivious to the buzz and the splatter, the mud, the groaning stink of horseflesh as it strained to carry more than its share of stuff and provisions to the stores and shops that supplied the multifarious bee hive of activity sweating away in that labyrinth of streets and lanes which all held secret dreams and passions, stories and fantasies that both Z and Maggie had struggled to encapsulate. Z sometimes saw that route as an uphill tributary of the Thames, a never ending stream that led from the city wharves to the dens of the East End; a special one that flowed not with water but with people - his people - and that reached back to Tilbury, back to the icy waters of the Channel, back to the ports of Hamburg or Bremen, back, back, back into the European heartlands which had vomited up a tidal wave of bodies, a vast, relentless, unstoppable torrent sweeping an endless supply of battered humanity along the path they walked that day.

And one after another, the streets, the lanes, the houses, the rooms, each with a density of animal matter which made them the most tightly packed bit of real estate in Europe – all these streets and lanes and houses and rooms had bodies that needed to be fed and souls that needed sustaining. Yet what intrigued him was not how many but how few actually starved there. How did it happen that more people weren't picked up from the street with bellies swollen from the fatal gasses generated through the last and bitterly ironic stage of starvation? As they packed themselves together, out of fear, poverty and protection, into rookeries, dank and demonic, how did they escape the plague of endemic diseases that often came with environmental hazard?

Maggie asked that question as they walked. Z avoided giving her a straightforward response as he had a deep and abiding suspicion of social reformers who came out of the so-called 'educated middle-classes', and thus he purposely constructed enigmatic replies that (he hoped) forced them to follow their reasoning into a paradoxical realm outside their boxed-in universe. So he told her, simply, that what's important is not what isn't but what is. Maggie being someone who prided herself on clear-cut thought found that sort of answer quite unacceptable (even if she bothered to consider what it meant, which she didn't) and said, in response to what she thought they were talking about – namely why a major plague had yet to occur in the East End - that a tinder box needs only a spark to set it off even if it sits quite harmlessly for a month, a year or even a decade. Which, she continued, is what liberal education brings to the service of civilisation – the ability to see the overriding nature of cause and effect. (A statement which only confirmed to Z that the horrid idea of a clockwork universe had become the abiding notion of 19th Century Britain.) But, she admitted, it was quite astonishing how the Jewish people could survive so well in such dire poverty. Which brought Z to explain to her his theory of the Farthing Shop. For without the Farthing Shop, he said, many more would have perished from hunger and malnutrition.

If one had a shilling, he explained, one could buy a decent piece of meat in any shop in London and have enough left over to purchase some bread and ale. But if one were living on pennies, there was a problem of what to purchase because most grocers were unwilling to service the poor (whose trade they neither needed nor desired). Whereas in Whitechapel the poor were the mainstay of the grocer's trade and so, in order to cater for them, a system was devised whereby this moneyless clientele could purchase anything for a farthing – though the quantity might be infinitesimally small. So if you came in with a penny you might purchase, when divided into farthings, not one thing but four. A penny's worth of herring might be the fish, but a farthing's worth might be the head or tail. Another farthing might buy you a half of a carrot, a slice of onion for another, and for the last one you might even have a thimble full of ale. So in the East End, a penny could buy you, in the miniature of course, an entire meal whereas in other parts of London you found yourself quite hard pressed to dine at all.

As Maggie had been living in the East End for several months herself, she realised that it was possible to survive on the cheap if one knew where to go, but it was just as possible to be gouged quite mercilessly if one didn't. And for the recent immigrants who were unfamiliar with the language and the lay of the land, the chances of being taken for a soaking and left hanging high and dry, were very good – except, of course, as the major language of trade in parts of Whitechapel was Yiddish, Maggie was as much the immigrant as those fresh off the boat from Poland. For, indeed, parts of the East End were like another country mysteriously transposed onto England. So who was really the foreigner there? It was a question that Z thought about most earnestly and Maggie thought about very little.

They walked up Commercial Road till they came to the corner of Flower and Dean Street, stopping before a warehouse with dull brick walls darkened with soot. Maggie pointed to the frontage door which led inside to a restaurant and told Z that this was the place Dickens had written about twenty-five years before when he had ventured within, attracted by a handbill telling of a cooking depôt for the workers in the district. He was a supporter of the co-operative movement, she said, but was well aware that it could be used as a mask to pay workers a pittance for their labour. In fact, before he gave his support, he asked to see their business accounts, and once satisfied they were fair, he was quite enthusiastic in recommending the place - writing in glowing terms of the well ventilated, clean and brightly painted dining rooms, the cheerful young waitresses and the nourishing, wholesome food which easily rivalled the rubbish served in the City's posh and pricey clubs. But what impressed him most was the dignity and spirit of those who ran this enterprise – which had only been up and running a week or so before he arrived.

They went inside and purchased some penny tickets at the kiosk in the vestibule before making their way to the main dining room and seating themselves at a table. The room still had an open feel, though the walls were no longer clean and bright as they were when Dickens had first come. Twenty-five years had given them a patina of age, the product of ten thousand days of boiled beef and mutton. The waitresses, too, were no longer young and cheerful. The smile had faded with their bloom and in its place a look similar, perhaps, to the walls where layers of time had been harshly embedded.

Maggie told him that she came on occasion as it felt comfortable to eat here alone. And for a few pennies she could have some nourishing soup and bread, though, of course, one couldn't linger too long over meals as the restaurant was always full during dinnertime and then seats were at a premium.

They ordered coffees and biscuits. Z liked the look of the place – it was a people's emporium without pomp or pretence. There were all sorts of characters scattered about the spacious room – artisans, elderly couples, unescorted women, a man dressed in rags whose hair stood up in spiky tufts and who kept reading the menu over and over again apparently without comprehension, another in a stiff white collar (a bank clerk perhaps?) played nervously with a teaspoon as his eyes focused on a charming red-head across the room who, herself, was glancing coyly at a sailor whose rolled-up sleeve displayed a tattoo of a naked dancer doing the koochy-koo every time he pumped his bicep.

Maggie asked him questions about this and that. She listened to what he said with interest. And Z, for his part, liked to talk. He enjoyed the art of conversation – for art it is – and could hold forth knowledgeably on a multitude of subjects. But she noted in him a sense of distance and, if not disdain, suspicion. That sense of him – his apparent lack of interest in her as a fellow writer – caused her some discomfort. For, in fact, she knew him as an author – she had met him once before at a party at her cousin Beatrice's flat, though she was certain he hadn't remembered even though she had complimented him on a story which she had read in a magazine that had just recently come out. And even though he didn't see her as a colleague, she wished she could speak with him about the profession and the craft. She felt that her male half, John, wouldn't have had that difficulty and she wished she could have metamorphosed into him completely, at least for a while, so the gap between the genders could be bridged.

But there she had him wrong. It wasn't her as a woman that he found difficult, it was her as an East End interloper – one of the many barging in those days with their pencils and clipboards taking notes and collecting figures, like wild, exotic butterflies, for their statistics, as if that could ever give them a true sense of what was going on there. In his mind, they treated the East End like one of their colonial

71

dominions, and the people like coolies or kaffirs who needed to be civilised before being given the privilege of offering themselves into the service of the Empire as fresh and pliant meat for exploitation.

And when they complained about the sweatshops run by greedy Jews who oppressed their own brethren, spouting out hackneyed rhetoric that sounded so very righteous, had they really thought it through? Yes, it was a brutal system without doubt. But was it as brutal as the factory where people were just replaceable units of labour to be hired or cast out at the will of some faceless financier who never left his country house except to go boozing at his club? The sweatshops in the East End were, in the main, small, family enterprises run by people who lived not much differently from the workers they employed. They spoke the same language, ate the same food and worshipped the same god. What's more, they taught the inexperienced and uneducated newcomers a trade – something the reformers for all their moaning and maligning did not.

But he had her wrong as well. She wanted to see the world from the eyes of the characters she met in the streets of Whitechapel. If only they would allow her to do so.

CHAPTER 7

THEY HAD BEEN conversing for a while before she brought the matter up. She felt he was the person to speak with about it, but she wasn't quite sure how the subject should be broached. However, being a straightforward woman who avoided any scent of pretence, she decided to boldly be direct. And so she asked him the question that was on her mind - whether he knew anything about what had come to be known as the Whitechapel murder case and the young man Lipski who was accused of that terrible crime. She had gone to Batty Street on that day, she told him, following the crowd of people who were drawn there so mysteriously. Something was in the air, something strong and powerful that took her over and, yes, was thrilling but at the same time very frightening. The world seemed suddenly askew, off kilter, and she felt a moment of terror when she found herself in the centre of the mob, swept up in blind emotion. She struggled with herself to regain that sense of detachment so important for her to see the event through the eyes of a journalist, through the lens of a writer, but the crowd was faceless and devouring and she couldn't escape the fact that she was part of it – that, try as she might, she couldn't detach herself from the essence of the beast, which itself was an organism, and being within it she, herself, had become simply an appendage. But later, when she had a chance to recollect, she realised that there had been a difference in the people – the native East Enders and the Jews – who were part of that mass and yet somehow separate. The native East Enders were braying for blood, they were pumped up and visceral, you could smell their juices like the sharp, acrid stink of animals in heat and

73

you could see the glint of unleashed frenzy in their faces. The anger of the Jews, on the other hand, was muted by a primal sense of fear. Perhaps they realised that if the others had been thrown a Jew just then, any Jew, and told he was the culprit, they would have happily ripped him apart – because he was a Jew as well as a suspected murderer.

Then the next day – and this is what concerned her - she started to hear the rumours, the ominous talk in the street, about the Jews being at it again and that this wasn't just any murder, but a ritual killing sanctioned by secret powers; that it was done to obtain the blood of an unborn child for the practice of some strange, demonic ritual - a grotesque and chilling notion but one which they believed quite strongly. But there was no truth in it, no truth at all... was there?

Z looked at her closely before he spoke, studying her expression. She wasn't unattractive he thought. She had a heart as well as a mind – he could clearly see that. But – justified or not – the suspicion entered his head that perhaps she was asking him for confirmation and the idea that someone like her could even countenance the notion of that dogged canard disturbed him. For this was the most terrible lie that maintained a tenacious grip upon the febrile minds of European peasantry and was so well exploited by those who wished to use it, for purposes of their own, as a spark to set the fires of accusation blazing. It was an especially powerful tool in the arsenal of the politically corrupt because it connected to those primeval fears that reached back into the dark expanse of ancient nights, echoing once more that cry of guilt, that basic charge of *juddenhaze*: the dreaded and most reprehensible deceit of the Blood Libel. And like the terrible Hydra of many heads, each one severed would be restored. It might take years or even centuries, but grow back it did, uglier than ever before. So ingrained in the psyche of primitive Christianity, so convoluted grew those roots in the subconscious soil of nightmares and netherworlds, nothing could completely extirpate it. Like the trunk of an ancient dark, demonic tree, it ran too deep into the ground, submerging cancerous tentacles into impenetrable soil, dank and diseased, always spreading its pustule seeds over newly fertile ground. But that these charges should emerge in his beloved England, that someone as sensible as her should ever dare to moot them, no matter how innocently, was especially troublesome. For these concerns, these fears, were not just another form of Jewish paranoia. They had a history spanning back to the dark medieval nights and continuing forward so close that Z could almost touch it.

In the third year of Victoria's reign something happened in Damascus that sent a seismic shockwave through the newly assimilated Jewish communities in Europe – which by then had only been accorded civil liberties for less than fifty years. News slowly filtering out of that region - once the pride of the Ottomans whose 500 year empire had fallen into terminal disarray – announced the arrest of several Syrian Jews who had been accused of murdering a Capuchin priest and using his blood as part of their rites in celebration of Passover. Though Blood Libel accusations had been common in Europe during the Middle Ages, this was the first recorded case in the Moslem world – though soon there was found to be a Machiavellian hand at work and, most shockingly of all (especially for those who began their evening prayers by giving thanks to Napoleon for their liberation) the hand was of a Gallic origin.

France, at the time, was trying to exert its influence in Syria, competing with the other European states to gain a Middle Eastern foothold, and seeing the newly politicised Catholics as their natural allies, they used the case, quite cynically, to what they suspected might be their advantage. England, however, having strong economic ties with the Jewish community there, supported negotiations with the Pasha of Egypt – the new titular leader of Syria – to sign a declaration absolving the Jews of that monstrous charge. And though the recently emancipated Jewish communities in Europe felt a renewed sense of confidence after burying those dreadful allegations (Thiers, the prime minister of France, was brought down partly because of this affair), there was still a lingering fear that the ghost might have been laid to rest but it was bound to reappear, perhaps at a time when they were much more vulnerable.

Perhaps he was being too sensitive. Perhaps she hadn't meant it like that. She had said it was a disturbing thought and she was trying to put it to rest, wasn't she? But 'Jew' was a word that had a multiplicity of meanings and thousands of years of historical resonance. And then there was an off-hand reference she had made – and she had meant it well – about how the Jews were able to lift themselves out of poverty, with the help of their wealthy brethren, and move on while others in the East End ghetto seemed to have resigned themselves to a life of misery and deprivation.

Statements like that only made him feel the tremendous chasm that separated him from someone even like her, someone who had taken risks that few women took with their lives, who had chosen to live among the poor and destitute and had given up the comforts of a quiet country life in order to pursue her mission. Even with all that he sensed a certain smugness, a kind of natural superiority acquired at birth as the right of any English Christian. It was something she couldn't see, could never see, he suspected, but it was there and was probably there, to some degree or other, in everyone of True English Blood who was born into the greatest empire

76

the world had ever known and had never questioned the raw and savage hand that gained it.

Yet Z himself was torn between two worlds – the one of the Jubilee and the one of the ghetto. That he was English, there was no doubt. He spoke the language of the Queen and could write it with the flair and fluency that few others could master. He enjoyed the company of a wide network of friends from many backgrounds and classes, most of whom were Christian. And he had even toyed with the idea creating a new Judeo-Christian liturgy which would take the ancient moral law and update it to modern times and the changing cultures born of the social melting pot.

But he was also a Jew whose parents came from Eastern Europe. He was the first generation to be educated into English customs and English ways – through the demands of the Board of Guardians supported by a network of schools and synagogues dedicated to the course of rapid assimilation. And Z, who went through that process, became as English as his antecedents had become German or French. Yet in his heart there existed another realm and another life that was attached to a curious lineage, one which was historical and metaphorical and sometimes more real and meaningful than the one he led in England. And to that extent at least, his Englishness was simply a useful façade – though he never, ever would have admitted it.

What was curious, though he had become quite used to it, was that Maggie didn't see him as a Jew, particularly. Certainly not one of those she referred to as the mysterious others who seemed to have special powers that she both feared and admired. It wasn't that he didn't look Jewish, whatever that meant. His features were similar to certain immigrants from the Russian pale (though some thought they seemed closer to what they called 'negroid'). He didn't wear 'Jewish clothes'

77

though the garments he wore were somewhat strange. It was, of course, his voice, his educated form of speech and his demeanour which could be as English as he wanted it to be – depending on who he was conversing with or what he needed.

Z was, therefore, an intermediary: a bi-cultural interpreter who could swim easily between two oceans. And, as such, Maggie saw him as neither fish nor fowl but a creature all its own. He wasn't of the stereotypical mould and even though she tried not to look at life with blinkered eyes, her thoughts and language had been shaped by the stories of her own antecedents.

When he finally responded to her remark it came in the form of a challenge – a way, he thought, of turning things around and making what seemed to be just another flippant statement carry the weight of its implications. For if the Jews had their protectors ensconced in the citadels of power, why was it that millions under threat of annihilation were so desperate to find a welcoming harbour? Why hadn't the wealthy of their tribe done more to help them than simply making token gestures? Could it be that these wealthy Jews – the Rothschilds, the Mocattas - would rather see them starve than encourage them on for fear of sending the wrong signal to the others who were anxiously waiting in the wings of Russified Poland? If history had taught the Jewish people one thing alone, he concluded, it was that the ordinary Jews, the masses, could depend on no one but themselves to help them – just like the ordinary Christian.

Lipski, he told her, was an example of this. His guilt had yet to be established, though the circumstantial evidence seemed firmly against him. But guilty or innocent, the Jewish establishment would rather let him hang than raise a finger to protect him, because, in the end, they were more concerned about their own place and position rather than the fate of some poor, Eastern European immigrant.

Maggie listened to him speak in fascination. She was in awe of his emotive powers, struck by his vulnerability and confused by his misinterpretation of what actually was going on inside her head. But Maggie was not someone easily intimidated and she would say what she had to say regardless of the consequences. So she took a deep breath and asked him the most obvious question that followed from his comment: if it were true that the Jewish establishment wasn't interested in protecting Lipski, where was all the money for his legal defence coming from?

CHAPTER 8

WHERE WAS THE money coming from? It was a good question, thought Z. And Maggie wasn't the only one who asked it. Even Mordecai could see it was a question that needed looking into – though quietly and discretely. If Lipski had found himself a good lawyer, who was paying for it? The young man hadn't a shilling to his name. Nor, as far as anyone knew, did he have any relatives or friends who were much better off than he was. And judging from the reaction on the street, given the rope and the opportunity, most people would have been happy to hang him themselves.

So in whose interest was it that Lipski be well represented? If Mordecai was any indication of how the established Jews were feeling – as he often was – then this case would be quickly dispensed with, disappearing into the dustbin of history before anyone had time to notice. For, Z suspected, the last thing the Guardians wanted was a grandstanding lawyer splashing the trial into the headlines and promoting the idea that if it wasn't one Jew who killed the pregnant angel then it must have been two.

Certainly there was more here than met the eye. And Z, who had been pondering the materials he had collected on the case for several days now, had come to realise that this was a story far more complex than he had first thought – complex and troubling. Several things bothered him about it and primary among them was the lack of a credible motive. Why would a quiet young man with no past history of violence, who everyone said was gentle and well-behaved, who was engaged to a proper young woman (one who supported his plea of innocence unswervingly), who was just starting to move up in the world – why would someone like that go into a penniless woman's room in the middle of the day knowing full well others were in the house just a few feet away on the opposite side of the paper-thin wall? Why on earth would he pour acid down her throat, pour some down his own and then crawl under her bed and wait to either die or be found? On the other hand, it was claimed that the bedroom door was locked from the inside. And at that time of day Batty Street was busy enough that two large men could hardly climb out the second storey window without having been observed. It was the paradoxical nature of the case that Z found intriguing; one which generated a multitude of questions - and the closer he looked, the more he saw.

Of his own circle of friends, when he told them of the case, one in particular found it of serious interest – though more as a conundrum than a question of justice. His name was Doyle, a young doctor living in Southsea at the time who came into London on occasion to visit the offices of Strand Magazine where his investigative crime stories using the diagnostic techniques he had studied while a medical student in Edinburgh were being enthusiastically published. He was one of the rising young stars of the new literary world descending on London then – someone Z's friend, Jerome, wanted desperately to bring on board the magazine venture he had planned (which with a little luck and much sweat and tears would soon get off the ground – or so he told Doyle during their occasional meetings in Soho). It was at one of those informal planning sessions that Z, who was also part of that motley circle, had given him a brief run-down of the case and Doyle had told him, first, never to take police reports at face value because they were so sloppy and rushed and all too often were motivated by political expediency; secondly, to take accounts of witnesses with a grain of salt since they

81

weren't trained observers and were exceedingly vulnerable to suggestion – especially by those they saw in authority; and thirdly, never to trust the locks on the doors of East End houses.

But it was Jerome who was to provide the most assistance. For Jerome, who at that time could hardly make ends meet through his literary enterprises, was still lingering on the fringes of the legal trade in order to bring in a few steady shillings.

The Factories of the Law, Z thought, were so different from the noisy pursuits of the artisan's shop with its constant din of people and machine, scrapping, hammering, pounding pliant matter into something marketable. In the legal trade there is quiet and peace, save for the scratching of pens which belie the nature of their intent, buried deep beneath the mounds of paper, which blandly registers in ink the consignment of some poor soul to the fires of Hell.

It wasn't to a solicitor's office, however, that Z was headed. It was another sort of building on a back street of the city amongst the charnel houses – a place lit from dusk to dawn with flickering oil lamps and coal fires that left an indelible stain of soot on all the windows. And inside men – no, shadows of men – ghostly, grey, crammed before desks five by five and six by six from front to rear. Some young, some aged, all squinty-eyed, they were the copyists – lowest of the low in the legal chain which led from this sad and sorry lot to dandified attorneys drenched in champagne and truffles. They were the legal equivalent of galley slaves, either rejects from solicitors' firms cast aside after endless years of service, or newbies – those without enough schooling or connections to start off as an articled clerk working their way upwards with the alacrity of ants caught in a pit of rancid butter.

82

Unfortunate enough to be literate and have a passable hand, they copied endless pages of script picked up from firms around the city at closing time and brought here, to the free-lance copy office to be ready at daybreak. By the midnight hour, shaky hands would reach beneath their desks for liquid stamina. Nearing dawn, red eyes would be rubbed in a vain attempt to stop the jittery movement of the script they sought to copy. After a few hours more, fearful of error - a blotch or smudge which meant the painstaking process must start all over from scratch again - it was time for one last drink from the bottle which was always at the ready. But then, alas, the jittery lines would take on a life of their own and start jumping from the page – letters of the alphabet flying all around like Russian Tartars and these poor, tired men whose stiffness could only be alleviated by another drink of dirt-cheap, rot-gut whisky, trying hopelessly to swat them down.

All this for one penny a folio of seventy-two words, thought Z. And he ran it through his mind again – one penny for seventy-two words. That meant 864 words needed copying before a shilling could be earned. And that without error or one needed to start over again. But then he wondered how many words had he, himself, written for naught? A thousand? A million? A writer's life was not a happy one – if happiness was found in pounds and pence. And yet there were no end of 'wallers' hanging around, his friend, Jerome had told him – men who lingered outside the copy offices leaning forever against the façade of buildings opposite in the hope that the master would look out the dirty window of the work room and see them. For, in truth, no matter how difficult and demeaning, a top-rate copyist working flat out could earn in a good week between four and five pounds. And then he could quit and have a decent binge until he was broke and had to queue up for that miserable work again. It was a way of getting through the winter. Come summer they might move off to Kent and pick hops instead. It suited some people, said Jerome, though it didn't suit him. For him it was just a way of quickly picking up a few extra bob till he sold another story to a magazine or newspaper.

Fortunately, Jerome was an eternal optimist – if he waited around another few decades till a certain children's book was written, he might even have been called a Pollyanna. Ideas shot from his fevered brow like the puffed rice breakfast cereal that was all the rage in the energised packaged food industry. Jerome had lots of ideas, he was a young man on the move. But right at that moment he was a copyist.

On more than one occasion he, Jerome, had said that it wasn't flamboyance they were after but a moderately good time, with articulate friends, decent whisky and aromatic tobacco. He had written an entire book (several, in fact) on this subject, praising the virtue of what he called 'idleness' – not laziness, mind you, but those enduring moments of space and time which nurture dreams and creativity. Central to this theme were the notions of respect and tolerance. Jerome had built his career on this simple idea, which led some people to think he was a sluggard. But nothing could have been further from the truth. As far as Z was concerned, Jerome worked harder than anyone he knew – with the possible exception of Z, himself.

Z trusted Jerome because, like Z, he had no one to fall back on but himself. And knowing that made a great deal of difference to Z because he felt that if Jerome said something, he said it with honour and if he said he would do something, he would do it with pleasure. In short, Jerome was someone Z could believe – not least because Jerome had once also lived in the East End and had been looked upon as an 'other'. Not an 'other' because of race, but an 'other' because he was different in his head. And that, Z felt, was the biggest 'otherness' of all.

Like Z, Jerome was a dreamer. You could see it in his eyes which sometimes would drift off into another land far away from the person sitting next to him. Those who knew him well (and few people did) would comment on how grounded he seemed, how self-possessed. And yet he himself didn't feel 'grounded' at all. Like many people with a strong inner life, he had a curious sense that there were things he was bound to achieve, that somehow, in a vague and ill-defined way, he had a unique purpose and that there were even vaguer spirits to guide him. And, yes, there were times he felt he was playing out a pre-determined role in the theatre of life – something reinforced during his years as a vagabond actor with a touring company.

But probably the same things could have been said of the other young writers in their circle – people like Doyle and Barrie, sometimes Shaw, and the blind poet, Marsden. They all were dreamers who had come up 'the hard way.' Nothing was given to them. What they had they had earned through sweat and toil and having had the courage to follow their dreams and listen to their own inner voices.

Perhaps, in a strange way, they were fortunate to be living at that particular time which the Jubilee represented. Though, for them (most of them, anyway – Kipling aside), it was just a lot of misplaced pomp and circumstance. A recently lettered public was emerging from the ill-lit offices with worm-eaten desks and the factories of some Dickensian Coketown into the dawn of a new and more open age where a multitude of penny magazines stuffed the shelves of railway newsagents providing unlimited fodder for the recently contrived class of commuters who consumed them voraciously as a means of all too briefly escaping their rapidly encroaching drudgery some twenty minutes down the track.

Yes, change was in the air. You could smell it along with all the dung churned up by the soon-to-be outmoded omnibus, but more especially by the new odours and sounds and sensations blaring at you from the walls, the stalls and the pages of papers like the Pall Mall Gazette. Suddenly (well, perhaps not so suddenly as all that) the stereotypical image of the Victorian lady and gentleman, prim and properly covering their piano legs with modesty socks, was being ripped apart with the vengeance one feels about a lie that's been allowed to fester just too long. The screen was being torn down to reveal a mirage that was never really there. But whatever was there - and that, of course, was open to interpretation - everyone knew it wasn't going to be there long.

It was an idea that was approaching with an unstoppable force that bordered on certainty. And like most ideas that brought with it the seeds of the new along with the annihilation of the old, the first thing to go was the language which propped up the ancient and outmoded – for there is nothing more sterile and stultifying than a language that has outlived its moment.

Was either Jerome or Z, himself, conscious of their role in this revolutionary reconstruction? Probably not. Marx's son-in-law used to chum around with them on occasion. And they all knew Eleanor, his wife. Who didn't? They were quite aware that the axis of the world was shifting - how fast, again, depended on whom you asked - but they weren't out to bang their drums (well, maybe Shaw but he did it with so much panache that nobody minded). And, Z, as we noted before, waited to bang his drum till later. Jerome never banged a drum at all, though after the War to End All Wars he wondered whether he should have.

The critics were not kind to them. Of course, critics are hardly ever kind – it's not their job, they would argue. But critics always have an axe to grind and a family to maintain – they either uphold the old regime or usher in the new. In either case their job is similar to the Praetorian Guards or The Young Turks who will soon become Praetorian Guards if their heads haven't been lopped off.

They, the critics, were especially unkind to Jerome (or would be, soon). They called him 'vulgar' and 'coarse' which was really quite curious for a fellow whose stories were so incredibly gentle. What they meant by that, however, was that he dared to write in what they called 'the vernacular' – throwing 'literary style' to the winds - or snobbish pretence, depending on which way you looked at it. But they did him and, by implication, the rest of his friends a great favour by giving them a collective sobriquet of 'New Humorists'. They hadn't meant it as a compliment but the rubric stuck, lifting them out of the great anonymity of amorphous faces and transforming them into a Movement - the dream of every half-baked writing group.

But back then, in the summer of 1887, they were still young pups chasing after bones. The bones, it is true, had become meatier and more frequently tossed so that, by then, both Z and Jerome were able to hear more clearly the Sirens' call. And, in fact, though they both would have many decades left in their writing career, it is of interest that the books each of them would be remembered for would be written in the following year.

It was Jerome that Z had come to see. Jerome knew who was who amongst the pack of braying lawyers (most of whom he discovered hadn't a thought in their head except what to eat for dinner) and, in fact, had studied for the law himself before he gave it up to write. It had been a difficult choice – law was boring, tedious, tendentious and much more interested in itself than justice, but it had a certain status and security that writing didn't. Besides, for a bright young man who was as personable and energetic as Jerome, the chances at success were high (or at least higher than writing novels). But Jerome was a dreamer who had a way with words. And a dreamer with a touch of magic was possibly what the world wanted then, he imagined. So he chose the route of least resistance, the one that felt right to him. It was risky, but so was everything in life. And Jerome, who had been orphaned before he was old enough to grow a moustache and had been responsible for himself ever since, was bound and determined to make his way in life. But he would do it in his manner – with a smile and a wink. After all, 1887 wasn't a bad time to be alive. Not if you were a young man like him.

They had a drink at the corner pub where Z told him about his interest in the Whitechapel murder case. Had Jerome heard anything over the grape vine? Did he know who was chosen to lead the defence? Jerome told him he didn't know for certain, but rumour had it that man was Geoghegan - a brilliant lawyer who wasn't afraid to take on the most difficult litigation. Maybe Z had heard of his defence of the Dynamitards? It was a brave and celebrated moment and, for a time, all of London knew him – or at least claimed they did. There was only one slight problem, though. Geoghegan was fond of drink, like most men of his ilk - overly fond, some said. He was honest, forthright and sincere, but he had been known to succumb on occasion – and then there might be problems, mightn't there? So it was a risky choice but, according to Jerome, there was none better.

CHAPTER 9

Z HAD A brother named Louis who was also a writer. Unlike Z, Louis was hardly known and wrote in self-imposed obscurity. Not that he particularly cared, for he was more of a bohemian and felt the idea of career was a 19th century bourgeois notion which had nothing much to do with art; he often said – to anyone who would listen – that an artist who made money from his work had probably succumbed to the call of mammon rather than the whispers of the muse. And so he wrote because he wanted to write and that was that. Anything else, he said, came from a false sense of pride. Of course these might have been sentiments that came from having a successful brother – one who people expected great and glorious things from. All the same, Louis wasn't really bothered. He travelled in his own world of like-minded artists. And together they would go off on jaunts across the Channel, for days of peripatetic philosophising and hazy, turquoise-coloured nights of rum and absinthe, even though they had hardly more than the price of the steamer crossing and a bare room in the garret of some cheap hotel on the Rive Gauche.

It was Z's brother who told him of Greenberg, a Jewish philanthropist of Eastern European origins who had worked his way up from poverty to become rich and well respected, if not extraordinarily wealthy, and had helped Louis out on several occasions. Greenberg was one of a small group of self-made businessmen who were nurtured by the ghetto and wanted to give something back to those they had left behind in the dank and dingy rooms of the East End. These were men like Herman Landau, himself a Polish Jew made good, who were willing to stand up and speak out against the xenophobic ranting that echoed not only on the streets but in the boardrooms and was being closely observed by opportunistic politicians who would tone down the language but not the intent in order to gain an active following they could exploit sometime in the very near future. They were few, but together they became a collective thorn in the side of the Guardians, who insisted on a 'softly, softly' approach to all things Jewish which came into conflict with anything Christian.

As it happened, Louis had gone to visit Greenberg just that very day and had found him deep in discussion with someone named Myers – a rather intense man, probably in his mid-thirties, who had the habit of mopping his sweaty brow with his handkerchief and then using it to wipe his glasses. Myers, it turned out, worked as the managing clerk for a law firm and was discussing a case that it seemed Greenberg, at Myers' urging, had placed with them. The case was a gruesome murder. The accused was named Lipski. And the law firm Myers represented was that of John Hayward, solicitor.

Louis wasn't able to stay very long as he had just dropped by on his way to the British Library, but, from what he could make out, Greenberg had already gone some way towards establishing a defence committee for Lipski, being convinced, for some reason, of the young man's innocence – as was Myers, himself. (Whether it was Greenberg who had convinced Myers or vice versa was something Louis hadn't found out.)

In a way, Z was surprised to hear that his brother had stumbled onto this conjunction of people and events at the same time Z, himself, was searching for it. But in another way he wasn't. Louis had a wide network of friends and acquaintances – most of whom were either artists or writers or those who liked being around artists and writers; that is to say his friends and acquaintances were all people wrapped up in words and images (people who some years down the road would be collectively termed 'the chattering classes'). Z was well aware that the 'Whitechapel Murder Case' – as it had come to be called – was the main topic of discussion among those who had anything at all to do with the East End, especially after the inquest when it had gone beyond the streets and into the more sedate living rooms of the Jewish intelligentsia. And as enough time had passed since the brutal facts of the murder had caused that initial frisson of vulgar excitement, people had started to consider the events themselves and the personalities involved and why an ostensibly 'nice young man' should have done such a terrible act – if, indeed, he had done it at all.

It was that first seed of doubt, that stirring of suspicion by those who looked just a few inches underneath the surface and thought that something didn't seem quite right – as if it were all too straightforward. And there was all that weight, all that enormous weight of circumstance, the viability of which had been camouflaged by the hounds braying for blood. Something smacked of the relentless march to the gallows that happened when the poor and powerless were trapped inside a bureaucratic nightmare of crime and punishment; a feeling most people who had gone through the refugee experience intuitively comprehended as that horrific process which severed them from the nurturing breast of humanity, degrading them into the lower ranks of the animal order to be herded, corralled and possibly slaughtered all in the name of stability. Yes, they understood that feeling quite well.

So was it at all surprising that someone like Greenberg, someone who had risen above the tumultuous fray but knew in his heart where that terror was coming from – was it at all surprising that he would have become interested in such a case? Z thought not. But, then again, Z was always a great admirer of the power of coincidence. Coincidence was all over the place and you could make of it what you wanted.

Louis was quite happy to introduce Z and Greenberg before going off on another of his travels – this time to Holland – and Greenberg was quite happy to meet him. He, of course, knew of Z and his work and realised that someone like Z could be quite useful. And it was through Greenberg that Z came to meet Myers, the managing clerk for Hayward's law firm.

So what did Z find out though his brief but fruitful meeting? He discovered, firstly, that there was a rump defence committee that had been set up. Secondly, that this committee was contacting Jews of some means who might be sympathetic to their cause (which, at this point, was simply raising enough money to provide Lipski with the possibility of having good legal representation). Thirdly, that this quest was not easy as most of the well-off Jews had been squeezed dry from never-ending appeals for aid and assistance to their unfortunate brethren. Fourthly, that most Jews of position were frightened of being identified with this case. Fifthly, though there was a general feeling that Lipski was guilty, there were a number of people of limited means who wanted him to have a fair hearing and therefore were willing to contribute a few hard earned shillings. And, lastly, though, as of yet, the defence hadn't any evidence that would contradict the prosecution's case Greenberg and Myers themselves were convinced of his innocence because they both had been struck by the young man's character and appearance. Myers especially was quite resolute in saying Lipski was simply another unfortunate victim of East End brutality coupled with incompetent policing and a rush to judgement. He was certain that a proper investigation would eventually exonerate him. However, as there wasn't enough time or money to launch a proper investigation of their own, they would have to construct a defence based on refuting the prosecution's circumstantial evidence as extraordinary pressure was being applied to have the case over and done with as quickly as possible. So, if they had any chance of saving this ill-fated young man, they would have to work fast.

CHAPTER 10

THE LIPSKI CASE had been handed over to the Treasury for prosecution (as most important cases were) – and for the next several weeks they and the defence (such as it was) went about preparing their legal disputations. There were, of course, the boring formalities to go through – the Magistrate's hearing, the Grand Jury indictment, the charges being read – all of which were routine and matter-of-fact (or matter-of-fiction depending one's perspective).

Z, meanwhile, had shifted his attention to other matters. The case had triggered something in his head, something that had been gnawing at him for a while. There was a crisis brewing. He realised that. But it wasn't the same crisis that many people, such as Maggie, had identified. It wasn't the crisis of poverty, degradation or overcrowding – not in themselves, at least. It had more to do with the ceaseless waves of refugees that were pouring in from the East, uprooted from their ancestral soil and sweeping across Europe, lost and friendless, in a desperate quest for sanctuary

Z is in his study, seated at his desk. He takes out a box of newspaper clippings and looks over several from the past few months. He glances through them, one by one:

'A wholesale expulsion of Jews is being carried out in Kiev, Russia. It is reported that the number has reached the enormous figure of 15,000...'

And the next...

'In reply to letters from Needy Jews wishing to go to Spain principally from Russia and Rumania, we warn them that they have not the slightest chance of succeeding and only starvation awaits them should they emigrate there...'

And the next...

'The anti-Semitic deputy Dr Schonerer, enlivened the last sitting of the Austrian Reichstag by presenting a petition against the Jews, which was signed by 40,000 persons. The petitioners abused the Jews at large without having any definite request to make of them...'

And the next...

'Some very bad riots at Pressburg in Hungary have had to be suppressed by the military. The foolish old story was raised about a girl having been decoyed away by a Jew that her blood might be used for sacrificial purposes and the house of the man suspected was besieged by a howling mob of 2,000 persons, who smashed all their windows and uttered threats of murder. The customary proposal was then made to go and wreck all the Jewish shops but the soldiers charged the mob with their bayonets fixed and, after some trouble, restored order...'

Then he focuses on one from the Jewish Chronicle which he had pasted onto a piece of foolscap so as to make some notations:

'The speeches at the annual meeting of the Jewish Board of Guardians last Sunday were mainly occupied with one problem – the increasing influx of foreign Jews to this country or rather the increasing difficulty of disposing of them when they do come here...'

He reads the article over once more and shakes his head in dismay. It is, he thinks, a typically mealy-mouthed response from the organ of the Jewish establishment. First, they tried to show how relatively little impact Jewish immigration was having on the economy while, at the same time arguing that 'each new family adds fresh units to the army of competitors who are bringing down the level of subsistence'. Then they blame the Russian political situation for making life intolerable for the Jews, yet they write, 'our very interest in their welfare would in many cases cause us to put obstacles in the way of their coming hither without prospect of earning even as scanty a livelihood as they can manage to eke out in Russia.'

But Z realises there is a problem, an enormous problem, which even that most pompous of newspapers identified. Whitechapel, for all its rookeries and boarding houses that seemed to absorb endless bodies, packing them into subdivided rooms of smaller and smaller partitions, in reality was only a very limited plot of land which was bounded by nature, in the form of the Thames, and by man, in the form of the railway embankments. It could not contain even a small portion of the enormous Russian-Polish refugee population, no matter how much they tried to squeeze themselves in. It was just physically impossible. Yet the tidal barriers had been breached on the Eastern frontier. And once breached there was no turning back again.

Z reads this article over one more time, rubs his eyes, sighs, and in the margin, on the foolscap, he writes, 'What will happen to them now? Where is our Moses when we so desperately need him?' underlining the questions three times with his pen. Then he puts the article back into the box where he was storing it and closes the lid. After placing the box onto the shelf above his desk, he takes a fresh piece of paper and sets to work on a story he's been commissioned to write on the people of the ghetto.

He has an image in his head. It's the image of a girl, a little girl standing in the queue at the Jews Soup Kitchen for the last of the watery soup and a loaf of bread which she must bring home to her invalid father. After a long and tedious wait she finally receives her allotment and is returning home again. But on her way back she is stopped by a man. He asks her for some bread, some soup. He's very hungry. But she needs the food for her father. What is she to do? He asks again, this time more forcefully. It's clear he'll take it if she doesn't give it to him. So she gives him some and he wants some more. This she cannot do. Infuriated, he reaches out to grab the loaf, but, in doing so, he causes her to spill the pitcher of soup. The little girl runs away, leaving the man who was the source of her distress, eating the crust he has stolen. But once he has a little food in him, he begins to weep, for now he suddenly realises what he has done. And he starts to feel never was there a man lower than him. Never, ever was there another man more abysmal than what he felt that day.

But this man, this thief, is not a villain. He is an immigrant and has recently arrived, just the day before. He is in London all alone, with no money and no place to go. When he left Warsaw there were a few gold sovereigns that he had sewn into the lining of his coat. But they were gone. How had he lost his meagre funds just a few hours after coming to London? After disembarking he was met by a man who addressed him kindly and offered to take him to a boarding house which was run by a cousin who would look after him, give him safe housing and food, deferring payment until he found work. The cousin did this out of the goodness of his heart as he, too, knew what it was like to have been a penniless immigrant. As it turned out, this gentleman, the man who met him at the docks, was not so gentle. He took him for a ride to the far reaches of town, took his money, and left him there to find his own way back. Back to where? He had no money and no place to go. Of course, there was never any cousin or, if there was, not one with a boarding house filled with immigrant Jews who were given a room and food out of the goodness of his heart. So, this man, this soon-to-be thief, struggles to find his way through the intricate maze of

London's streets and byways, back to the East End without a single word of English at his disposal. At least in the East End he can make himself understood, so it's there he belongs. That's the way he feels.

It is almost night when he arrives and he is very cold and hungry. His valise with his few personal possessions has been taken as well, so he has only the clothes he wears. He sees a few beggars plying their trade but he is still too proud to beg. But he is very hungry – he hasn't eaten for several days - his head is beginning to feel light and the world around him is starting to spin. He prays to God and wishes he was back in his little Polish shtetl and thinks that even the Russian army from which he has escaped couldn't have been worse than where he is now. He walks through the fading light, down narrow streets smelling of sewage and rotting food which he cannot see because if he had he would have eaten it. Finally, he reaches a quiet alley and, feeling he can go no further, leans himself against a dirty brick wall, wet with slime and spittle, and then slowly lets his body slide down until he lies, exhausted, on the edge of the dirt road. An older man, a bit unstable from drink, comes down the street and must climb over him because his body is blocking the path and the older man curses him as he climbs over this unfortunate creature lying huddled on the ground who, at that moment, feels like a piece of rubbish that has been tossed from the window of one of those warm houses across the road. It is as if he, himself, has been tossed out to rot. This is how he feels. Life is elsewhere. Life is inside those warm houses, not within his mortal being, for he is dead – dead to himself and dead to the world. But at that instant, just when he feels the cold claw of Azrael tighten around his chest, at that very moment he sees a girl coming down the street. He sees her like a little angel, a vision of the most astounding beauty, surrounded by a phosphorescent glow radiating sparkles like a gossamer of gold. The girl is dressed in shabby clothes, but, to him, she wears the robes of a fairy queen. She is holding a pitcher of hot soup in one hand and a loaf of bread wrapped in her cape, the folds of which she clutches in the other. She slows her pace as she nears him, somewhat suspicious perhaps but saddened that another human creature should have been brought to that awful state, lying helpless on the grime encrusted ground just inches from the human filth running through an adjacent ditch into an open sewer. And yet perhaps she saw something in him, something about him that was special because as she comes closer she seems to lose her fear and gives him a sweet and tender smile. Entranced with this magical vision of an angel which he now believes has been sent from heaven to save him, he rises up, till on his knees, and reaches out his hand in supplication. The little girl, who has allowed herself to feel sympathy for this man because she senses he is unlike the multitude of beggars she has seen every day of her life as she walked up and down the road, tears off a bit from her precious loaf and hands it to him. It is just a tiny piece, a crust, which is hardly enough to satisfy his hunger. He holds out his hand for more. The girl now is torn with conflicting emotions. She would like to give this man more bread and perhaps even some soup but the thought of her hungry brother and father, too ill to rise from his bed, suddenly takes over from the sympathy she feels for the strange, frightening man worshiping on his knees before her. The expression on her face now changes from tenderness to terror – both of him and herself, for what she has done and the danger she has brought to her family's sustenance. She edges herself backward, and as she does, the man's vision of the angel suddenly transforms into that of a demonic vixen tantalising him with tasty desire. Now all he sees is the bread and he reaches out and grabs it. Horrified, she tries to pull away. But the man tenaciously clings to it like a drowning swimmer grasping at a bit of flotsam keeping him afloat. The girl cries out. The man by now is oblivious to her and thinks only of the food. The raw desire to satisfy his brutish hunger gives him strength. He pulls and the bread with the girl attached to it comes closer to his swollen lips. The girl cries out again and tugs once more at her loaf but in doing so, she loses hold of the pitcher which slips from her grasp, falling to the ground, its watery contents forming a little stream which slowly oozes along the ground towards the sewage ditch. Aghast, the man falls to his hands and knees and tries to lap up the steaming liquid before it is absorbed into the ground. But it is already hopelessly mixed with the filth of the pavement. The girl takes advantage of his distraction to grab the fallen pitcher and the rest of the bread and runs off, weeping, to her dingy room just a few houses down the road. The man, meanwhile, is on all fours, like a dog, trying to lick at the soup which has already become mud. Even in this state he can still see her and later her image comes back to haunt him – the figure of a small girl, silhouetted in the moonlight, a frightened child, sunk in gloom and despair, who had failed her father and her brother because of a simple act of kindness. And when he thought about it later the man felt as if a knife had gone through his heart and through his soul – a knife that he, himself, had plunged inside his chest; an invisible dagger that would stay there, inside him, forever.

Z put down his pen as he finished writing. Why had this image come to him, he wondered? He knew the girl for he had written about her before. But the man – the man was a stranger. Who was he? And the tragedy, was it really such a tragedy? After all, it was only a loaf of bread and a jug of soup. A loaf of bread and a jug of soup - it was nothing to anyone who ate regularly, who had no idea of hunger. But to those who had tasted the terror of starvation, a jug of soup and a loaf of bread was everything there was in the world. And this man who Z could hardly picture in his head – he knew his soul. He knew this man well. For Z, himself, had once been without bread and soup. And he understood that everything he held dear and cherished came to nothing once hunger had taken him over. And once hunger had taken him over he was capable of anything. Anything. Even... Even what? He wondered. No, there were limits, though he hoped he never had to put himself to test.

Where was this taking him? It's the little girl he was interested in, not the man. The girl whose innocent eyes he had borrowed to view the ghetto so it could be understood as only a child could understand it – as a world unto itself, a world of poverty but also one of humour as well as deep emotions. She was bringing the soup and bread home and would, he thought, trip upon opening the door, fall and spill the contents of the jug herself onto the floor whereupon the soup would leak through the floorboards onto the wedding dress of the young woman who was preparing for her nuptials in the apartment below. The young woman from below would then bound angrily upstairs to berate the poor child for damaging her trousseau, totally oblivious of the tragedy which meant the family would be without their evening meal. And it would be her little brother licking the floorboards to get the last of the broth before it seeped into the cracks, not that mysterious man who just seemed to appear out of nowhere.

PART II

Week 5: The Trial

CHAPTER 11

ON FRIDAY MORNING, July 29th, Z found himself outside the largest of the Old Bailey courtrooms along with the milling crowd of expectant observers all dressed in sombre tones touched with a dash of the frivolous, giving the appearance, he thought, of something between a Jubilee Ball and a Jewish funeral. They waited patiently (or not) for the great, sanctimonious doors of authority to open onto the culmination of what had become an epic every bit as large as a ghetto version of a Shakespearean drama (at least they hoped as much, even though few if any of them had ever heard of Shakespeare – 'Maybe he's the *shmata* man on Wentworth Street between Moishe-the-butcher and the Horwitz–the–*gonif*?') Though only a few would actually get inside the chamber itself, the rest would be close enough to feel they had - if only vicariously - and, thus, to have participated in the moment. For to participate in the moment is to be, rather than not to be. It is fulminating with the present. You are, therefore, alive – even though tomorrow you may be dead. Like Lipski.

But something was wrong. Z could sense it immediately. There was an acrid scent in the stale courthouse air: the unmistakable smell of barely contained panic. Where was it

coming from? He noticed a circle of men gathered to the side
– professional men from their appearance. He couldn't hear
their words but he could feel the intensity of the emotions
like the urgency that might have been felt on the field of
battle when someone had forgot to bring the cannon.

One of the men – there were three and he was the
leaner (thin as a string-bean too long in the sun, someone
once said of him) - was gesticulating, wildly, with his hands,
like convulsive supplications to a god who, it seemed, had
become significantly less beneficent than twenty minutes
earlier. Another rather corpulent man, was thrusting out
a pointed finger toward a humble-looking figure opposite
him. The corpulent man had a face that was red and was
growing even redder.

The man being fingered, at first glance looked to Z like
a human sponge whose sole purpose was to soak up any
emotional detritus thrown at it. But the slight enigmatic
smile he wore was in striking contrast to the pliant, rather
unctuous-looking figure the large man with the red face was
hectoring. It was that sense of curious contrast along with his
foggy spectacles which he had removed and was wiping with
his stiff white handkerchief, that made him recognisable to
Z as Myers, the man he had seen the other day at the house
of Greenberg. And catching his eye, Z saw him squint, in a
painful sign of recognition.

A moment later the other two men walked off. The one
who had pointed a threatening finger was Hayward, Z
thought. But, he was wrong. Hayward, as it happened, was
the bean left out in the sun. And when he found that out, he
realised at once why Myers was so very important to a man
like Hayward. It was as clear as light through crystal, neatly
refracted into its true colours, that Hayward desperately
needed someone like Myers who was calm under stress and

104

could, in the most trying circumstances, persevere no matter what was thrown (or pointed) at him.

As Myers had been left alone to ponder - Hayward and the mysterious corpulent-looking man having gone off - Z took the opportunity to approach him. It was a delicate moment. Myers, Z understood, was not made of stone. But he knew others of this sort; others who had learned that time-honoured technique of apparent servility – finessing a need but inside feeling the sharpened blade of history twisting in the dark reaches of their gut. Yet for people like Myers, there were two dignities they possessed – one for the Jewish and the other for the Christian world. The one for the Christian world was pliable – it could be bought and sold. The one for the Jewish world was held in a mental sanctuary many thousands of years old. And it was that duality – among others – which made someone like Myers an extraordinary man who could maintain his honour while being treated like a dog. For dogs are dogs and men are men, but survival meant that sometimes one had to play the mongrel even if it was a momentary invention.

Coming up to Myers, Z had the feeling that there was something the law clerk would have liked to have told him, something he would have gladly shared, to lighten the burden bearing heavily on the slightness of his frame, envisaged by his shoulders, stooped as they were, which appeared to carry a mighty but invisible weight upon them. Yet the wrinkling of his forehead indicated there was something else, some other mysterious reason why he couldn't freely speak. That there was trouble, Z had no doubt. Trouble was in the air. Z could feel it, taste it, smell it – it had absorbed through his skin and into his lungs like a toxic mould, too fine to see, but easy enough to ingest - though that venomous taste might also have been caused by a persistent image which had intruded

105

into Z's imagination; that of a shadowy figure with a waxen face swinging, limp, at the end of some carefully knotted rope made out of jute, hemp or sisal (the actual construction of the hangman's noose was something he had made a note to find out about).

Myers was in a hurry - he didn't want to get into a long conversation, but there was something he needed to tell him. It was about Geoghegan – Geoghegan, the barrister with the silver tongue who had courageously defended the Dynamitards; Geoghegan, the hero of the oppressed; Geoghegan the saviour of the underdog – Geoghegan, Geoghegan, Geoghegan - what happened to Geoghegan? Myers lifted an imaginary bottle and put it to his mouth as his lips took on an ironic twist.

So who would present the defence? Couldn't there be a postponement?

There would be no postponement. The defence was to be presented by a man named McIntyre with Geoghegan's limited assistance.

And who was this man named McIntyre?

Oh, a very good barrister by repute. Also in Geoghegan's chambers. They say he's a fine commercial lawyer.

A fine commercial lawyer? Has he ever tried a criminal case?

Myers's face looks pained. There's no reply. Z thinks that Myers wants to say something more but feels he can't. Not yet, anyway. Why does Z suspect this? He's not sure. Perhaps it's a look, something in his eye, a movement of the hand, a curious tilt of his head. How does one account for intuition?

So there it was in a nutshell – but from what kind of nut? A commercial lawyer brought in at the last minute to defend a poverty-stricken Jew accused of murder while the people's champion of misplaced justice bows out due to a

106

marinated liver. There must be something in that, Z thought – something sublimely metaphorical. Poetry could always be found in the grotty grime of life; how else had his people survived for so long, he asked himself.

Z had wangled a seat in the area reserved for 'the gentlemen of the press'. Actually, Mordecai had wangled it for him. Wangling was something Mordecai was good at, even though one wouldn't have thought so by looking at him. Mordecai had many connections in small and mostly unimportant circles. If you wanted a select piece of kosher meat, Mordecai was your man. Getting a seat in the press box at an important trial, Z thought, was probably out of Mordecai's league, but apparently it wasn't. Perhaps there was a Jewish link somewhere in the courthouse, a minor civil servant who might have exchanged small favours with him. That's how Mordecai's world was constructed - a favour here, a kindness there; it was the petty cash of the newspaper trade, even for one as miniscule as the Record.

He was seated between a dandified man from the Times and a boyish chap (who could easily have been a short haired girl in trousers) sketching the trial for London Illustrated. The man from the Times smelled equally of cologne and brandy; the boy from London Illustrated reeked of turpentine and charcoal.

It was the aura of the place that struck him. Z had never been in court before, let alone the likes of the Old Bailey, with its Bastille walls of dark granite and its awesome rooms of mahogany and leather. The boisterous anarchy of the corridors vanished once inside the hallowed chambers of the law. Settled in the public galleries, as the mighty doors had shut cutting off all and sundry from the world outside, a sacred space was created where everything great and small

107

was under the discipline of protocol, precedent and the elliptical pathway of the planets.

And suddenly Z found himself in a different world, one which he neither understood nor appreciated. It was a world more akin to the stage than real life, except here fantasy and reality were merged in a brew that would end in a conclusion about someone's death and someone else's existence. Roles would be played out, speeches would be made and in the end twelve men would pass judgement upon some unfortunate nonentity who would find himself either dangling from a rope or free to go on his merry way as if it were all a bad dream and he had finally awoken. It was, therefore, theatre with the direst consequence. So all the pomp and circumstance, the granite, the mahogany, the finest leathers - they were all part of the production which enabled this particular kind of performance to be taken seriously by those who would otherwise smash the place up, ripping it apart, stone by stone as had been done not so many years before by ordinary people on the other side of the channel.

The reverent hush, therefore, that occurred when the clock struck ten and Mr Justice James Fitzjames Stephen entered the room dressed in his finest horsehair wig and his blood bright scarlet robe trimmed with the fur of a skinned ermine, proceeded by a series of dignitaries including the Lord Mayor and the London sheriff – this hush, was it not similar to the one that took place before the raising of the playhouse curtain? Could not this procession have been seen as similar to the parade of actors who came on stage prior to a medieval pageant? That there was power in these vestments of authority, Z could not deny. But looking at them with his metaphorical eye, nurtured on the visions of the ghetto, he could only see the farce – even though underneath lurked the dark face of tragedy. And he wondered if monkeys had

108

been dressed in ermine and scarlet and bestowed with horse-hair wigs, whether they would have been given the dignity of court like those who trouped in that day with countenances so grave and solemn.

The architecture of the trial chamber was of a curious design, Z thought. The spectators, the jurors and onlookers, on one side of the room faced the attorneys, the defence and prosecution, seated at the other. Against the third wall was the judge, seated magisterially at his dais, facing the prisoner, at the other extreme, standing lonely at the dock. Four sides facing one another: the observers, the attorneys, the prisoner and the judge. Each side was separated from the other; each had its boundaries, each had its purpose. It was a formulaic show, Z thought – one designed for ritual; devised to create a sense of awe and reverence. And in that it well succeeded. For all the rough and boisterous banter in the halls ended abruptly when the processions of wigs and robes trooped in leaving in its wake a raptured silence.

The boy from the Illustrated was sketching furiously, for all he was worth, splashing out frantically with his pen. He had set up a contraption, rather like a collapsible easel that sat neatly on his lap with little built-in perches for his various inks containers. The position of the easel made it easy for Z to glance at the work and as he watched the lad construct the cast of characters that surrounded them, he realised how different a vision the young man had of the people he sketched than Z, himself, was verbally drawing in his head.

The quick sketch of the judge, for example, Z felt, was barely recognisable save that both the drawing and the man were clean shaven. He had managed to get the general shape of the head but missed all the details of significance – the straggles of hair jutting wildly from beneath the wig; the thickness of the lips, the slackness of the jowls, the heaviness of the chin, the lethargy in the eyes behind the smudgy, oval-shaped glasses.

The lawyers were slightly better drawn he felt. Geoghegan, with his drooping moustache expressed little more than tired exhaustion. McIntyre, his replacement, had a quiet biblical look of studied patience. The sketches of the prosecutors weren't bad at all. He had captured the bland, look of Sims – expressing well that tedious feel of the lifelong civil servant. Queen's Counsel Poland, however, was the best of the lot, he thought. The lad had somehow managed to capture the strange lines of his magnificent nose, with the wire spectacles clinging precariously to the brim, his angular features and the rough cut of his beard, all of which together gave him the appearance of a stern headmaster at a school for rowdy children.

But it was the prisoner, the accused, standing behind the glass partition at the dock that he missed entirely, Z felt. There was hardly anything about it recognizable to the figure Z had captured in his eye as soon as the young man had ascended the platform which rose above the court room like a pillory from which the accused looked down, powerlessly, onto the forces which would soon control his destiny. The lad from London Illustrated could hardly get close to the sense of the accused, to the tragedy, to the terror and so he just made a few lines and blotted in some ink around the profile as if a black cloud of gloom had somehow descended into the courtroom to hover over the prisoner's head. But what he missed entirely was that look of boyish innocence – for whether or not Lipski was guilty of a most horrendous murder, he exuded a sense of honest bemusement. And the lad doing the drawing missed that entirely – he missed the freshness of the face and the gentleness of the eyes and the overall expression of quiet wonder, like that of a young man caught up in a strangely persistent nightmare, waiting patiently for it to end so he could he could get on with his life and do whatever it was that God had fated.

CHAPTER 12

GENTLEMEN OF THE jury, look upon the prisoner and harken to his charge. He stands indicted by the name of Israel Lipski, that Israel Lipski on or about the 28th day of June, 1887, in St George's in the East, in the County of Middlesex, unlawfully murdered Miriam Angel. Upon this indictment he had been arraigned, and upon his arraignment he hath pleaded not guilty. Your charge, therefore is to inquire whether he be guilty....

Z GLANCED OVER to see what the brandy soused gentleman from the Times was writing. He was, it seemed, taking down in shorthand the words of the judge as the prisoner stood and the jury listened in rapt and reverent silence. But what did that leave out? Here was the paper of record, the newspaper which informed public opinion and disseminated information throughout the British Empire, around the globe – and what was their man doing? He was simply taking shorthand notes that amounted to an edited transcript.

But what about everything else? What about the things that really mattered? What about the things unsaid? What about the fact that the jurors were never questioned, that their names were simply announced by the clerk and no one asked if they had a relationship to the victim or the accused? Well, probably they didn't, Z thought, but certainly they could have heard about the case. Perhaps they had already formed an opinion or had a personal prejudice that would get in the way of a proper judgement. Maybe they knew the investigating police detective or one of the other witnesses. Or, perhaps they hated refugees, especially immigrant Jews, and thought they should all be hung no matter what. But maybe they were all decent, clear-thinking, unbiased men, sound-hearted and true. Maybe they were, but no one asked so no one knew.

Z studied the men seated in the jury box. They were shadowy figures all dressed in dark and muted clothing; their faces were blurry, indistinct. They seemed to him an amorphous mass. It was as if they formed a single organism all its own with one ear and one brain. And this amorphous mass, this organism, could never be seen or understood by the man from the Times as he meticulously took down the words, the words, the words that droned forth, practiced many times over with only the names that were changed to fill in the blanks.

It was Mr. Poland who opened the case for the prosecution. Harry was his name. Mr. Harry Poland with a very important 'QC' appended. And Z thought, how ironic, how ironic indeed, that Poland should be prosecuting a man called Israel who had come to England seeking refuge from that same benighted nation. But Poland, QC, was more than a name, he was a loyal servant of the State – the State in the form of the Queen, who, herself, at that very time, was still in black and still in mourning, as she had been for the last twenty-five years of her rule. But the Empire that the Queen represented and thus that Harry Poland, QC, served, was more than a person and more than the state: it was an idea. And within that idea of Empire, Victoria was not Queen but Empress. It was as much the Empire that Harry Poland, QC, served as he did Queen and country. This realisation which Z found both fascinating and horrifying, was promulgated by another Israel – though that Israel was of Sephardic roots and thus had the required D, apostrophe, with the suffix 'i' (meaning 'of the Israeli people' – though as it became Anglicised the apostrophe was lost, leaving only the Christianised form,

'Disraeli').

It was Poland who opened the case in his slow, ponderous, methodical manner. Lanky frame, features chiselled out of granite, expressionless eyes peering over the wire frame of his spectacles, he was the very image of a modern, major prosecutor (as William Schwenck Gilbert, himself trained as a lawyer, might have said).

The man from the Times took down his words in summary fashion, thankful for Poland's unhurried delivery which allowed him to make adjustments to his pen. Because of the manner in which he had positioned himself, it was quite easy for Z to see what he wrote.

So what were the significant points the man from the Times thought worthy to mention? These were the ideas that Poland stressed:

1. That the prisoner entered the deceased's room for some purpose, locked the door on the inside, and being discovered by the deceased he battered her with his fist and then administered the nitric acid to her. When finding that she was dead, he took a portion of the acid himself but the quantity he took was not sufficient to kill him.

2. That it was clear the prisoner could not have gone into the deceased's room with the door locked on the inside for any proper purpose.

3. That the prosecution was not suggesting the prisoner bought the nitric acid for the purpose of administering it to the deceased, but having it in his pocket at the time, he used it.

4. That the statement made by Lipski to the police, accusing two others of the murder, was most improbable and with reference to the sovereign he had claimed to have given them, it was the very same morning that the prisoner had asked the landlady to lend him five shillings and she had

114

refused.

Z jotted down these points himself, and as Poland finished his languid speech in the direction of the jury box, without passion, without any sense human feeling whatsoever (he could have been speaking to statues made of salt), Z considered the essence of the case which the prosecution was to present and thought to himself that it was rather flimsy. Point 1 indicated that the prosecution had not decided on a motive. Point 2 depended on the door actually having been locked from the inside – a fact the defence was bound to question. Point 3 suggested that this was simply a crime of opportunity on Lipski's part without any rhyme or reason. And Point 4 challenged Lipski's statement on no other basis than it seeming to be improbable. And, again, the improbability depended on the door having been locked from the inside. (The point about the sovereign didn't make sense to him at all since Lipski might well have needed the sovereign plus five shillings more to purchase his supplies.)

The first witness to be called was Sergeant Bitten who produced a series of drawings – diagrams of the Angels' room, the house and the surrounding neighbourhood. Bitten confirmed that 16 Batty Street had three storeys and that the ground floor was composed of two rooms – a bedroom and a kitchen, which faced the back. There was a passage running alongside the rooms that led to the yard without going into either of the rooms. A short staircase of nine or ten stairs led up to the first floor which, again, consisted of two rooms. Then there was another short staircase which lead to the top floor which was composed of one room only. Bitten testified that the height of the first floor window from the pavement was twelve feet and that after close examination no marks were found on it, indicating that there was no evidence that anyone had used that route as a means of escape – further confirmed by a workman in the house opposite number 16 giving evidence that he had seen nothing unusual.

Z watched in fascination. The detailed sketches, diagrams, measurements – what did they mean? What did they prove? Had they codified and analysed everything about the house so they could present a dispassionate and scientific investigation? Or was this a tried and true way to lead the jury step by step in the direction the prosecution wanted? Was this a method of determining truth or was it a way of selectively choosing facts to bolster their hypothesis?

It's what came next that made Z wonder where the prosecution was trying to lead the jury – what idea they wanted to implant. And looking over at the scribbling reporter next to him (Z fortunately knew shorthand himself), he saw that man from the Times had picked up on the significance by the way he had underlined the following questions and their response:

Did you go up the staircase leading from the first floor to the second floor?

Yes.

It is a fact, is it not, that there is a small window through which you could look on to this bedstead from the staircase outside?

Yes. Commanding a full view of the bed.

A muslin curtain was there?

Yes, but it is a very thin muslin, so you had just the same view.

Thin muslin you say?

Very fine muslin.

Did you see it?

I saw through the muslin.

You could see through the muslin, and get, as you have said, a full view of the bed?

Yes.

116

And of any one who was lying on it?

Yes.

So, thought Z, it wasn't true that the prosecution was avoiding the issue of motive. They were planting a seed – and a vile one, at that. Glancing over at Myers, who was sitting with the defence, he saw him cringe, as McIntyre stood to cross-examine and simply asked about the specific times the diagrams were constructed. Nothing to question the implicit accusation of lust that the prosecution so blatantly suggested. Nothing about how anyone could live in an East End house, with hardly an inch of privacy, constantly stepping over people in various states of dress. How on earth did the prosecution expect to get away with such blatant innuendo? And then looking at the man from the Times, he realised it didn't matter. It didn't matter at all. For this wasn't the boring details of how many steps led upstairs or the exact distance the window was from the ground - this had to do with a fantasy that his readers could secretly relish, something to get their pulses racing fast enough so they could be bothered to read on and maybe even buy the paper again tomorrow (being the Times, of course, nothing more than a titillating suggestion could be broached – but those fine men who prided themselves on reading the Newspaper of Record, those fine men, one and all, would love to have secretly stood on the darkened stairs and furtively gazed through a muslin curtain to salivate over the half clothed body of a woman, Z suspected, no matter if she were fat, pregnant and unattractive. It was the idea itself that they would find exciting, because they had nothing else to bother their addled minds about. The fact that a poor man in a crowded house, half starved, working night and day simply to survive would probably have neither the time, inclination nor desire to take a few precious moments to leer through a dirty widow at a sleeping woman (especially

117

since he could see all the sleeping women he wanted to see through open doors) never entered their minds because they assumed everyone lower in their rigid hierarchy had baser morals than they had, themselves, even though, most likely, the opposite was true, Z felt.

CHAPTER 13

KARAMELLI, THE INTERPRETER, was a stocky man with a bloated face, a walrus moustache and a tight fitting jacket that served as a corset to push his beer-inflated belly into his barrel-like chest giving him the appearance of an overfed and underpaid non-commissioned officer. He spoke German as well as English and pretended to know all the dialects including the one used by the Jews - which Karamelli translated with contempt. He had no patience with that linguistic abomination which he considered to be the lowest of low German spoken by illiterates producing truly horrible sounds that assaulted his senses. To his mind, it was as if the Jews had purposely taken that sweet language of Goethe and Schiller and had run it through a meat grinder simply to annoy him. In short, he had no patience with it. However, since he earned his living as a translator, hired by the court, and since he was registered as one of those who could interpret all dialects of German, and since 'Jewish German' (otherwise known as 'Yiddish') was one of the dialects listed, he translated it when called upon – but without any joy or happiness.

Z, on the other hand, loved the Yiddish language. He loved the words and he loved the sounds and he loved the expressions. That is to say, he currently did. When he went to the Jews Free School they had tried to beat it out of him – not physically, but through mental intimidation, attempting to convince him that this was the language of the uneducated immigrant masses and that if he ever hoped to become someone, anyone – a man of substance and respect – then he would have to come to understand that this pseudo-language,

Yiddish, was nothing more than one of those pidgin dialects used by cargo cults to trade breadfruit for opiates. This, he was told, was part of the Anglicisation process – a process of re-education which meant that he would have to give up the tired and old in exchange for the new and the shiny; a process whereby he could, in time, become a credit to his father, his people and, most especially, his Queen, in whose reflected glory he would bask like a diamond in the sun (or quartz under street light in his case perhaps). But first he would have to stop using that horrid language – which came from neither God nor Caesar and which identified him with those long bearded men in scruffy black cossacks and oversized hats, the dress of the Polish peasantry - and only speak his mother tongue (not of his biological mother but that of her adopted land), the glorious and most perfect language of English (with, perhaps, a smattering of French, Latin and few other linguistic predecessors thrown in with it).

That aspect of Z which identified him as a modern man and a member of the new Jewish intelligentsia beginning to take root in the European capitals of London, Paris and Berlin, immersing itself in the values of the age of Enlightenment and looking upon the likes of Spinoza not as a heretic but as a model – that aspect of Z, perhaps, found Yiddish something of an embarrassment. But the other side of Z which established him as the 'Poet of the Ghetto', that side of him cherished Yiddish in the way one might treasure an aged ancestor whose face, wrinkled and worn as it may be, conveys in its multitude of lines a pathway back in time and thus becomes a precious artefact in which resides the crucible of self discovery.

Isaac Angel, the next witness called by the prosecution, gave his evidence in Yiddish, interpreted by Karamelli so that,

120

while the simple facts came through hopefully unscathed, the subtleties of phrase, largely remained unknown except to that part of the gallery who understood his languid words without the questionable help of the accidental translator.

What information, then, did the prosecution ascertain? That Isaac Angel was the husband of the deceased; that he was a boot riveter by trade; that he had come from a village near Warsaw; that he had been in England for ten months at the time of the murder; that his wife was only twenty-two years of age; that he and his wife had moved into 16 Batty Street about a week before Whitsuntide, towards the end of May; that they occupied a furnished room there on the first floor at the front; that on the day of the murder he had left for his job at George Street, Spitalfields, at about a quarter past six in the morning; that up till the day of the murder he had never spoken to the prisoner nor, to his knowledge, had his wife…

Z made a note of this last statement. Could that really have been the case? 16 Batty Street was a tiny house with a communal kitchen. Is it possible that neither Angel nor his wife had met Lipski in all that time – not even bumping up against each other on the staircase?

On the evening before the morning of the murder, Isaac Angel testified that he returned home about nine o'clock. His wife was waiting for him at the door. They spent a few hours together, eating their meagre supper before going to bed around half past eleven. What did they speak about, Z wondered? What did they say? 'This was their last meal together,' he scribbled. 'If only they had known…'

Next morning at about six he awoke. It would take him about fifteen minutes to walk to his job at the boot making shop. He made her breakfast, as was his custom. What did they have? Some bread? A small pat of butter? Some jam?

She didn't eat with him. She was awake but stayed in bed. Her pregnancy, perhaps, had made her tired, lethargic. If she needed to rest, so be it. He would pick up their dinner on his way home. He asked her what she would prefer. What did she reply? He didn't say. What was he going to pick up that day for the dinner they never had, for the child that was never to be? What had they planned for their dinner? It was questions like this that the prosecution never pursued. It was questions like this that Z would have asked. For these were the tiny details at the essence of who they were; details about a special moment that would never come. But the prosecution wasn't interested and Karamelli couldn't have translated it into the language of the court because it was an irrelevant fact and it meant nothing to them. But it meant everything to Z because it was a minuscule hook that would give him insight into an unfathomable mystery being haltingly articulated by a large, ponderous man, ill clothed, coarse and uncultured, who lived a brutal and impoverished life along with his wife he had brought here from Poland, happily pregnant, and now she was dead and he was alone with only her memory and that of an unborn child.

His wife was still in bed when he left the house that morning. She was awake. Did she go back to sleep? Probably. Who knows? Maybe she lay there, half asleep, half awake, a hand placed on her swollen belly, feeling the movements of the life within her. But she was well. Was she cheerful? That was a question the prosecution asked. Cheerful? Who was cheerful in that place? Cheerfulness is something only the middle classes might aspire to – and maybe children who know nothing yet about life. But is that a word for an impoverished immigrant – no matter how hopeful?

He was asked if he noticed the position of the table when he left. The table? It was at the window. Where else would it

122

be? That is where he sat to say his daily prayers. Why would he move it? But if the table had been left there, could two bulky men have used the window as an exit?

And then the prosecution got to the crux of the matter, Z thought. It was the question Z was waiting for them to ask. Did Isaac Angel shut the door when he left the room that morning? Did he remember if the key was in the lock? Had he locked the door that night when he went to bed? Did he have to unlock the door in order to get out?

Yes, to all of those questions. Yes.

And was it a good lock? Did it work well?

Why not? It was a new lock, wasn't it? He had complained about the door that was difficult to shut, so finally after having lived there for six weeks and eight days they put in a new one. For six weeks and eight days the door wouldn't shut. Now, finally, it did. And, thought Z, after it was fixed she was murdered. Maybe they would have been better off with the broken one.

It was noon when he was called home. Mrs Levy, another of the boarders, had come to get him. What did she say? What did she tell him? What did he think when he saw her? Did he look up from his work, riveting, riveting, riveting, his boring, tedious work, riveting, riveting, riveting, boom-ka-boom-ka-boom-ka-boom, hammer, hammer, hammer. Fingers thick and stubby but trained after years to be smart and quick. Rivet, rivet, rivet, again and again and again. From six thirty in the morning till nine at night. Rivet, rivet, rivet. And never look up, never look up, never look up. But when the rhythm took him over, boring as it was, sometimes he entered another world. His work was so automatic that he could dream. He could dream. He could dream of a day by a quiet stream when he would be fishing with his son. And it was so misty, so hazy, he could hardly make him out. But then once he did. He saw his face. He saw his face. He saw his face, and he smiled. And it was at that very instant, that very moment he heard his name. And he looked up. And he saw her. It was Mrs Levy. Mrs Levy? Mrs. Levy from the Batty Street house. What was Mrs Levy doing there? What did she want? Their eyes met, thought Z. Maybe their eyes met. Or maybe not. Maybe she said simply that something has happened and he must come quick. Was it his child? His unborn child? That must have been what he had asked himself.

When he got home did he not find his wife was dead? That is the question the prosecution asked. It was a sad, brutal question and at first Isaac Angel just stared at Karamelli, as if it were the translator, himself, who had the temerity to ask him that.

Of course he found his wife was dead. But what did that mean? Did that have anything to do with what he felt on that terrible day - the 27th of June? He fought his way through the crowd, still in a daze, still hoping this was part of a dream, and those terrible faces that had surrounded the Batty Street house were just part of a grotesque, nightmare. He pushed his way up the stairs only to be stopped by a phalanx of police from going into his own room. They had sealed it shut. He couldn't even touch the bed or the few possessions they had shared in their meagre life together. He couldn't even say goodbye. All he could do was stand in that narrow corridor, hold his bulky head in his rough, calloused hands (the same hands that riveted shoes fourteen hours a day and would have cradled his new born son) – all he could do was stand there and weep and pray that he would soon wake up again.

The next to take the stand was Philip Lipski. He was the husband of Leah Lipski and held the lease on the Batty

124

Street house, renting it from a Mr. Peters, who was the real landlord. Z knew well how the brutal property market worked in the ghetto. An immigrant arrives in Whitechapel and rents a room. He works for a sweater for however long it takes to save enough to start his own workshop. Then, if he were lucky enough to save a bit of cash, he leases a house from another immigrant who is one step up on the ladder and has leased the house from someone else slightly above him who also has a lease on the very same building. And so the chain of leaseholders could be infinitely long, each creaming off a little profit from the series of sublets as they worked their way down to the poor, unlucky man who was at the bottom. Thus Whitechapel property, no matter how mean and grotty, was some of the dearest to be had in London.

Though Philip Lipski was just one step up from the bottom, he was working and settled and, if life was far from easy, at least he had a house with enough space to partition off into little rooms sufficient to give him a few shillings a week over and above expenses. What's more, he spoke English well enough to dispense with Karamelli, to the relief of both the translator and the Yiddish speaking Jews in the crowded courtroom.

Z quickly sized him up, this bland, unhappy man, as someone he was quite familiar with, not personally, of course, but as a typical character of the ghetto. Stoic, sad, a man devoted to his family but fated never to achieve whatever minor dreams he might have had before being crushed in the heaviness of his brutish existence. In short, he was a *nebbish* - a word from the dialect that Karamelli so detested. But that word, like many others, could not have been properly translated into English even if Karamelli had been so inclined since it refers to a cultural entity that has no equivalent in the English mind. For a *nebbish* from the Jewish

125

ghetto isn't simply a failure, and thus reprehensible because he is without value in commercial terms; he is still a man and part of a community which understands life is hard but also unpredictable and that sometimes there are heroes and sometimes there are *nebbishes* but *nebbishes* can also be heroes and heroes can also be *nebbishes*.

What did the prosecution hope to gain by calling this *nebbish* to the stand, Z wondered? It was, of course, the lock. A new lock had indeed been put in after Angel had complained for six weeks and eight days. But not by Phillip Lipski, who, by the look of him, could hardly hammer in a nail let alone be trusted with the intricate fitting of such an important device as a lock. No, it was Mr Peters who had done the job. Mr Peters, the landlord of the landlord, who had grumpily put the new lock in after six long weeks and eight long days. And Mr Peters, was he a locksmith? Of course not. He was a tailor. You want a lock? I'll give you a lock. But locks are not trousers and trousers are not locks. So what's to worry? A door is a door. It opens and it closes. If it closes, then it's shut. And why would anyone want to lock it anyway? What was there to steal - some rags in an egg crate?

So the prosecution ascertained that Mr. Peters put in a lock. Whether it was a good lock or a bad lock, that was another question. But that the landlord's landlord put in a lock, there was no debate. However, once on the stand, the defence, in the undemonstrative form of McIntyre, quietly established that, yes, the prisoner had been a well-behaved young man during the time he had lived at Batty Street and, yes, he had been steady, honest and industrious. Also, yes, he was engaged to marry a nice young woman. But, no, he was not a relative even though he was called by the same name.

All this information was verified by McIntyre without fuss, without bother and in a manner which was bound to make

126

the jury forget about the *nebbish* with the same name as the prisoner. Especially since the next witness called to the stand was the one everybody had been waiting for - the very man Israel Lipski had accused of stitching him up: the man called Rosenbloom. For after Rosenbloom had testified, thought Z, who would remember what the *nebbish* had said?

To compare Rosenbloom and Lipski was to contrast brashness with diffidence. That's what first popped into Z's mind when he saw the self-possessed man neatly dressed in suit and tie take the witness stand. Rosenbloom had the slicked-back hair and thinly pencilled moustache of the classical roué. But his eyes had the bemused look a man accused unjustly.

The prosecutor fixed him in his gaze. Did he live at 27 Philpot Street? A questioning look was thrown back. 27? A bad start, thought Z, as the prosecutor looked down at his notes. Did he live at 37 Philpot Street? Ah, yes. 37. And was he a native of Poland? Wasn't everyone? Yes, yes... And had he been in England for eighteen months? Maybe, not quite. And had he been married for ten of those eighteen...?

Ah, so Rosenbloom was newly married. That did not bode well, thought Z. Slicked back hair and pencil moustache or not, it gave the impression of homely stability.

Did he work as a stickmaker for Mr. Mark Katz of Watney Passage, Commercial Road? And during that time was the prisoner working in the same employment? Yes, yes, yes. Until the 20th of June. Till Jubilee Week.

Until Jubilee Week. And then they were laid off. All of them. The stickmaking business depended on being what it always had been, what it always was. And that was wet. For Katz's sticks were made for the umbrella trade. And there was nothing that dampened the umbrella trade more than lack of rain and blazing sun.

127

Was that not ironic, thought Z. Two men sweating in the heat to make sticks for umbrellas and praying for rain. While the great celebration for the Empress, for the Queen, continued on and on and on, they prayed for rain. Not because they held her ill. Not at all. They prayed for rain so they would keep their jobs. And the organisers of the Jubilee? They prayed for sun. So two groups were inexorably vied one against another: the Royal retinue who prayed for sun and the umbrella makers who prayed for rain. And what of the Queen, herself? She probably had stopped praying long ago, thought Z. Whether it was rain or sun, she would be carted out - the only difference it would have made to her was if the top of her carriage was up or down.

Thus, at the very moment the proud and pompous defenders of the realm were parading through the city, smugly declaring a new age of prosperity, Rosenbloom and Lipski had been thrown out of their jobs. In a certain way they were brothers under the skin, thought Z. Both were recent immigrants from Poland. Both were victims … but victims of what? Of the Jubilee or of the weather? Whatever it was, it was the same. Under the skin, they were definitely brothers, but brothers who could hardly have been any different.

The prosecuting attorney, the man named Poland, did not like Rosenbloom, thought Z. Neither did he hate him. But having decided that Israel Lipski's story was the desperate fantasy of a guilty man, Rosenbloom had become a vital cog in the engine of conviction. Poland, therefore, was methodical, drawing out each piece of information, bit by bit, like nails to build a coffin.

Had he met the prisoner on the Saturday of Jubilee week? Yes, he had met him and, yes, they had conversed. Z tried to picture it in his head. The diffident young man, Lipski, slight of build and the bigger, rougher, older Rosenbloom, with the pencil moustache and the slick-back hair. Lipski is building a workshop in his attic and wants Rosenbloom to work for him. Rosenbloom studies the waif of a figure before him, small, slight, boyish in looks. Why should he work for such a man – a boy who knows less than he does, himself? But both are out of work. Both need to eat. Does Lipski have any money? He has raised a little. How much? A little. Enough to make a start. Rosenbloom, what does he think? He thinks, of course, that there's nothing else on offer so something is better than nothing and who knows? Maybe there's an opportunity. Because opportunity, no matter how infinitesimally small, is everything when you are poor and are struggling for survival.

Had he been to Lipski's place before he had started work on that Tuesday? Yes, he had been there on the Sunday before the Tuesday. He went there to help set up the workshop and to start making samples. So he had been there before, thought Z. And he found that very interesting. Rosenbloom had been to Batty Street on the Sunday before the murder. He helped to get the workshop in order and had stayed there long enough to make some samples. So he was familiar with the house and with the layout. He, too, had climbed the stairs. He, too, could have looked through that tiny window and peered through the muslin gauze into Miriam Angel's room. But not having lived there, he didn't know something that Lipski must have been aware of – he didn't know that the Angels were poorer than church mice, that they lived from hand to mouth and spent all their meagre earnings on rent and a bit of food to put on their table. Of course most of the Whitechapel immigrants were poor. But 'poor' is always a word that's relative to the one who uses it. So many people in the ghetto appeared like the Angels and lived like them but had a few sovereigns stashed away – sovereigns that were acquired farthing by farthing in a process that was painful slow and disciplined. It was all a matter of time. The longer they were there, the longer they were able to sweat out their labour, the more chance they would have saved a few precious sovereigns. It was all a matter of time. And what Rosenbloom didn't know was that the people in the room beyond the little window were still greeners, they had only been in England for little more than half a year. He couldn't have known that. But Lipski did.

So when Rosenbloom came that fateful Tuesday morning at 7 o'clock he already knew the house since he had been there before. He knocked at the door and waited. Who answered? It was Lipski. Lipski was the one who had answered the door. He was working upstairs in the attic but he heard the knock at the door and came down to answer it. Of course he was waiting for his worker to come but he heard the knock all the way up in the attic. Noise travelled easily through the paper-thin walls; there was no barrier for sound – you could hear everything everywhere. (Z used his pencil to underline this fact.)

Lipski came downstairs in his trousers and his shirt. He was barefoot, Rosenbloom said. The house seemed to be empty and quiet as he followed Lipski up the stairs. Did they chat? Were there any pleasantries exchanged? What did they say to each other? The prosecutor didn't ask. Rosenbloom didn't say. When they reached the attic Lipski set the stronger man to work bending the metal points that would eventually go on the tips of the walking sticks they were making. The sticks, themselves, were still in a raw state. They would have to be finished and then the metal tips would be fixed at the end and filed smooth while clamped in a vice. But there was only one vice, so only one man could work. And Lipski told him that another man would come, a 'filer', he said, therefore he

130

would need another vice.

Who was this man, this other mysterious 'filer'? Lipski didn't say. According to Rosenbloom the other man was nameless and this nameless man would come to work, eventually. Then Lipski put on his boots, his jacket and hat, preparing to go out.

The prosecutor, Poland, handed a jacket to the witness. The jacket he handed him had blotchy stains from some corrosive substance. Then, pointing to the jacket that Rosenbloom now was holding in his hands, he asked him whether Lipski had worn a jacket similar to that. Rosenbloom stared at the jacket he was handed. Yes, Lipski wore a jacket similar to that. Similar but not exact. For the jacket Lipski wore had no stains on it. Not that he could see, anyhow.

So Lipski left in an unstained jacket and soon he came back as the shop where he went to buy the vice was still closed. What time was it that Lipski returned? Rosenbloom didn't know. Why was that? Because there was no clock.

What happened then? Where did Lipski go? According to Rosenbloom he went up and down the stairs, up and down the stairs until the boy returned. What boy? Then Z recalled. Of course, there was a boy who Lipski had hired on to do odd jobs. A boy named Pitman. What time did the boy, Pitman, come to work? Around eight by the clock. That is what Rosenbloom said – around eight by the clock.

Z looked back at his notes. But Rosenbloom had said just moments before that there was no clock so he couldn't say what time it was that Lipski returned. Rosenbloom's time-telling capabilities were, at the very least, somewhat inconsistent. But those little details hardly troubled the prosecution, who, in the dogged guise of Poland, continued to plough on.

So Pitman came and then Lipski went out again. This time

to buy a sponge for the boy to varnish with. And that was the last time Rosenbloom saw Lipski until he was found, half dead, under Miriam Angel's bed. But where was Rosenbloom all this time? He remained up in the attic room, he said. Up in the attic room with Pitman, the lad. And one other person was also there. One other man. A big man. A strong man. The man whose name he didn't know – Rosenbloom had said – but only found out later. His name, as it turned out, was Schmuss. 'Schmuss.' Z wrote it down again. 'Schmuss.' It was one of those unfortunate names that innocent people had to bear and sometimes not so innocently. How much do people come to resemble their names, Z wondered?

But this man, Schmuss, was like a ghost. He came and then he left. How long did he stay? Simply a few minutes. There was no work and so he left. And then there was just Rosenbloom and Pitman. Only Rosenbloom and Pitman in the attic room, alone. And while they waited, just below, a vile murder was enacted. A vile murder, just below them. While they waited.

Alone? The two of them alone? But Pitman left, didn't he? Yes, he left. He left sometime after the man, Schmuss had gone. When was that? How long did the boy stay after Schmuss had left? An hour? An hour and a half? Rosenbloom couldn't say because there was no clock. But, yes, the boy named Pitman did go off. He went to get his breakfast. And after he left Rosenbloom was alone. Alone in the attic workshop. Just by himself. And where was Schmuss? Schmuss had disappeared. He had simply vanished.

So Rosenbloom had stayed in that attic room from seven in the morning till the alarm was raised in the room downstairs when the body was found. The boy, Pitman, was there as well, except for the time he went to have his breakfast. And when did he return? When did Pitman get

132

back? Rosenbloom could not tell. There wasn't a clock. But Pitman did return, sometime, and stayed in the attic with Rosenbloom filing away, filing away, filing away the handles. Until they heard the sounds, the terrible sounds, from below, from the depths of the house. And then they ran downstairs, together.

McIntyre now rose to cross-examine. Z watched with interest. Rosenbloom's speech was well rehearsed and filtered through Karamelli's translation, it seemed calm and reasoned. The original words, however, were not quite as straightforward. Like the Yiddish language, itself, they hovered in a different realm where certainty is no longer certain. Because what means certainty when you're always an alien in a world that is constantly shifting? In Yiddish, you can only be certain that today will be different because nothing is ever exactly the same as it was yesterday and tomorrow you might be somewhere else (which is why the Yiddish speaking Jews of Eastern Europe never bothered to paint their houses).

But for McIntyre, the commercial attorney, who dealt in contracts and bill of lading, both God and the Devil lay in the detail. When he rose to cross-examine, therefore, he was only interested in getting Rosenbloom to say what he had to say with more precision, even though, with Karamelli as the intermediary, that was like pulling teeth from a toothless donkey.

McIntyre, however, persisted. Did Rosenbloom know Schmuss before? No, he didn't. Did he ever see him before? How could he see him before if he didn't know him? Did he tell the boy, Pitman, that he knew him? How could he tell the boy, Pitman, that he knew him if he didn't know him? Besides, he didn't speak English and the boy, Pitman, didn't know Yiddish. So Rosenbloom didn't speak English? Not a word? No, not a word. Was he sure? Yes, he was sure. And he didn't say to the boy that he knew the strange man who came to work in Lipski's attic? No, he didn't say that to the boy at all because he didn't know Schmuss and he didn't know English.

Then McIntyre led Rosenbloom, step by step, through Lipski's statement: Wasn't it true that he, Rosenbloom, and the strange man was standing at the door of Miriam Angel's room when Lipski returned? No, he was not. And wasn't the door of Miriam Angel's room partly pulled open at that time? No, he didn't see. Would he swear that he was not there when the door was partly open? Yes, he would swear it. He would swear it in Temple, if need be.

The judge, impatient at this verbal imprecision, now intervened: Did Rosenbloom at any time that morning stand before Angel's door? No. Except, yes, he was there when the alarm took place.

McIntyre took charge again: Was Rosenbloom not standing just outside the door and the strange man just inside the door of Miriam Angel's room? No, he was not out and he had not seen the strange man before he came up to the attic room. Did he not catch hold of Lipski by his hands or wrists? No, he did not catch hold of him at all. That was lies, all lies. Did he and the mysterious man not throw him down?

Here the judge intervened once again. What purpose was being served by going though all this, he wanted to know. Isn't it all quite useless?

Useless? Z wondered what he meant by that. Was it useless to have Rosenbloom respond to Lipski's accusation? Perhaps it was, if you believed that Lipski was guilty and all this was simply taking up precious time that would be better served by having lunch.

However, McIntyre, to his credit, doggedly went on: Did

Rosenbloom force open Lipski's mouth? No, he wasn't strong enough to do that. Didn't the other man hold Lipski down? The other one was not there. Lies, all lies!

Then McIntyre stopped. The courtroom was quiet. Nothing could be heard, not a sound. And then: What part of Poland was he from? From Plotz. Was that near Warsaw? Seventeen or eighteen Polish miles.

And that was that. The witness stepped down and McIntyre returned to his bench.

CHAPTER 14

THE TRIAL BROKE for lunch. Lipski was taken away to a tiny holding cell below the courthouse, hardly bigger than a coffin stood on end, where he would patiently wait while up above the Judge and the Lord Mayor sat down to an opulent feast catered by the Sheriff, Sir Henry Isaacs, in the Judge's private dining room.

Z wished he could have been a fly on the wall, first in Lipski's cellar cage where the prisoner sat alone, eating, if he had any appetite at all, a piece of stale bread, some watery soup, served to him in a metal cup slimy from second-hand drool and then flitting up to the finery of the Judge's private chambers where the three high ranking servants of the Crown were tucking into their meaty fare after popping the cork of some decent claret in order to toast the long and profitable reign of Her Majesty, Queen Victoria.

What would they be talking about? What was going on inside their heads? Upstairs where they were toasting the Queen, they would be praising their good fortune and marvelling at the weather. But down in the cellar, behind the bars of frigid steel, Lipski would have no one to talk with except himself. It was a time, a quiet space, perchance to dream. To dream within a dream within a nightmare. His body might have been confined inside that cell, but Z suspected that his mind had drifted elsewhere - across the water, across the choppy sea, hovering over the filthy docks of Hamburg infested with its rats and rabid dogs, before floating on through vapid memories of Prussia, Pomerania, of wooden benches, midnight trains, nostrils filled with soot and dung, the barking, guttural sounds of black booted bureaucrats, and then soaring beyond the River Oder, into the Polish heartlands, across the planes, the never-ending fields of rich, golden wheat, ripening in the summer sun, the mind's train rolls on and on and on… Hush little baby, hush… The chicken's in the pot, the Shabbat candles are lit, your father has made you a basket of straw. And I will rock you fast asleep in the safety of my arms.

Z sat there thinking in the emptiness of the courtroom. The people all had left – the reporter from the Times, the artist from London Illustrated, the jurors, the myriad of observers, all had gone to have their meals, to be watered and be fed. And Z stared out at the mahogany walls, staring out into the emptiness, out into the echoes of the past and he wondered – he wondered what on earth he was doing there and what in heaven's name was going on.

And then he saw her. She was standing near the back of the chamber, by the door. Alone. And he realised that she was waiting – waiting patiently for him.

There was a quiet pub around the corner from the courthouse. Maggie knew of it. After they had settled themselves in a wooden booth, she began to speak. It was clear from the beginning that there was something she wanted to tell Z - something she wanted to say.

What she had to relate was one of those curious coincidences, she told him, very difficult to explain. Quite by chance she had, that very weekend past, been invited to accompany her cousin, Beatrice, to a garden party at the home of a gentleman Beatrice thought might be helpful to her journalistic career for, besides being a scholar of some repute, he edited the Dictionary of National Biography, a job which had given him access to the Great, the Good and the

Despicable. His name, Maggie told him, was Stephen Leslie Stephen. And it was his brother, James Fitzjames, who was presiding over the trial they were witnessing this day.

And she continued, for this curiosity was not all: once there she had met a child, a little girl with a very long face, enormous bright eyes full of wonder and dark hair that fell impishly down the back of her starched, white frock. Her name was Virginia and Maggie had taken to her at once, seeing, as it were, a kindred soul in the body of a child much more to her liking than all the others who seemed to feel that pretence and formality were required even in a lovely garden on a warm, sunny afternoon.

The little girl was Leslie Stephen's youngest daughter and the garden was her own special wonderland. So, it seemed to Maggie, she felt somewhat annoyed that these people – these stiff and sober guests of her father's (not hers) – had taken over her neat, protected world. But of all the annoyances the little girl felt, one was supreme. It was that of her cousin, the son of her father's brother, some many years older, whom she detested because he took such delight in tormenting her. Maggie, herself, had witnessed this when she saw the very same mean-spirited lad come over to the child and pointing back toward the thicket where she liked to play, say with a wicked grin, 'A wolf is going to eat you, Virginia if you go into the woods today!' To which she replied, defensively, 'I'm not afraid of wolves! In fact, I'll marry one some day!'

And then, grabbing Maggie's hand, the little girl headed back into the thicket that was her own special patch behind the house. She tugged her along a path, Maggie told him, that led beside a bubbling brook, till they came to a little summer house – a quiet retreat where Virginia stored her fantasies. But as they came close it was clear someone was inside the hut – a fact that quite annoyed the little girl since she imagined the place as her own special hideaway. Though Maggie tried to restrain her, Virginia quietly made her way up to the window that overlooked the rushing stream and through which a shadowy figure could be seen.

There was something malevolent in the air, Maggie told him. Something she could feel. And sensing the danger, she went closer to the summer house to fetch the child who had placed herself before the open window and was standing on her tiptoes peering in. A gentle wind was stirring up the leaves and the branches of the trees began to sway. Inside, through the gauze-like curtains, a figure could be seen reclining on a sofa, lost, it seemed, in dreams. On the table next to him a clay pipe still burned, noxiously, and the odour, as it wafted though the air, was something Maggie knew from her pharmacy days. And just before she pulled the child away, she managed to get a closer look of the man who was slumbering in that state of great abandon which was the effect, she understood, caused by his indulgence of a substance which took away the pain of worldly cares and transported the users into a trance which opened up to them, they felt, the portals of Valhalla with all its timeless mysteries and took them on a voyage so seductive that they wished only to remain.

Then looking into Z's eyes, she told him that she had seen that man again today. She saw him, she said, sitting on the bench, with drooping jowls and eyes that spoke of languid reveries. It was the man Virginia had said was her uncle and who Maggie had recognised once more in the courtroom, overseeing a trial where he would eventually pronounce sentence on some poor unfortunate soul, perhaps dispatching him, with the full authority of her Majesty, the Queen, to a place where dreams no longer matter.

139

Back in the courthouse, Z thought of giving this information that Maggie had passed on to Hayward's law clerk, Myers. But he was nowhere to be found and, Z thought, what end would it serve? Whatever Maggie felt the moral implications might be, there was nothing illegal the judge had done; nothing that would impact on the trial as no one was accusing him of being drugged while on the bench.

Still, it did cause Z to look at the judge differently as he watched him ascend to his director's perch overlooking the courtroom playhouse, his belly full of blood rare meat, his lips still showing traces of spicy mustard, his crimson robe invisibly stained (Z imagined) with splatters of ruby wine - so well fed, well boozed and well pampered he was ready to get this shabby affair done. And yet what sweet, seductive memories rushed through the judge's brain, relics of his commune with the angels? Or was it not that way at all? What else had been unlocked inside that aging head, nodding with torpor caused from such overabundance that only the fattest mandarins could ever imagine? Could it have been the fear that somewhere, sometime this whole charade would pass and, like Shelley's *Ozymandias*, nothing would remain except the lone and level sands onto which the ruins of Empire have crumbled? Could it have been the terror that on those sands one day he would stand naked? What stark and dreadful thoughts went on inside that addled cranium? And in his mind Z imagined some future Macbeth holding it aloft, that skull now bleached bare to the bone, and sighing, 'Alas, poor judge, I knew him well...'

These thoughts and images, however, quickly passed into oblivion as the sound of the judge's gavel resonated sharply through the chamber bringing all and sundry to their senses with its emphatic thud, enforcing the dictate, by dramatic exclamation, that the court was now in session and this space,

140

however small, was once again under the control of Her Majesty, the Queen, in her guise as head of state and ruler of the law.

CHAPTER 15

THE YOUNG LAD who took the stand had that gawky look of boyhood in the process of change but still in the chrysalis stage so that the metamorphosis hadn't yet completely taken place. He was, according to his mother, only fourteen years of age though he, himself, had added two years to this figure in order to make himself employable. And, indeed, who was to quibble? He was willing and able and needed to work and so Katz had hired him to do the little tasks that boys are best at doing – running here and there on errands, sweeping up and generally making themselves useful without the need for life enhancing skills or (more importantly) a wage that was even semi-liveable. And, yes, it was there at Katz's he had met the prisoner, Lipski, who, it seemed, had taken a liking to the lad – perhaps seeing in him the boy he never was allowed to be himself. But whether or not that was true, Z thought, was entirely irrelevant – though not entirely to him. What was relevant, to the court, was that Lipski had asked this lad – Pitman was his name – to come work for him and help with the tasks that were needed in creating a workspace in the Batty Street attic.

Looking back at his notes, Z recalled that Pitman was said by Rosenbloom to have been in the attic room that morning of the murder. He had gone out for his breakfast but then had returned and had remained with him until they heard the shouts from below after the discovery of the brutalised body of Miriam Angel lying lifeless on her bed. But how long had Rosenbloom been left upstairs alone? When he had been called as a witness, Rosenbloom could only estimate the time for he hadn't access to a clock – or so he said.

The prosecution lost no time, however, in having Pitman confirm his statement: What time did he arrive at number sixteen? Eight o'clock. Was that his regular time for coming? Yes, it was. Did he go upstairs to the attic? Yes. Was the prisoner there when he arrived? No. Then who was there? Rosenbloom. Had he ever seen Rosenbloom before that morning? No, he hadn't. How long had he remained with Rosenbloom before he left? About an hour. So he arrived about eight o'clock and stayed there till somewhere about nine? Yes. And during that time did the prisoner come into the room? Yes. What did he say? He said that he had gone to buy a vice but the shop was shut. Was there anything more that he remembered? Yes, that in a little while after that he went out again saying that he was going to have another try at buying the vice. And then did he go out? Yes. And what time was that? About five minutes past nine. And after Lipski had gone did a strange man come into the room? Yes...

Z watched as Schmuss was summoned into the room, escorted by a court attendant. He stood there, his large bulky figure, thick and heavy, trying to force an impression of studied nonchalance but projecting a sense of malice just by his very size.

Pitman was asked to identify Schmuss as the man who had come up to the Batty Street attic. Did this man speak to Rosenbloom? Yes. They spoke together for a while? Yes. In a language he understood? No. So how long did Schmuss remain? About five minutes. And then what became of him? He went out. So you went out after him? No, before him...

Z looked over at the notes the man from the Times had taken to see if he had heard correctly. But he needn't have bothered for the prosecutor, himself, noticed the discrepancy and reminded the lad, who had begun to look quite nervous, that he had just said Schmuss had remained in the attic about five minutes and then had gone out but that Pitman, himself, had left before him. Was that correct? Yes. So he had left Schmuss there behind him? Yes.

Then how could Pitman possibly have known how long Schmuss had stayed, Z wondered?

Once again the prosecutor asked Pitman to confirm his statement. Did he actually go downstairs, leaving Rosenbloom and Schmuss upstairs together? Yes. And then he went home for breakfast? Yes. And how far was his house from Batty Street? About a quarter of a mile. And he saw his mother when he returned home? Yes. And he had his breakfast? Yes. And he came straight back to Batty Street? Well, no...

No? No. Actually he stopped to play in the street for a while. He was only a boy, after all. He was only fourteen. So how long did he play in the street? Oh, about a quarter of an hour. And then he went back to Batty Street? Yes. And when he went back, did he go up to the workshop? Yes. And who was there at that time? Simon Rosenbloom. Anyone else? No. And how long did he stay there with Rosenbloom? About an hour. And then what happened? Was there anything to call his attention downstairs? Yes, in about half an hour Lipski came in...

Again the prosecutor stopped and stared at the boy. He clearly had expected Pitman to have said something about hearing a shout or some other disturbance indicating the discovery of Miriam Angel's body. He asked the boy to confirm that's what he meant – that a half hour after he got there the prisoner came in. Pitman, doggedly, stuck to his story.

So Lipski came up to the attic room about a half hour after Pitman returned from having his breakfast. What time was that? Z went back to his notes. Pitman left around nine. He walked back home, about a quarter mile, had his breakfast, walked back but stopped to play for around a quarter of an hour. Therefore he must have been away about an hour in total. That would have made it ten o'clock when he returned to Batty Street. Ten at the earliest, Z suspected. The boy then said he saw Lipski come up to the attic about a half hour later – 10:30 according to Z's calculations.

What did Lipski say when he came back up to the attic? What did he do? According to Pitman, Lipski said nothing and did nothing. He just stood in the room. He stayed for about five minutes and then he left.

But what about the stranger? It was the chance for the defence to cross-examine the witness and McIntyre wanted to know about Schmuss, the mystery man. Did Rosenbloom know him? Pitman thought perhaps he did. Why? Because of the way they spoke to each other.

The Judge, however, wasn't going to let that remark pass unquestioned. Did Rosenbloom actually tell Pitman that he knew the man Schmuss? From the boy's expression, Z thought the Judge's annoyance must have been interpreted by him as anger. He answered nervously, but firmly. No, Rosenbloom hadn't said that.

But McIntyre had Pitman's statement written down before him. Hadn't Rosenbloom said, 'I know that man; I have been in his company before'?

Pitman confirmed that was correct.

This annoyed the Judge even more. Didn't the boy just tell the court that Rosenbloom didn't say he knew the man? Flustered, Pittman admitted that he had forgotten his words.

So did he remember that Rosenbloom told him he knew the man Schmuss? Yes, yes, yes…

And did he tell him that in English?

It was all too much for the boy, who now began to cry. But

145

even through his tears he still managed to confirm that yes, Rosenbloom had told him that in English.

McIntyre was hardly moved by the boy's sniffles. This was his moment and he wasn't about to let it be undone by mere emotions. So looking down at his document again, he asked the boy to confirm that Rosenbloom hadn't told him once, but twice, that he had known Schmuss before. And he asked him to again confirm that he had said those words in English. And that Rosenbloom had also told him Lipski had gone to buy another vice and he had said those words in English as well. This the boy did. And satisfied he had exposed Rosenbloom as a liar on at least three counts, McIntyre sat down.

Poland, however, wasn't about to let the boy off so lightly. He rose from his seat, unfolding his angular body, uncoiling himself like a cobra that sensed its prey was within striking distance. And when he focused his fearsome gaze on the lad, now quite shaken from all that happened before, Z could almost see the shiver traversing the boy's spinal cord, down through his legs to his twitching toes.

So Rosenbloom had told him that the prisoner was going to buy a vice, did he? Yes. And he spoke in English? Yes. What sort of English? Half his own language and half English. Could the boy understand him always? Not always. And when the boy said that he thought Rosenbloom knew the man Schmuss it was because they spoke the same language? Yes, that was right. And then when Rosenbloom told him, 'I know that man because I have been in his company before where he used to work,' did he say that all in English or part in the foreign language? Half in English and half in his own language.

Now the judge stepped in again. Could the boy tell him exactly which part he said in English and which part he said in his own language? The part he said in English was, 'He had been in his own company before.' And how about, 'I know that man?' What language did he say that in? The boy thought a moment and then offered that half was said in English and half in his own tongue. But the judge reminded him that he had said half of all Rosenbloom had said was in his own language. Yes, the boy agreed, that was correct. So did he mean that Rosenbloom talked like a foreigner or a man who did not know much English. And the boy confirmed that Rosenbloom did not know much English and only told him what he could understand but that he could make out what he meant.

Poland, following on from the judge (who may or may not have been helpful to him, Z thought), asked Pitman whether he could make out all of what Rosenbloom had meant. And the boy stated that he could. But how about the part in the foreign language? He couldn't make that out, he supposed. No, the boy agreed, he couldn't. So he was quite clear that they knew each other when they spoke a foreign language? Yes, he was.

Poland allowed a trace of smile to cross his arid lips. Then, nodding at the jurors, he sat down.

What had the jurors made of all that, Z wondered? Poland had twisted the boy's words so that, in the end, the confusion had been compounded to a point of nonsense. Poland, of course, was trying to get the jury to see the boy as a child whose words were not reliable. But the fact was that Pitman gave the strong impression Rosenbloom and Schmuss had known each other previously and had been left in the attic room alone together while he went off to get his breakfast.

CHAPTER 16

THAT EVENING, BACK in his room, Z looked over his notes of the testimony from the various witnesses that had been called to give evidence that day.

After the boy, Pitman, came a man named Schmidt whose small shop on Backchurch Lane sold hardware goods of various descriptions mainly suited for the small artisan workshops that abounded in the area. Schmidt, himself, had been a stickmaker for seventeen years before evolving up the ladder from sweat-shop worker to sweat-shop merchant. According to Schmidt's testimony, his shop also served as a makeshift hiring hall where odd-job men would come in hopes of finding a day's employment. In fact Lipski had gone there that Monday before the murder not only to see about purchasing another vice but also to find a man to do the filing of the metal tips after they had been hammered into place on the bottom of the walking sticks which were to be produced in his workshop the very next day.

Lipski, Schmidt said, had come that Monday afternoon to ask for a man who could work as a filer. At the time, there were four men at the shop, hanging around, waiting for an offer of a day's work. Schmidt said that Lipski could choose which one he wanted. Lipski then had gone outside with the four and had spoken with them so Schmidt hadn't heard what he had told them. And then Lipski left and Schmidt hadn't seen him again until Tuesday, the morning of the murder, when Lipski came by to offer him some money for a vice – too little, however, for Schmidt to release such a precious bit of his inventory to the young, inexperienced sweater.

But that small piece of equipment, Z thought, was vital

to Lipski's operation. Certainly Schmidt must have realised that. And furthermore, Lipski was starting a business that would have meant more trade for him. So when Lipski had made him an offer for the vice, couldn't a deal have somehow been struck? Couldn't Schmidt have released the vice with the proviso that Lipski could pay him the balance later? Unless, of course, Schmidt felt that Lipski was bound to fail. In which case, it would have been money down the drain for him. For he could always sell a vice to some new greener who had big ideas and a few more shillings in his pocket. But to recoup a bad investment – that was another matter.

Z looked down at his notes again. There were four men Lipski spoke with outside Schmidt's shop that afternoon. One was Schmuss. Another was a man called Barsook. The third was named Robinski and the fourth Schmidt didn't identify. Schmidt had testified that three of the men had worked for him but Barsook didn't – he was just with the others. Did Schmidt get a percentage of their wages for connecting them with work? And, if so, was it in Schmidt's interest to protect his men's reputation least his own good name be stained as a result?

The shopkeeper testified that he saw Schmuss once more on the Tuesday of the murder at about noon. By that time news had already swept the neighbourhood about Miriam Angel's murder. But curiously Schmuss hadn't heard about it even though throngs of people had been drawn to Batty Street and the crowd was still swelling as Schmuss made his way to Backchurch Lane. At least that's what Schmidt testified. And yet, apart from that, there was no evidence of unusual movements or strangeness on Schmuss's part. Nothing to indicate he had just helped to commit a vile murder – or two if the acid forced down Lipski's throat hadn't been pumped from his stomach that terrible day. In fact, according to the

149

shopkeeper, Schmuss continued to come to his shop on a regular basis until he left for Birmingham that following Sunday.

But then there was that curious revelation McIntyre had brought out in his cross-examination. The four men who were at Schmidt's shop all had a trade – they all had an expertise. McIntyre had suggested to Schmidt that as he seemed to know these men, perhaps he knew their business. And Schmidt agreed. He did. All four men had a similar craft. It seems they were locksmiths – they knew all about locks, how to make them and how to fix them. But there were too many locksmiths in London so they were reduced to doing odd jobs for people like him.

And then Isaac Schmuss had been called to the stand and he had given evidence that he had recently come from Elisabethan Graff, near Odessa, that he was a locksmith by trade but now worked as a slipper maker in Birmingham after having left London a few weeks before.

Z studied his notes. Schmuss had testified that he had gone regularly to Schmidt's hardware shop in Backchurch Lane in hope of finding employment. There he met with three other Russian Jews: Barsook, Robinski and the third was Totakoski. He said that Lipski had spoken with him that day – the Monday before the murder – and had asked him if he thought he could file sticks for him. Schmuss had never done that kind of job before but he said he would be happy to try as he was so desperate for work. Then Lipski had asked him to come along with him and they had walked to Batty Street, which wasn't far, so Lipski could show him the door of number 16.

The next day Schmuss had come as arranged. The door to number 16 was open and he walked in. The time then was about a quarter past eight. Lipski had met him in the passage and sent him upstairs, asking him to wait there while he went out on an errand. Schmuss then went up to the attic where Rosenbloom and Pitman were already working. He spoke with Rosenbloom briefly in Yiddish, remained there for ten or fifteen minutes and then left, a minute or two after Pitman. At least that's what Schmuss said to the court.

Why did he leave? Schmuss testified he left to eat his breakfast. But he never returned. Why was that? He needed work and there was clearly nothing else on offer – not that Schmuss said, anyway. When he was cross-examined by McIntyre he explained that he didn't feel he had a great chance of work there, so he left. But Rosenbloom had remained. And Lipski had told him that there would be work. Why then did he decide there wasn't work to be had? Clearly the workshop was being set up. Rosenbloom was already working on some sticks. Pitman was also busy. So how had Schmuss come to the determination that it wasn't worth his while to stay? Was it something Rosenbloom had said? Or was it something else?

And what about this man Totakoski who Schmuss had arranged to meet at Schmidt's on the morning of that fateful day? Lipski had needed only one more man – not two. Why had Totakoski planned to meet him there that morning?

Schmuss had left Batty Street around eight thirty, according to his testimony, and had gone home for breakfast. Then, over three hours later, he turned up at Schmidt's hardware shop, unaware of the murder. Where was he during that three hour period? McIntyre had never thought to ask Schmuss to account for his movements. And then, on Sunday, Schmuss had left for Birmingham. McIntyre had made much of that but Z didn't find this information particularly suspicious. After all, Schmuss had found a job working in a slipper factory there. It was five days after the murder that Schmuss had left. He hadn't tried to go into hiding. No, going to Birmingham seemed a reasonable option for a man with no work in London who had limited prospects. But why had Schmuss left Batty Street after waiting just a few minutes? And where did he go after that? These questions McIntyre had left unanswered.

Then Leah Lipski had given evidence that she had last seen the accused, her young lodger, at about 8:30 when she went to fetch his coffee. It was then he had asked her to lend him five shillings. She had suggested that he try his future mother-in-law but he had replied that would be difficult since he had borrowed twenty-five shillings from her just the other night.

The prosecution, Z, suspected had been trying to lay the ground for robbery as the motive for the murder, but McIntyre, cross-examining, had brought out the fact that it was common knowledge in the house the Angels hadn't any money. Furthermore, the reason the landlady couldn't lend Lipski five shillings is that Miriam Angel had borrowed that same amount from her only the day before in order that she could pay her rent.

McIntyre also got the landlady to testify that the replacement lock in the Angels' door had left a hole where the old lock had been large enough to stick her fingers through (though she admitted she couldn't have reached the key on the other side well enough to turn it).

Mrs. Levy, another lodger, Dinah Angel, the murdered woman's mother-in-law, and Mrs. Rubenstein, the landlady's mother, were all called to give evidence about the movements in and about the house that morning and the discovery of the body of Miriam Angel. Z found nothing in their testimony to give him further insight into the case.

Another witness to the events was Harris Dywein, a friend

of the Angels, whose shop was around the corner from Batty Street and who had come to the house shortly after the body had been discovered. He had gone into the Angels' room before it had been sealed off and testified he had seen Miriam Angel lying on her back with her face toward the wall and her hair helter-skelter. He had covered the body up before Piper, Dr. Kay's assistant, had come and he told how then Piper had cleared the room and had, with difficulty, taken the key from the inside of the door and had used it to lock the door from the outside until Dr. Kay arrived. Later he had accompanied Piper and Kay back into the room where Kay had him search for a bottle that might have contained the acid which had been forced upon the victim. Dywein had searched underneath the bed – pulling out first an old coat and after that an egg box which was used to store clothing. Once all that stuff had been cleared away, he had noticed something else, something too far to reach. Dr. Kay, he said, then jumped atop the bed and pulled away a pillow which was against the wall, and, through the crack, saw a man under the bed, pushed up against the corner. The bedstead was then pulled away and the man was recovered – he was found lying on his back, his shirt sleeves rolled up and his waistcoat unbuttoned. Dr. Kay had felt his pulse and, seeing he was alive, slapped his face in an attempt to bring him back to consciousness. Dywein was then told to call a constable. But going over to the window and trying to open it he found it was stuck. However, he was able to call out through the top of the window and two constables eventually came up to the room and helped prop the man up against a corner of the walls so as to hold him aloft while Dr Kay attempted to revive him.

Dywein then assisted one of the constables in searching for the bottle which contained the aqua fortis which was finally discovered on the bed underneath the covers. Cross-examined by McIntyre, Dywein admitted there were other people in the room by then – one of whom was Simon Rosenbloom who had helped in the search for the bottle.

Z wondered if Rosenbloom could have been that clever, that self-possessed to have assisted in the search if he had just moments before helped commit these brutal acts? Then, again, could Lipski have been able to stuff himself underneath the bed, behind an egg crate filled with old clothes and other odds and ends after having swallowed a quantity of acid? Dywein had testified there was an overcoat that had to be removed before the egg crate could be pulled out. Z couldn't understand how that was possible. How could Lipski have pulled a large crate in after him and then have put an overcoat in front of it? But, if it wasn't him, who was it?

William Piper, Dr. Kay's assistant, then gave evidence that he had been stopped in the street at about half past eleven, shortly after the body was found. When he arrived he had found several people in the room, including the three women, Dywein and Rosenbloom. He then had cleared the room, as Dywein had testified before, locking the door behind him. But Piper also indicated that he found the lock had a 'queer look' and finding himself unable to close the door properly had to go back inside and turn the key so that the bolt was retracted. Piper also gave evidence that it was Rosenbloom who pointed out the location of the bottle where it had been hidden in one of the folds of the feather bed. He also testified that there was still a little acid remaining in the vial.

Piper was followed to the stand by Arthur Sack who was the first constable who had responded to Dywein's shouts and had come up the stairs. He testified that after Lipski was carried from the room he was placed in a cab and then taken first to Dr. Kay's and then to the police station and finally to London Hospital where he arrived about three quarters of an hour later.

There were three other witnesses that afternoon. Alfred Inwood, another constable, who gave evidence that he found Lipski's coat at the foot of the bed near the wall, underneath the bed on the floor with another coat, a newer one, over it. Then the leaseholder of the house, Charles Peters, told how he had put in a perfectly good, brand new lock as a replacement for the bad one in the door of the murdered woman's room and that he was satisfied that it was in perfect working order. The final witness was a man who had been working in the house across from number 16 who testified he had noticed Lipski only once that morning at about a quarter to nine, wearing his hat and coat and going inside the house carrying a very small parcel. The man said he hadn't seen him again after that.

CHAPTER 17

Z CUT HIMSELF a thick slice of black bread and placed on top a piece of cheese and a ring of raw onion. The cheese was English. The black bread was Russian. The raw onion was a habit picked up from his father who had come from the northern part of the Pale in what was once the Kingdom of Lithuania. His mother had come from Poland, or what had been Poland before it had been ripped apart by its land-greedy neighbours. Countries and borders were constantly changing, constantly in a state of flux. They always had been, he supposed, but there were times when things had been a bit more stable.

Four hundred years before the Jews had first been invited to settle in that region by a Polish King anxious to have the great forests and empty fields of his realm populated and a moribund economy energised by trade. Z's people, the Jews, even then were recognised as a cheap economic catalyst. And as the resource rich but cash poor countries of the Baltic North watched in envy while the countries of the South amassed greater and greater wealth from their voyages of plunder bringing ever more galleons of gold and silver back from mines dug deep into the far reaches of the world, the invited Jews - those useful intermediaries of commerce, whose trail led everywhere because nowhere were they allowed to stay for long - were gratefully exploited.

Their sojourn in the joint kingdom of Poland and Lithuania was a relatively happy one. Four hundred years is time enough to feel at home, to feel that sense of place so long denied them in their wanderings throughout the European heartlands. These Jews, of course, were a breed apart from those who had lived through that exquisite moment of grandeur in Moorish Iberia, whose ancestors found succour in the Empire of the Ottomans. Unlike the Ladino speaking Sephardim, the Ashkenazi, the Yiddish speaking Jews of Eastern Europe, were thought to have come up from the German Rhineland but, in truth, they were a strange and hearty mix of tribes - of peasants, traders, nomads and scholars – some whose forefathers travelled up from the Caucuses and ancient Khazaria others who began their journey as far west as Narbonne.

But ingrained in all Jews, no matter where they may have originated from, was a sense that no place was really home – no place but one. And that place was not a place at all, not in the physical sense, at least. It was more an idea planted deep in their collective subconscious (as the young man who had recently returned to Vienna from the Salpêtrière hospital in Paris and who was also of these tribes might have said). That idea which resided in the head of those Jews who called themselves Jews, even though they might have looked differently, spoken differently and prayed differently – that idea was called 'Israel'. For according to the most learned of the Rabbinical scholars, a Jew might live in Poland and, if he were devout enough, prayed enough and was patient enough, could at the same time reside in Israel. For Israel, in their way of thinking, was a state of mind.

Now there were those who disputed this notion, saying that Israel was indeed a place locatable on the world map and that it was written the Jews would not find true peace and salvation until that physical space determined precisely in the Bible be re-populated again by them. But these people, who were beginning to be known as 'Zionists', were very small in number.

Z, himself, had read the writings of Theodor Hertzl, and

157

was much impressed by the man. But he also understood the enormous implications of having the Jews form a state of their own – especially in an area which was already populated by other tribes who prayed to a different god and had staked their own claim to that territory.

Yet the quandary existed and there was no getting around it. Hundreds of thousands of Eastern European Jews were being forced out of their ancestral homes with no place to go. As the crisis deepened, the pressures mounted. Those countries like England and America which had opened their doors to these impoverished refugees, were being overwhelmed with hungry bodies and, in the case of England, without work to provide for them.

So what to do? What to do? Z only knew that left to the established order, groups like the Board of Guardians, tiny plasters would be used for massive haemorrhaging and the patients most in need would be allowed to bleed to death while the Guardians, wringing their guilt laden hands, would cry that they had really done their best.

Z's own father was one of those pious men who had found Israel both in his heart and in his head. A pedlar by trade, he would take the train each morning with his case of goods, travelling to the outlying districts where certain products were still rare and competition for selling them was minimal. One day Z's father left for Jerusalem, giving up his family, his home and his worldly dreams (if any he still had) for a life of meditation, prayer and poverty. Z partly admired his father for his spiritual determination, but he also never forgave him. (Indeed, what son could ever forgive a father who abandoned him, for even the most noble of reasons?)

Educated, acculturated and, by now, becoming a writer of some repute admired by both Jews and Christians, Z was still trying to come to terms with his sense of self. Who was he,

158

really? Where did he come from?

Like most Jews, Z could trace his ancestors back to his grandfather and perhaps his great-grandfather. But after that, family genealogy became lost in the mists of time as personal histories were subsumed by stories of the tribes and of a 'people'. Maggie, on the other hand, could have traced her own ancestry back for a number of generations through birth certificates, land grants, deeds and all the other paper records which the State maintained. But, of course, she too would reach the time, not too many hundreds of years before, when even that trail would peter out and lineage would resort back to tribal wanderings; for it is only the State and the Church that defines a pedigree just as long as the particular State and Church are ascendant.

Z understood that lineage and power were intricately related. Slaves took on the name of their master and immigrants tended to adopt family names more congenial to the countries they were living in, thus severing forever that convenient link with their most direct line of ancestors (who, in fact, had done the same thing in their voyage from nation to nation). So, for the newly assimilated Jew, the question of who you were and where you came from could hardly be solved through tracing a family tree, for ancestral names meant nothing. The answer to this question could only be broached by looking not at individual family members but rather at one's people in a wider sense - either that or by wiping the ancestral slate clean and starting afresh.

This understanding, however, only created more intricate problems. For who defined the history of his people? Who were the keepers of the stories which gave him insight into his particular lineage? Who were the keepers of the collective memories? Was it the Board of Guardians? Was it the Rabbis? Was it the writers and the artists who passed on to the future a certain song or picture – artefacts which gave meaning to life in the past? Or was it the tales of his own father and mother (or, in his case, his grandmother) that were told and retold throughout the generations?

It was simpler, Z realised, to re-invent oneself, especially in a place like London and in a time like his when different worlds were being created and old economies were being shifted to make room for the new. Z had adopted a language and a literature and had made it his own. He had even toyed around with a different vision of God – a God more suitable for this period of modernism and assimilation. But, try as he might to detach himself from his past, in the background lurked another language, another literature and another God, more austere, more primitive perhaps, but one he knew with an intimacy that the amalgam hardly could possess.

Z's thoughts drifted back to a time earlier in the year, in April when the Anglo-Jewish Historical Exhibition opened at the newly complete Albert Hall, where the Guardians, as part of the Jubilee celebration, proudly displayed the ancient artefacts of Jewish culture and civilisation dating back to the time of King David and spanning the great epochs from Nebuchadnezzar to the long sojourn in Moorish Spain. In its grandness and opulence, this exhibition was a statement by the richly cosseted Jews of England (those who had long been anglicised and had profited bountifully from Victoria's reign through their participation in the running of Empire) of their glorious past displayed in Biblical magnificence, like jewels from an ancient crown, as if to say, 'We, too, have royal blood and thus are worthy of your gracious trust and forbearance.' There were no klizmere bands, nothing in Yiddish, no Hassidic dances or songs. All dirt was banished. The splendour of the past all pointed south; everything to the east was simply ignored as an embarrassment.

For Z, the highlight of this exhibition had been an appearance by Heinrich Graetz, the noted Professor from Bresslau and Jewish historian, now old and feeble, who braved the hazards of the Channel to present a paper. Seeing this old man, this legend in the twilight of his years, was a moment of inspiration for Z. The paper, read haltingly, by this gentle man, was on the subject of the Wandering Jew, a myth which came into existence in Germany as late as Reformation times, when scepticism first made its appearance in European thought. The idea of the Wandering Jew, he said, was invented as a foil to this growth in rationalism. For if he existed and would bear witness to the crucifixion Christian faith could be saved. In the German form he was a degraded outcast, but in the form in which it reached France the figure of the Wandering Jew was ennobled and began to symbolise the idea of wandering Judaism that stands on a lofty turret, and from this position surveys the rising and falling billows of the world's history. It speaks all tongues for it has been in all lands. It escapes, in a manner which must be regarded as a miracle, all dangers and terrors. It is the youngest brother of time. It has a mighty memory of all the events of the thousands of years which have passed before it. The historical memorials of Judaism are, therefore, the most extensive of all nations and its history forms a history of the world in miniature.

This idea of Judaism as separate only by conception, but serving, because of its special historical path, as a reservoir of collective memories for all humanity, was something that quite appealed to Z. It was an outward looking notion which was nurtured in contemporary ideas of the brotherhood of man. It was a concept that could, once and for all, break down forever the gates of the ghetto by recognising the Jews as a people who represented the multifarious trials of

161

humankind.

Assimilation, after all, had brought its rewards and, as far as Z was concerned, there was no turning back. The difference Z had with the Board of Guardians, wasn't on the idea of assimilation itself but how it would happen and whose interests it would serve. For, in Z's interpretation of Graetz, the history of Judiasm wasn't just the relics on display at the Anglo-Jewish Historical Exhibition; it also included the Eastern experience with all the cultural richness that brought forth. If one looked beyond the economic poverty of the Polish refugees there was a great spiritual wealth every bit as glorious as King Solomon's temple, he would argue.

For the Guardians – in Z's mind, at least – assimilation meant a severance from those cultural roots; banishing Yiddish literature and theatre and the bitter-sweet stories of the shtetl. It meant the abandonment of the schuls, the tiny local prayer houses through which newly arrived immigrants maintained links with their former villages or towns, and the acceptance of the great temples of worship with its rabbinical hierarchy (called 'ministers' in deference to their British hosts) and, most of all, acceptable models of cleanliness, deportment and manners, which, along with a certain standard of language, would give them true entry into the English world. They would become English citizens – Anglicised Jews – gaining all the privileges that entailed.

But what would they lose? Somewhere in the ghetto resided the heart and soul of his people. What it was – what one would call it –was still a mystery to him. Yet it was a mystery he needed to explore. And somehow, in a strange way, this trial of Israel Lipski, with all its horror and grotesqueness, seemed to be related to this quest.

162

CHAPTER 18

MAGGIE ARRIVED AT the courthouse early but still not early enough to avoid the crowds of mainly Jews who had taken advantage of their single day of rest coming in their hundreds to witness this extraordinary event which was evolving in theatrical form as an East End saga played out by characters they had seen in their everyday lives; neighbourhood people like themselves, who had been given a part in this highest of dramas which would climax with a final and sublime moment of decision whereby a single word spoken by one of twelve anonymous men meant an ending of either life or death.

The previous day she had been crushed near the back of the courtroom lost in the swell of the crowd but today she was noticed by one of the guards who immediately saw by her appearance, her costume and, most of all, her demeanour, that she was not like the rest of what he thought of as 'the smelly mob', but a fragrant English lady; therefore he pushed his way through the rabble so as to escort her to a seat reserved for special guests of the court – that is to say, those ladies and gentlemen who, for some strange reason, wanted to observe this bizarre ritual of the uncultured versus the unwashed.

Maggie knew she was receiving special treatment by being given a preferential seat in the crowded courtroom while others who had arrived there before her were forced to wait in the disordered queue. But she didn't object. Why would she? Although she had democratic instincts and wrote powerfully about women's rights, she accepted the meagre privileges her class and sex would allow, not so much because she thought it her due but rather as a way of gaining whatever tiny advantage she might accrue to help overcome the massive deficit of being a very clever woman alone in a world dominated by thick-headed men.

The first day of the trial had left her somewhat bewildered. Though she was familiar with the types who had paraded before the witness box, she still had a clichéd notion of them. Many of the men looked the same to her – their clothing, their build, their unshaven and shabby appearance. But mostly it was the way they talked in a language she barely understood even though she had a smattering of words and terms picked up from her time in the East End; there was an intonation and rhythm of speech that made them all sound, to her, like one another.

Still, she was able to tell the protagonists well enough apart – Lipski, Rosenbloom and Schmuss. She was impressed with Lipski's calm demeanour (though she detected a sign of nervousness by the twitching of his hands) and his boyish look of bewilderment. Rosenbloom appeared to her as a scoundrel but not a murderer (though she had no idea what a murderer might look like). But if, on the basis of appearance, she was forced to choose the one who could have possibly done that unspeakable act of pure barbarity she would have selected Schmuss because of his great hulking presence. Yet that look was not unfamiliar to her in her work with the unemployed labourers of the East End. And she had found more than once that outward appearance often belied the workings within. The lowest of labourers might look fearsome but they were not necessarily base of heart – even though they were assumed to be so by many of their 'betters.'

The first witness called that morning was Inspector David Final of the Metropolitan Police who was at the Leman Street police station when Lipski was brought in. Maggie's

164

feeling about the police had always been similar to most of the British middle class who saw them as fine and worthy upholders of law and virtue – occasionally a bit dim though generally incorruptible. But over the last few years her opinion about the police had begun to shift. Initially as a reporter witnessing the sheer brutality that occurred during protests organised by the Social Democrats where several demonstrators were nearly clubbed to death. Then, of late, having followed the case of a woman who had been hounded and harassed by several constables who had arrested her on a charge of soliciting simply because she had been walking alone on Regent Street. This particular case – of a certain Miss Cass who was employed as a shop assistant in the area - had been taken up by the Pall Mall Gazette claiming a blatant disregard for natural justice as the police seemed to have gone after that poor woman with a vengeance, becoming a law unto themselves. So even though Inspector David Final's evidence was generally straightforward, Maggie felt a lingering sense of doubt.

Inspector Final confirmed that when Lipski was brought to the Leman Street Police Station he was still partially insensible and was seen by the divisional surgeon who gave him some mustard and warm water as an emetic for the acid Lipski had ingested, though it failed in its intended effect of making him sick. His clothing was then searched and some coins – three silver shillings and some coppers – were found along with a pawn ticket which, according to Final, were all replaced in his pocket before Lipski was then transported to London Hospital.

After disposing of Lipski, Final then went to Batty Street where he entered the room and examined the lock, stating that the appearance of the screws jutting out from the wood indicated that the door had been forced open, though the lock itself seemed to be in perfect order except that the bolt was shot.

He also confirmed that one of the constables who had been at the scene had brought him the coat and hat which had belonged to the prisoner. Final had searched the pockets and had found a card from the United Stick and Cane Dressers Protection Society in the name of J. Lipski along with a pawn ticket for a silver Geneva watch made out to John Lipski for the amount of six shillings from a broker on Merdle Street.

So, thought Maggie, the name he used to conduct his business wasn't Israel at all, but John. How very strange she thought. For that was the name she had selected for her own male self. Was that to be his English persona, she wondered?

McIntyre's cross examination had been rather pathetic, she had felt. He had simply focused on having the Inspector review Lipski's condition when he had arrived at the Leman Street police station and tried to get Final to clarify his assertion that Lipski was only partially insensible whereas on his oath before the magistrate he swore that Lipski had appeared insensible without any such qualification. It was, she thought, a minor point of semantics and only served to get the judge into a tizzy, causing him more than once to admonish the hapless attorney for the defence.

What interested her more, however, was how it seemed clear that the police had assumed from the beginning Lipski had been the murderer and treated him as such from the moment he was discovered underneath that poor woman's bed. Their job, as she suspected they saw it, was to build a case for conviction rather than investigate if there wasn't a possible alternative. So when the interpreter – a man with the unlikely name of Smedge – accompanied Inspector Final to the hospital that evening after Lipski's fiancé had come to say that her man had wished to give a statement, he was obliged to issue Lipski with a translation of the official caution, 'You are not bound to say anything, but what you do say may be used as evidence against you...', before accepting to take down his version of the tragic event. (Though McIntyre made it seem that this mandatory caution may have been stated incorrectly – opening up the possibility of some technical defect.)

In court the transcript of this statement was read out sentence by sentence, by Inspector Final stopping after each line so that the words could be translated by Karameli into Yiddish for the benefit of the prisoner. It was strange and arduous, Maggie thought. But then she realised how curious it was that prior to this, Karameli had translated nothing into Lipski's tongue – only the reverse – Yiddish into English, for the purposes of the judge and jurors. Lipski, she suspected, hadn't understood most of the testimony that was issued against him, the questioning of the attorneys nor the judge's intrusions, because of his poor knowledge of the English language.

But, in the end, Lipski had been firm. When the charge was later read to him at the Lehman Street Police Station, translated by Smedge, he had looked the interpreter in the eye and said, '*Ich habe nicht gehalhret, ich habe nicht getahren*' – 'I have not murdered her, I have not done it.'

Maggie stared up at the figure standing at the dock. The boyish face had been transformed over those two days of trial, she thought, and had aged as if two days were two years or even two decades. She tried to imagine his look when he was being questioned that day at the Lehman Street police station, when he was being formally charged and had spoken those words - '*Ich habe nicht getahern.*' Who believed him then? The police? Inspector Final? And who believed him now? She glanced over at the jury – those twelve men good and true. Dressed in dark and sombre clothes, they looked the very model of the straight and proper burgher celebrating the Queen this year in Jubilee England. But who were they? Who were they really? Each of those men had a life, a job or a profession, and, perhaps, a wife and children waiting for them at home. Each one, alone, was an individual with his own trials and tribulations. Yet together, in court, they looked so much the same. They looked so ... what was the word she was searching for? Respectable! Yes, that was it - respectable! And that was the problem, wasn't it? They were blinkered with respectability! What did they see when they looked up at the dock? Did they see a frightened young man (for Lipski must certainly be frightened, she thought) on trial for his very existence? Or did they simply see a murderer who the police, in their efficiency, had quickly identified and charged, thereby launching the mechanism of which they were now a part - like the chorus in a drama by some ancient Greek tragedian.

After Inspector Final came Dr. Kay whose surgery was on Batty Street at the corner of Commercial Road, just a stone's throw from number 16. Maggie had seen him before at the inquest and had taken an immediate dislike to the man as he reminded her so much of those stiff and starched, impossibly pompous men of the medical profession she had the misfortune to have known during her years of training as a nurse. Most of the hospital doctors she had become acquainted with were little more than butchers, she thought, unconcerned with the feelings of their patients and prescribing cures that were often more terrible than the disease. Neighbourhood surgeries were little better, separated from the community by deep chasms of class with swaggering doctors looking down on their filthy flock like feudal lords. There were exceptions, of course but Maggie's intuition told her that Dr Kay wasn't one of those saintly figures she had come across occasionally

– those selfless ones whose mission brought them to the depths of human suffering and who ministered to the body as an enlightened priest might tend the soul. Kay was more a pay-as-you-go man; pay a shilling, pop a pill and out you go. His function was more bureaucratic than medicinal – a private adjunct of the State making sure his little patch was free of weeds. He was, in that way, part of the magnificently intricate apparatus of control that allowed the Queen to look upon her England with the benign tenderness of one who is secure in the knowledge that hereditary privilege and power would always be hers.

Kay was led by the prosecuting attorney, step by step, to describe his observations when he first had been called to the Batty Street room by his assistant: how he saw the woman lying on her back, dead, with her hair dishevelled. Her mouth had a stream of yellow coming from the corner on the left-hand side. Her neck had two or three splashes of nitric acid as did her breast. And her hands were covered with stains of that dreadful substance called, in deference to its terrible corrosiveness, 'aqua fortis.'

The dead woman was under a duvet which covered her up to her breasts. Kay had turned it down to see if 'any violence had been offered to her' (a phrase Maggie copied verbatim onto her notepad because of its extraordinary euphemism. What did it mean to 'offer' violence to a woman? Why couldn't they just say what they meant?). The dead woman's chemise was pulled up to the breast and the body was exposed. He noticed blood on the duvet – splashes of blood mixed with acid, suggesting that the effect of its administration would have been to make the woman cough quite violently. However, there were no marks of violence on the lower part of the body, he confirmed.

From the temperature of the corpse, which was growing

cold though rigor mortis hadn't yet set in, he estimated that the woman had been dead for about three hours more or less, taking into account the size of the woman – for she was quite stout – and the warm weather.

After inspecting the body a search was begun for the bottle from which the acid had come. It was during this search that the prisoner had been discovered lying on his back underneath the bed. He was in his shirt sleeves, Kay said. He looked pale and his eyes were partially open so Kay could observe the whites and part of the pupil. Kay then felt his pulse and, confirming that the man was alive, put his finger on his cornea to see if he was unconscious. Deciding that he was insensible, Kay slapped him on the face, whereupon the prisoner opened his eyes wider.

Kay now instructed the police to help him get the man to his feet and accordingly Lipski was pulled across the floor toward the window and then lifted and propped up against the corner where the two walls met. As the police held him aloft, Kay tried questioning the man and gaining no response, shook him and tried questioning him again – in English - to which he received no response and then in German, again receiving no reply. The police then took charge of him and carried him away.

The next day, on the 29th, Kay carried out a post mortem on the corpse, finding it to be a body of a well-developed young woman about six months pregnant showing no sign of having had recent intercourse. He noted several violent blows to the head, with the right eye discoloured and swollen. The right temple was also injured with the muscle underneath pulped and bloody from what he could only conclude were very violent blows, though the brain, itself, was not congested. However, in his opinion, the force of these blows would have been sufficient to render her unconscious.

It was also Kay's opinion that the acid was administered after the woman was beaten unconscious; the greater portion appeared to have gone down the windpipe so that the actual cause of death would have been suffocation. He estimated the amount of acid ingested would have been about half an ounce.

Cross examined by McIntyre, Kay confirmed that there had been no evidence of recent intercourse. McIntyre also questioned him about Lipski's state when discovered. Could that have been from the effect of the poison? Not simply from the poison, Kay agreed, Lipski hadn't ingested enough of it. Kay thought it was due to the prisoner's mental perturbation. Wouldn't that have been rare, for a man to have gone unconscious from mental causes? But suppose Lipski had been seized by two men who had knelt on his chest and forced poison down his throat by prying open his mouth – could that have not more easily caused his state of insensibility?

These were good and proper questions, Maggie thought. But they seemed to be lost, evaporating into the air with all the other good and proper questions the defence had so hesitantly brought out.

William Calvert, the house surgeon at London Hospital who had examined Lipski shortly after he had arrived found that the fingers of his left hand had been stained with nitric acid. Also he noticed scratches on the backs of both hands and on the right wrist as well as the forearms. The skin, he noted, had been rubbed off both elbows.

Was Lipski left or right handed? Maggie wondered. Did the stains on his finger-tips come from pouring acid down the woman's throat or from fighting off the attackers who had tried to force the substance down his own? And the skin abrasions on the elbows – did they come from dragging Lipski

171

out from underneath the bed or were they the consequence of two strong men throwing him onto the ground and roughing him up whilst he lay on his back?

Calvert indicated there were no significant marks of violence on Lipski's person other than the scratches and abrasions. But what about his throat? McIntyre had asked. Wasn't there evidence of injury inside the mouth such as might have been caused by a piece of wood used to pry it open as Lipski had stated? Yes, Calvert admitted, there was certainly evidence that a foreign substance had been thrust inside his mouth.

Then Thomas Redmayne, another of the house physicians, was called to testify that he had used a stomach pump on Lipski and that the injuries noted in his throat could well have come from this procedure – especially as a tube needed to be forcibly inserted down through his oesophagus.

But could the injuries in Lipski's mouth and throat have been caused by violence of another sort? McIntyre didn't pursue this question and Maggie was left to write a simple note to herself regarding the nature of fact and circumstance. Authorities always presented fact as if they alone had a God-given right to determine the nature of occurrences. For these fine and upright gentlemen, everything eventually fit together neat and tidy and it was their job to make sure it remained like that.

But it was the vial of nitric acid, aqua fortis, the contents of which had been forced down the throat of two victims (for, in Maggie's eyes, Lipski was a victim even if he was a casualty of himself), splattered on clothing, hands, bed and floor in a never-ending stream, that the prosecution focused on. All that corrosive acid, what seemed like oceans of the stuff when the resulting damage was surveyed, had come from one tiny vial containing a single ounce. And where did that vial come from?

Maggie recalled the testimony of Dr Kay saying that Lipski was found when searching for the missing vial which had contained the poison. It was subsequently located in a fold of the bed covers, pointed out, she recalled, by Rosenbloom.

Now a man named Charles Moore was called to the stand. He was the manager of the shop in Blackchurch Lane where the origin of the substance had been traced. Moore testified that he remembered a man coming into his shop that fateful morning at around nine o'clock who asked for a pennyworth of aqua fortis. Moore had weighed it out for him – one ounce in weight – and had poured it into a two-ounce vial the man had brought with him.

It was Friday morning, several days after the murder, that Moore was brought to London hospital and taken to the ward where Lipski was being held in order to identify the prisoner.

But how was he identified? Moore had been escorted to the Hospital by a police inspector and taken to the ward where Lipski was kept, watched over by a constable who sat guard at the foot of the bed. There lay a man of foreign appearance with bandages over his head and a policeman standing watch. In such circumstances was an identification fair? After all, as McIntyre ascertained, hadn't Moore's shop been especially busy that morning? Hadn't there been a half dozen people asking him for different things and competing for his attention?

A circumstantial chain had been constructed by the prosecution, Maggie thought, which looked to be straightforward. But it all depended on belief – belief and interpretation. Maggie, herself, was well versed in taking facts and ideas and spinning them out in various ways in order to create believable fiction. Sometimes things fit together easily,

173

sometimes they were forced. But she could always create a number of different stories from her material.

Anyway, it had come out in the evidence that nitric acid was often used by stickmakers to stain their wood. Therefore, it wouldn't have been unusual to find a vial of the stuff in a stickmaker's shop. And even if Lipski had purchased an ounce of aqua fortis that morning in question, did that mean he had used it to murder Miriam Angel? After all, there was a flood of acid to be accounted for, not merely an ounce.

When Moore had completed his testimony and had left the witness box there was a moment of confusion as if something was supposed to happen but, for whatever reason, hadn't. Maggie glanced around. She heard a sound like the rustle of leaves that portends something in the woods, something unexpected. The audience was restless in expectation. Was there something they knew, she wondered? Something she didn't?

And then she saw her, being escorted down the aisle which led to the witness box next to the judge. She was a plain and simple woman, someone who would have easily faded into the crowd at Petticoat Lane; thick of leg, slightly hunched, a face worn over by the years and eyes without an inkling of twinkle, without even an echo of the glint that comes with youth. Whatever there had been had dried away like arid dessert ruts that once were cool blue streams but left no trace after years of blistering heat and stifling dust. This woman, thought Maggie, had at one time been a girl even though it was hard for her to imagine. And she had been a baby once, someone whose parents had showered with love and looked upon with faithful eyes of hope. What imponderable events had robbed her of that? Who was this poor creature? Why was she being called to court? What manner of beast would force this sad, ungainly thing to play a part in such

174

grotesqueness?

Her name was Anna Lyons. And hearing the surname, Maggie suddenly understood. For this was the woman whose daughter, Kate, had been engaged to the young man who stood on the other side of the room and gazed out with hollow eyes that were expressionless.

Anna Lyons spoke English and answered the questions put to her by the hawk-nosed prosecutor in a languid tone but without hesitation. Her daughter, she said, had been engaged to the prisoner for six months. On Monday, the 27th of June, her future son-in-law had come to her house about one o'clock to eat his dinner and had asked whether she would be kind enough to lend him some money. But, she had no money left to lend him that day. So she had taken her brush and her ring to Church Street to pawn in return for twenty-five shillings.

Maggie gazed at the woman with tired, tired eyes and thought about pawning a brush and a ring. A brush and a ring. How would she brush her brittle hair? What would she wear on her thin, barren fingers?

She pawned these things for twenty-five shillings and then... and then...

And then what? Maggie thought to herself. And then what did she do?

She took it there. Where? She took it there to his house and gave it to him, to Mr. Lipski. She called him that – 'Mr. Lipski'. She pawned her brush and her ring and took the money there to his house and gave it to him - to Mr. Lipski.

Oh, how sad, Maggie thought. How very, very sad. A brush and a ring. Pawned for what? For hope. For the future of her daughter and the promise of offspring. She pawned her ring and her brush for the promise of life after death. And now it was gone. Gone was the ring. Gone was the brush.

175

Gone was the twenty-five shillings. Gone was the promise of grandchildren. Gone was hope. Gone. All gone.

Did the prisoner say anything about repaying her? The hawk-nosed prosecutor wanted to know. Repaid? Of course she would be repaid! She was to be repaid ten times over. Repaid by the promise of the future of her daughter. But, yes, he said, 'Saturday, please God, I will take in the work, or finish the work. I shall pay you all I owe you.'

Had he borrowed some before? Of, course, she said. The total had been two pounds and five shillings. And had any money been given back? Nothing. Nothing back. But on Saturday, please God, he would take in work or finish work and pay back all he owed her. That is what he said. And that is what he meant to do.

The prosecutor waved his hand as if to say what more could be added to such a story: an old woman who pawns her ring and her brush to lend money to a murderer.

Then McIntyre came up to cross-examine. Had she known Lipski long? Oh, yes - for two years. Ever since he had been working for her son-in-law. (Another son-in-law, thought Maggie? Had she also pawned a brush and ring for the first one?)

Was he a man of good character, asked McIntyre? So far she couldn't give him a bad character as he always behaved himself. But left unsaid, the words lingered in the air: Who knows? Perhaps he is a murderer…

And did she know that the money she had lent him would be used for the purpose of fitting up a workshop? Yes, she thought so. Yes, she did. And did she know what kind of work he was doing? Yes, horn work. Stick work? Yes, horn work and stick work. And did she know that he was working for a Mr. Lewis in Aldermanbury? No she didn't. And others? She didn't know them.

176

Then McIntyre, with a flourish, handed the judge a list of names of the people for whom he worked; for whom Lipski would be making sticks. So there it was - hard evidence that the sticks would indeed have buyers. There it was in black and white. God willing, on Saturday, Lipski would really have paid his future mother-in-law back the money that he owed her.

CHAPTER 19

Z COULD HARDLY believe his ears, as if they were impacted with wax causing a distortion of sound, transforming the intricate codes that allow the magic of comprehension to be short-circuited and thus changing the nature of meaning into gibberish. But today impacted wax wasn't the problem and so he stared out at the pathetic figure of McIntyre with disbelief, wondering if what he said could possibly be correct.

Poland had just announced that the case for the Crown had been concluded. Now McIntyre stood before the judge and spoke in the monotonous tones of a commercial lawyer more used to unravelling the Gordian knots of arcane contracts tied neatly with pink ribbons and smelling of eau de cologne than dealing with strange-sounding foreigners living in stinking slums and occasionally killing one another as starving rodents might do when faced with a shortage of edible dung. To Z's horror, McIntyre stood there and said that the defence did not intend to call any witnesses.

No witnesses?

Not a single one offering alternatives to Lipski's curious injuries or how he ended up stuffed underneath a bed behind an egg crate, a jacket and a smelly old coat or questioning the workings of that ridiculous lock (and thus the idea that Lipski had bolted himself in) or, even more incredibly, disputing the lack of any significant motive that might engender such a horrific crime in a pauperised house where a swollen woman lay like a lump in bed in a room where there was nothing of value – not even herself? Was there no one to query why a young man of good reputation, engaged to be married and just starting a business of his own, would brutally kill a hapless being such as that, without a penny to her name and six months with child, by pouring acid down her throat? Could Z actually have heard correctly? Did McIntyre really say that the defence would call no witnesses?

In fact, that is exactly what McIntyre said. And having said what he did, the defence rested. So, apart from the final summations, the trial was essentially over. And, as if to emphasise this fact, the judge banged his gavel and the court broke for lunch.

Z, still confounded by the rapidity of events, stared out at the courtroom as if in a daze. What he saw in the scurry of bodies headed for the exit door, was the image of the uncomprehending prisoner, a look of utter confusion on his face, being led away to the darkness of the cellar. And then his eyes scanned the room, searching for a particular face which he located in a scrum of lawyers. Their eyes met – his and Myers. What message was transmitted? Confusion? Despair? Or was it betrayal? And if so, betrayal of what? Betrayal of whom?

He waited behind as the courtroom cleared, the buzz and clatter becoming progressively lessened, like a crowded train watched from a station moving off into the distance. Then he stood there once more alone. Except for her. She waited for him again by the door. Quietly. Patiently. And yet, as he walked towards her, he could see that she was brimming with emotion – but so contained. How unlike the ghetto, he thought, where emotion flowed ceaseless from every pore. She had the outward appearance of statuesque tranquillity until he studied her face and saw the slight twitching at the corners of her mouth. Like climbing up a peaceful hill, he thought - peaceful until one looks down into the cone of the volcano

She wanted to know what was going on. Couldn't he

interpret for her? After all, these were his people.

His people? Well they were, weren't they? And yet they weren't. They knew nothing of the poetry of Keats nor the tranquil air when boating up the Thames on the way to his beloved Kew Gardens. What did they know of all that – those people who thought that life revolves around the schul and the market? What on earth compelled him to come to this dreary place? Who was that man Lipski anyway? Why did he care what happened to him?

Myers was waiting outside the courtroom door. He was in a rush – couldn't stay to talk. But things weren't as bad as they seemed. No, not at all. There was method in the madness. The prosecution hadn't proved their case. The ball was in their court, so to speak. It was up to them to show that all the supposition and coincidence was enough to hang someone. That now depended on how convincing Poland would be in summing up. If McIntyre had called a single witness, then the prosecution would be allowed to address the jury last. Ridiculous, of course, but until the law could be changed, that's the way it was. So the defence, considering their options, thought it better to retain their rights and have the jury leave with McIntyre's words ringing in their ears instead of Poland's.

Maggie thought that possibly Myers was right. The case certainly hadn't been proved beyond a reasonable doubt, she told him as they sat in the same wooden booth at the same pub they had come to the day before.

Z thought of McIntyre and pictured him just moments before droning on emotionlessly like a statistician giving a lecture on the number of beans it takes to cleanse your bowels. Was it the cold light of reason or logic that would save Israel Lipski's hide? He suspected not. In fact, Z felt himself beset by a strong premonition of doom.

180

Maggie on the other hand felt that there was still hope. For, despite everything, she had a basic, elemental and deep seeded trust in British justice.

CHAPTER 20

Z'S PENCIL FLEW fast and furiously as he watched Poland expound to the jury, his face of chiselled stone expressionless, but his eyes like those of a hawk focused intently on its prey.

Poland's summation was short, forceful and to the point. After scribbling his notations, Z inserted some parenthetical comments so as to underline questionable aspects of the case:

"The facts were so simple and clear that the jury could come to only one conclusion. The prisoner and the deceased were the only ones in the room and on that day the prisoner had purchased the acid which undoubtedly was the cause of her death. The question of motive was not material (*why not?*) but it was reasonable to suppose that the accused might have intended to outrage the deceased *(really?)* or to commit a robbery *(what was there to rob?)*. The prisoner's answer to the charge was that the crime was committed by Rosenbloom and Schmuss. He asks the jury to believe that even though they were unknown to each other *(are we certain?)* these two men combined together to kill Mrs Angel in broad daylight and that even though the woman was unknown to them and was in such poverty that she had to borrow five shillings the day before to pay her rent. *(They didn't know that, but maybe Lipski did.)* The prisoner was an active young man and if he had struggled for dear life with those two men, didn't the jury think he would have marked them in some manner while they were seizing him and opening his mouth? *(Perhaps not if one held his arms from behind.)* But neither man had any mark, neither did the prisoner have any marks such as he would have had if there was the struggle he had alleged (*How about the marks on his elbows and in his throat?*) The marks he

182

did bear were such as he would be likely to get in a struggle with a woman *(how come?)* and this was all the more likely to be the most feasible explanation when they remembered that he uttered no cries for help. *(How could he cry out if they had gagged him? Why didn't the woman cry out as well?)* At first there was a little mystery in the case, the man Schmuss having gone away, but it was now proved he went to Birmingham for work and that he made no secret about going...*(Indeed! So what does that prove?)*'

The jury had listened to Poland carefully, noting his every word and seemed not to flinch at any of the inconsistencies or suppositions neatly contained in this off-handed summation which Z had annotated with the terse comments above. They appeared content and satisfied with no trace of scepticism on their collective brow. If anything, they seemed quite pleased that a gentleman like Poland would address them with such courtesy – asking them to believe, not actually demanding. It was, after all, up to them to verify what the good gentleman claimed was so obvious. But would the good gentleman have claimed that if it wasn't?

Maggie also focused attentively on Poland's summation. But her eyes were directed somewhere else. She was gazing at the prisoner in the dock and trying to intuit how much he understood. He knew more English than he let on, she thought, noticing his eyebrows twitch after Poland spoke about the absence of any signs of struggle because the prisoner showed no serious trace of marks. No serious trace of marks?. One only needed to look at his boyish face which wasn't boyish anymore. Over two days his features had hardened and his face had become that of an ageless man. Oh, yes, he was marked, but not in the way Poland meant it!

And then McIntyre stood to make his final address. He stood for a moment, quietly, as if deep in thought. It might

183

have been his finest hour. It might have been the moment of his career when suddenly words of brilliance would leap into his head and he could speak them with a golden tongue. It might have been. But who, after all, was he trying to defend? What, really, was in it for him?

When he finally spoke, his words were restrained and his tone was almost apologetic. That he was forced to have put forward a defence which had implicated others was a painful duty. But whether or not they were convinced of Lipski innocence, he had to submit that the prosecution had not made out such a case against the accused as would justify his conviction upon this fearful charge. What motive did the prisoner have? He had first thought that the prosecution was trying to imply that the prisoner had entered the woman's room for an immoral purpose, but the medical evidence entirely destroyed that contention and the prosecution had given it up.

For a moment, it seemed to Z, there was a light in McIntyre's eyes and a little wind, however slight, had buffeted his sail. But just as he had established a bit of connection with the jury, just when they had started to perk up, hearing something of interest beyond the drone, just at that moment...

Mr. Justice Stephen interjected. In a voice that bristled with authority he instructed the jury that the prosecution had not given up the motive of immorality – certainly not! It was only that they hadn't attempted to prove adultery had taken place!

All eyes had shifted from McIntyre to the judge. And when Justice Stephen had said what he had to say, venting his annoyance, all eyes shifted back again to McIntyre, who now looked that much smaller. It was like pricking a human balloon. For a moment, thought Z, he had almost flown, but now, admonished by the judge, he had been well and truly deflated, fluttering haplessly to the ground.

McIntyre cleared his throat and continued: The alternative motive suggested was robbery, but the accused was known to be a man of exemplary character. He did not conceal his movements on the morning in question and must have been aware that there wasn't much to be gained by plundering the deceased's room. In fact, the circumstances seemed to indicate that the murder was the work of two men not one. If the prisoner had indeed attempted to outrage the deceased she would have certainly struggled and called out for assistance. But had there been two men, one could easily have gagged the woman while the other administered the blows, preventing her from calling out in alarm. It was asserted that the door of the room was locked on the inside when the prisoner was found under the deceased woman's bed. The evidence, however, showed that the door was easily opened by the women pushing from the outside, which would indicate that the lock had merely stuck. If the door had been locked, what reason could there possibly be for the prisoner locking himself in? The fact that the accused was found under the bed in an insensible condition was far more in keeping with his statement that he was attacked by two men than with the theory of the prosecution. Given the contradictory aspects of the evidence, certainly the jury would find it too inconclusive to justify finding the prisoner guilty of this awfully serious charge.

And then McIntyre sat down. And the courtroom fell silent.

It wasn't that McIntyre failed to bring out some crucial points, Z thought. It just seemed to him that this man, this tired commercial lawyer, was simply going through the motions. There was nothing forceful in his speech, nothing that would make the jury sit up and listen. He said what he had to say – interrupted, of course, by the judge. And that was that. The jury would have to make up their minds based on reason and logic in a method not too dissimilar to analysing a contract. That is what McIntyre probably wished to see happen, Z suspected. But the problem was, it didn't seem to work like that.

Maggie sitting a few rows behind, had stopped taking notes. She found herself too horrified. She simply penned: 'These men aren't interested in justice, they only want to win. It could be cricket, it could be a footrace. It just so happens that a person's life is at stake. But they're not interested in that, they simply want to festoon their careers with peacock feathers and plaudits; to line their mantel- piece with trophies and nail hides onto their walls to remind them of their conquests...'

CHAPTER 21

Z UNFOLDED THE note that had been passed to him and quickly read the contents. 'The prosecution hasn't proved their case,' it said. 'No jury could possibly convict him.' Then neatly refolding the slip of paper along the original creases and sticking it into his jacket pocket, he glanced over at the small man sitting near the defence table. Myers caught his eye and nodded.

And then spoke the judge. This is how Z described the moment:

'Mr. Justice James Fitzjames Stephen, with his haggard face and his drooping jowls, cast a weary eye over his small domain and thought that life was simply a Biblical allegory destined to be repeated over again until the great sands of time swept all and sundry from this wicked world. Until that bitter-sweet moment, it was only the likes of him that kept the universe from collapsing in onto itself and so, understandably, his sense of duty was enormous. It was as if he was destined to carry the weight of Hercules on his stooping shoulders. But it was a burden, however onerous, that still fascinated him.'

In a voice devoid of passion, yet resonating with the authority of Her Imperial Majesty, the Queen of half the earth, the judge intoned:

The cause of death of the deceased was one of wilful murder. There was no doubt that sometime between the hours of six and eleven on the morning in question the deceased woman was murdered by some person or persons. There were only two motives which could be put forward for the commission of the crime – passion and avarice. There was nothing taken from the deceased's room because there was nothing to take and the circumstances did not seem to support the motive of avarice so it was more probable that passion was the motive for the crime and if that were so it would likely be the act of one man rather than two. As it was shown that the prisoner had not been acquainted with the deceased and her husband, if it was indeed the prisoner who committed the act it must have been under the influence of a sudden temptation, there being a window from which a view of the deceased's room could be obtained from the stairs. However, the prisoner was a man of good character and was engaged to be married and these were circumstances which the jury should take into consideration in favour of the prisoner. The man Schmuss remained in London for several days after 28 June and then went to Birmingham for work, writing from there to London, and his conduct certainly did not look like that of a man who had committed a horrible murder. There was evidence that the prisoner had nitric acid, but that no one else had. The prisoner's statement was a highly important part of the case and the witnesses Schmuss and Rosenbloom had been cross-examined as to its truth. One could hardly imagine that two men who were strangers to each other should walk down from the workshop and go into the deceased's room for the purpose of committing an assault upon her and it was almost as difficult to imagine that they should go into the room of a woman as poor as themselves for the purpose of taking a few clothes, which after all they did not take, and why should they rob the prisoner? How could they reconcile the prisoner's statement with the fact that the door was locked on the inside? The locking of the door was a circumstance of very great importance supposing the jury were of opinion that it was locked. The observations made on the part of the defence as to the improbability of the prisoner having committed the crime were of very great importance and should be carefully considered by the jury. However, if the jury came to the conclusion that the prisoner was the person who committed the offence, then the natural inference was that he attempted to commit suicide afterwards.

It was a summation that left Z aghast for it was not a summation at all, but an invitation for the jury to convict the prisoner, Israel Lipski, of wilful murder. And he wondered what Myers, whose face had turned quite ashen, now thought of the strategy the defence had set up to place the burden of proof upon the prosecution. There was a fatal flaw in that approach, thought Z, a fatal flaw that Myers, had probably only just considered, and that was the Queen's factotum who sat so smugly on his cushioned seat overlooking his surrogate realm. For say what they might, the last word belonged not to the defence but to the judge. Whatever assertions might have been spoken in the prisoners behalf, whatever doubts, whatever queries, were suddenly all wiped out, like dusting chalk marks from a classroom blackboard, by his terse, authoritative and commandingly sanctimonious summation.

It was a quarter to five when the jury retired. Eight minutes later they returned. Eight minutes later; time enough to walk to the jury room, cast a vote and come back out again. Time enough to simply confirm what everyone knew by then was the predetermined outcome.

The foreman rose and announced that the jury had reached a verdict. He announced it without anger, without pleasure, without joy, without malice. It was simply an announcement – simply that.

The verdict he announced was that Israel Lipski was innocent and free to go and live his life and marry Kate Lyons whom he would take as his wife...

That is what Maggie heard. That is what Maggie wanted

189

to hear. That is what she would have written.

But in the other universe which she was forced sometimes to recognize, that gruesome world which hardly conformed to romantic visions, the foreman stood and said what everyone (even Maggie) knew he would say: that the prisoner, Israel Lipski, was guilty as charged.

The jury had done their duty and the judge, well satisfied, put a black cap on his head. He put a black cap on his head and said:

'Israel Lipski, you stand convicted of the crime of wilful murder. By the law of England the punishment of that crime is death. I have only to say to you, prepare to die...'

'Prepare to die.' That is what the judge intoned. That is what he said. And Z looked up at the prisoner in the dock, the child, the boy, the refugee, the man, and thought – is he prepared?

'And the sentence of the court is that you be taken from hence to a place of execution, that you be there hanged by the neck till you are dead, and that your body be buried within the precincts of the prison in which you shall have been last confined ...'

And finally. And finally. And finally, almost as an afterthought, he said, 'May the Lord have mercy on your soul.'

A hush fell over the courtroom, over the audience, as Israel Lipski was led from the chamber back to Newgate Prison where he would be placed in the cell for the condemned. It was a reverent hush; a quietness of finality like that which occurs in the great wastelands of Antarctica after a strange, exotic animal, washed up upon the shore, has expired.

PART III

Weeks 6-8: The Aftermath

CHAPTER 22

THEY WALKED TOGETHER along the gravel path in Victoria Park until they came to a bench overlooking a little flower garden. Sitting down, the two of them gazed out onto a sweet display of honeysuckle hues and fragrant foliage, transporting themselves somewhere else. For within this tranquil space they were no longer in the East End of London, but in another realm far away from all the tumult and the grime which existed outside the narrow boundaries of this tiny urban oasis for the working classes.

Both had felt that unsteadiness of spirit which often comes in the wake of a great event for, like a mighty wave crashing from the sea, it is only in the aftermath that one sees the devastation. And so it was with them. Though they held a brief moment of hope that it would have turned out differently, that some brave soul on the jury might have questioned the basis of the shaky framework used to build that unfortunate young man's gallows, there came a time when each of them knew the game was up. The consequence of the verdict, though, was just beginning to dawn on them.

But was that it? Was there nothing to be done? And, if there was, how should they respond? It was here the two of them diverged. Maggie, for her part, had come to believe

191

that the young man was innocent – not so much because of what she heard at the trial (for she didn't really know what to make of that), but rather because she intuitively felt it to be so. She had stared into his face, into his eyes and had formed a curious bond with this soon-to-be executed child-like man (or man-like child). Somehow, she was convinced he was not an ordinary person, but someone very special. And she felt strangely connected to him on the basis of his 'otherness' – a quality, perhaps, they both shared. But beyond that nebulous emotion, and probably something she felt even stronger, was an inherent sense of outrage at the blatant disregard for the sacrosanct values of natural justice that came out in the process and procedure of the trial which she had witnessed.

Z, on the other hand, didn't know what he felt about Lipski's actual guilt or innocence. And being a Jew, himself, he had no inherent faith in Christian justice, even though he had come to value it in theory. But he did believe that the case against Lipski had remained unproven. And even more, he felt that something else was also going on. He didn't know exactly what, but it lingered like a vague, disturbing aftertaste. It had to do with something deeper and more essential than simply the question of how an impoverished young woman, six months pregnant, had come to be murdered on a hot summer's morning of Jubilee June.

So there they sat, each caught up in emotions of their own, yet bonded by a commonality, a unity of feeling that some great offence had occurred which they had witnessed and that, in effect, they had been ordained with a certain responsibility to rectify a wrong.

In such a way like minds connect. Nothing really need be said. All is understood instinctively. A sense of powerlessness mixed with outrage can also be empowering. There was a force for decency, they believed in 1887. For it was just thirteen years till the 20th century, bright, new and beckoning. And only one hundred years after that till the glories of the millennium. Certainly they were living on the cusp of a New Age when all things would be possible. They breathed the air of hope for the crack and fissures within the stultifying Empires were there for all to witness. One only had to peer across the Channel at the senile confusion of the Hapsburgs, the creaking dissolution of the Ottomans, the frantic death throws of the Tsars, the renewed risings in the Balkans to see the dance of progress but also crumble and decay. And as the 20th Century approached, was it so outlandish to believe that upon the wreckage of the old, a new architecture would appear? Something good. Something better than before. For this they did believe. This they understood. Each in their own way, of course. Each in their own way, but based on a faith that true principles of justice would prevail.

Nothing needed to be said. Nothing needed to be spoken. But they both knew that something needed to be done. It wasn't yet clear what that something was, but they knew that they were now employed by forces beyond themselves to act. How they would act precisely wasn't clear, nor did it need to be. The only thing that was important was the idea that they were somehow responsible for saving Israel Lipski swinging from the gallows on Monday morning, the 15th of August, just two short weeks from then.

Earlier in the day, Z had been at the British Museum doing some research on hanging. He hadn't ever considered the idea before; it wasn't something he was very interested in. He knew they happened occasionally but there were many ugly things in life. Why dwell on them? But now he needed to know what actually happened. This is what he found out:

'...the inmate is ordinarily weighed the day before the execution, and a rehearsal is done using a sandbag of the same weight as the prisoner. This is to determine the length of "drop" necessary to ensure a quick death. If the rope is too long, the inmate could be decapitated, and if it is too short, the strangulation could take as long as 45 minutes. The rope, which should be 3/4-inch to 1 1/4-inch in diameter, must be boiled and stretched to eliminate spring or coiling. The knot should be lubricated with wax or soap to ensure a smooth sliding action. Immediately before the execution, the prisoner's hands and legs are secured, he is blindfolded, and the noose is placed around the neck, with the knot behind the left ear. The execution takes place when a trap-door is opened and the prisoner falls through. The prisoner's weight should cause a rapid fracture-dislocation of the neck. However, instantaneous death rarely occurs. If the inmate has strong neck muscles, is very light, if the "drop" is too short, or the noose has been wrongly positioned, the fracture-dislocation is not rapid and death results from slow asphyxiation. If this occurs the face becomes engorged, the tongue protrudes, the eyes pop, the body defecates, and violent movements of the limbs occur...'

Was this what would happen to the young man with the bewildered look who had quite remarkably managed to keep his dignity over the two days of trial? Was this what would happen to the lad whose gaze had penetrated into Z's dreadful nightmares? Could Z imagine Lipski dangling from a rope, his bloated face cyanic blue, his gentle eyes thrust demonically from their sockets, his tongue protruding starkly from a contorted mouth, as the body's final defecation oozed down his legs, lingering on his rigid toes before dropping onto the arid ground beneath that corpse swinging silent in the summer heat of August?

The flowers, they shimmered in the bright. The air was crisp and pure, oxygenated by the foliage in this piece of

194

green protectiondom. Two conflicting emotions beset him –
one of beauty, one of fear. The beauty was fading with the
setting sun. The horror, though, had just begun.

CHAPTER 23

HAYWARD'S OFFICE WAS just off Cheapside, tantalisingly close to Old Jewry Street, an ancient road that dated back to the Norman Conquest, surviving in name the Jewish expulsion of 1290 by the first and most ruthless of the Edwards. It was a simple chamber, not great in size, as Hayward worked alone except for Myers and several junior clerks who managed to look invisible. On first sight, Z thought the place a shambles – even compared to the Record's remarkable state of derangement – but he soon became aware that what appeared as disorganisation was simply the outward manifestation of too much work and too little room. Myers, in fact, was a brilliantly obsessive systematizer who kept Hayward's little ship afloat despite the overwhelming ballast of paper which threatened each day to sink them into the underground river that people claimed ran mysteriously below.

A small wooden table had been cleared of its boxes to provide space for the conference which had been called by Myers on Hayward's behalf after the initial shock of Lipski's conviction had worn off and, in its place, the determination to save an innocent man. For, it seems, both Myers and Hayward had been convinced that the jury would find their client not guilty as charged – until the final moment of the judge's summation. What ensued was a sense of outrage and anger coupled with a tinge of guilt that somehow, in some way, they had been culpable.

But how were they to have known that Geoghegan would leave them in the lurch? Their strategy had been based upon the notion that the prosecution's case would fall apart for lack of concrete evidence. But that had depended on an articulate attorney who could passionately underline this fact to a weak-kneed, lily-livered jury that otherwise would be playing the prosecution's poodle. It also depended on the judge's adherence to the letter of the law without introducing his own moral conjectures which, as Z had realised, was essentially an invitation to convict quickly so he, the judge, could don his black hat, pass sentence, and still be home in time for dinner.

As the solicitor and chief clerk, Hayward and Myers were helplessly obliged to watch these rogue events mischievously play themselves out. And as Lipski's hired solicitor, Hayward was the man primarily responsible to his client - which ordinarily would have been neither here nor there, but in this case presented a serious problem in that Hayward sincerely believed in Lipski's innocence, as did his most valued and trusted employee, Myers. And being someone both honest and honourable, Hayward was truly devastated by what he saw as his failure to provide the best possible defence to save a seemingly virtuous man from the gallows.

Maggie had come along with Z, not at his suggestion but because when they were in the flower garden at Victoria Park and he had told her of this rump gathering which had been set up to initiate the fight for an appeal, she had insisted.

The tiny room was thick with smoke when they came in – smoke of all sorts from cigars, pipes and the new-fangled cigarettes which that very year had fallen drastically in price as the expensive hand-rolling by nicotine stained 'cigarette girls' was replaced by the Bonsack machine which spat out 12,000 little white tobacco-filled cylinders in a single hour.

In the centre of the plain deal table were several bottles of whisky and some small tumblers, most of which had already been partially filled and in the hands of the various men who were seated.

The meeting was in full swing by the time Z and Maggie had arrived. It was Myers who had let them in and, after discreetly questioning Z about his companion, had introduced them to the others.

Besides Hayward and his managing clerk there was Greenberg, the organiser of Lipski's defence committee, whose house Z had gone to some days before; a man named De Souza, who Z recognised as the mysterious figure he had seen the first day of the trial in close conversation with Hayward and Myers; a Scottish MP named Cunninghame Graham and, finally, someone called Krantz who edited a Yiddish weekly.

No one objected to Maggie's presence. Perhaps with all the smoke in the air they couldn't see she was a woman. Or perhaps they were too wrapped up in their heated conversation to care. Despite any secret misgivings, along with Z she was passed one of the tumblers full of whisky and a lacquered box of cigarettes, which she gratefully accepted out of nervousness rather than compulsion, extracting a hand-rolled Turkish Philip Morris which was then lit by De Souza, the corpulent gentleman to her right, from the tip of his amazingly big cigar.

Hayward was just going over the question of reprieve. He said that, as the law presently read, it could only be determined by the Queen on advice of the Home Secretary but, in reality, it was the Home Secretary, himself, who decided – his office becoming, in effect, the single court of appeal.

So what were the possible grounds on which to base their plea? According to Hayward there were three main principles the Home Office used in reaching a decision. The first was compassion, the second was the possibility of an unjust decision having been reached in the trial, and the third was a judgement of mercy based on evidence that there was no intention to kill. It seemed to Hayward that the Lipski case could fit easily into any of those criteria. In fact, he seemed to think their chances were good as nearly half of all those condemned to death over the last few years had their sentences commuted.

But was it as straightforward as all that? Greenberg argued that there were other things they needed to consider. This case, from its very outset, went beyond a simple act of murder. Its ramifications, he told them, reached the very heart of government because of its inherently political nature. The 'Jewish Question' had become a major issue over the last few years and was nearing the boiling point. The domestic economy was bad and foreigners – namely the Jews – were being held up to blame. There was a great pressure to legislate some sort of barrier to close England off to the flood of cheap labour pouring in from Russia and Poland. Consequently, the Anglo-Jewish establishment were quaking in their boots, frightened that the loyal, hard working and enterprising image of the Jew which they had been trying so hard to instil into the British mind was being threatened by a situation growing desperately out of control. The government, they feared, could easily go down the route of those who have found it quite in their interest to unleash that primal hatred to detract from real economic and political embarrassments.

Cunninghame Graham told them he feared that from the government's standpoint, Lipski's hanging would be welcomed as a ritualistic bloodletting which was needed from time to time in order that the social pressure valve of pent-up proletarian fury be vented. He, himself, wasn't as interested in the Jewish question as the human one. There were some serious issues relating to English justice that the trial had raised and he would be happy to direct a question in that regard to the Home Secretary in Parliament.

Krantz, the man from the Yiddish weekly, suggested that a petition urging the Home Office to grant a stay of execution be immediately drawn up. There may be no great love for Lipski amongst the Jewish workers, he said, but as the dust settled it would become clear that some grave injustice had been done. He had already heard murmurings on the street that led him to believe many in the community would already support a movement for appeal.

De Souza cautioned everyone about stirring up a hornet's nest (though his words were meant primarily for Krantz). Things needed to be done quietly. An open campaign that pitted Jew against Jew and Jew against Christian would be counterproductive.

Maggie, for her part, was intrigued. She was fascinated by these exotic men – especially Krantz, with his impassioned eyes smouldering, darkly, in the wake of something she could never know or even hope to understand. He seemed far more interesting than De Souza who might have been from the tedious English upper classes (except for something swarthy, almost Latin, about his appearance), though she, herself, felt that De Souza's plea for prudence was not entirely mistaken.

These impressions of Maggie's were somewhat intensified by both the urgency of the situation and the stimulation of the rich tobacco coupled with several sips from her tumbler of flavoured liquor. Not that she was pure as the driven snow with regard to those particular vices (or pleasures, depending on which direction one was coming from). She and her cousin Beatrice had been known to put their feet up and share a smoke and a glass of gin together on occasion. Certainly she was not one of those who were known in 18th century France as *prudefemmes* – those seemingly virtuous women who cast a disapproving eye on the wayward ways of the world whilst harbouring a bevy of secret lusts. But observing the effects of alcohol on family relations in the dismal streets and alleys of the East End had made her cautious about that substance which was capable of inflicting so much misery. (Although she found it of interest that Jews were rarely the ones who seemed to suffer from it – except as the brunt of a drunken mob.)

Z agreed with Greenberg that there was a larger story being played out and to comprehend the Lipski case one needed to look further and deeper into the miasma of great events sweeping across Europe. But there was also a real life at stake and the hands of the great celestial clock were moving inexorably toward the zero hour when all life on earth would cease – at least for Lipski. So what to do in the few days that remained? A petition was all well and good as was a question in the House of Commons. But it would take something more dramatic to stop the Death Angel in its tracks.

It was Myers who said it, for Myers was indeed a natural organiser. Z was right. It would take something forceful and dramatic to halt the dreaded juggernaut. But that needed to be coupled with a campaign at the highest of levels to convince those in power of the facts. Myers then suggested a dual approach: letters would be written to those in authority pleading for a respite and outlining the main issues which indicated a miscarriage of justice and, at the same time, a campaign would be launched immediately to gain public support – through petitions, a pamphlet and articles in the press. Time was short, so things would have to happen fast. Greenberg would be in charge of the defence committee – raising funds to keep the investigation going and, hopefully, bring more facts to light regarding the case. Krantz would lead the petition drive. De Souza would attempt to mobilise support amongst the community leaders and those who might have some influence behind the scenes. Cunninghame Graham would organise a Parliamentary opposition.

And for Maggie and Z? For them Myers had something special in mind.

CHAPTER 24

THE CAFÉ ROYAL stood rather pompously like a regal icon on Regent Street – though the iconic nature of this garish rendezvous had more to do with Louis XIV than Victoria. It was, most definitely French in both food and fashion. That its back door opened out onto the fringes of Soho, however, meant there was another side to the place perhaps a bit more disreputable – appealing to that combination of opposites, the Bohemian Prince or the High-minded Pauper. The Café Royal catered to both of them, the rich and the raffish, upstairs in its elegantly expensive restaurant or down below in the madcap bar where the prices were cheap (or, at least, cheaper). So it was not unusual on the same night to have General Boulanger, the despised traitor of the Republican cause, dining upstairs with his retinue on truffles while downstairs in the aptly named Domino Room, exiles from the days of the Commune were downing bottles of cheap claret while plotting to de-trufflize the Boulangers of the world.

The fact that a Gallic Grand Café could be both royalist and republican was not something that the traditional English mind could easily absorb. However, there it stood, defiantly, in the middle of London's West End as a magnet to the new class of intelligentsia spewed out by the overheated engine of late Victoria and its unrealised (and ambivalent) quest for Modernism. Is it any wonder then that artists like James Abbott McNeill Whistler, fresh from Paris and imbued with a heady mixture of Courbet and Baudelaire, should have used the Royal as a base in his battle against the Ruskinites and their visceral horror of the dreaded Impressionists. (Or, for that matter, why the Marquess of Queensbury could so easily have confronted Oscar Wilde over his son's love that dared not speak its name – because where else would that paunchy boozed-up reprobate be having his dinner?)

When Z had come there after his first sojourn in France, soaking up the language and the culture (a requirement for any would-be writer in those days), he both loved and hated it. What he loved about the place was the buzz and the energy and the fact that somebody who was anybody in the arts was always there in the flesh to see and be seen. What he hated about it was exactly the same thing. There was, of course, a great deal of posturing and pretence – of cocks showing their cockades. There was also wit and brilliance and viscous verbal bantering that often gave lie to the soft and succulent words reserved for the vellum of the page. And Z could partake in this tournament of male vanity, valour and vulgarity along with the best of them. But afterwards he often felt an ache both in his stomach and in his head. Sometimes he found it easy to go along with the game, seeing it as young men doing what young men do, letting off steam and having good fun. But other times he found the whole charade abhorrent – feeling a moral revulsion to this daily bout of ubiquitous consumption and of drunken knives being sharpened on slobbering tongues. (This virtuous nausea was best summed up to him by the sight of a minor poet who was noted for his routine of taking a small golden cross from his waistcoat pocket and dipping it ceremonially into each successive glass of absinthe prior to drinking it – until, as often happened, he would slide slowly from his chair to end up, legless, underneath the table whereupon someone would complete the ritual by placing the absinthe-soaked cross onto his forehead.)

Not that Z came here very often. He preferred the

smaller cafes around Soho and the British Museum. They were quieter and the artists and writers he knew who went there were more down-to-earth people. Perhaps they weren't blazing stars hoping to ignite the heavens, but they were serious about their work and they all, in their own manner, had something important to say – or, at least, thought they did.

But he was at the Royal today on a mission. Through Myers a meeting had been arranged and Z held in his hands an envelope that contained the peculiarly grotesque item of trade that clinched it. It was a rather macabre deal, Myers had told him, but it had to be done. So he – or rather Hayward – had seen to it. And that was that.

Now Z held the envelope in his hand and waited. He held it firmly between his thumb and forefinger as if, somehow, it could escape if he didn't hold it tight enough. It felt leaden and cumbersome even though it only contained a single sheet of paper. And he wished the gentleman it was meant for would come soon so he could get rid of it.

Fortunately, he didn't have to wait for long. When the gentleman from Society Magazine finally arrived he wasn't alone. He had with him another man, somewhat older and far more serious-looking. The older man was introduced to Z as W. T. Stead, but the introduction, though formally required, wasn't really necessary as Z already knew who he was. In fact, judging from the number of heads that turned when the two men entered the Domino Room of the Café Royal, there were many more than Z who recognized him.

Stead, however, was the type of person who would have turned heads even if no one knew him. He had that curious presence that tends to disrupt the delicate balance of a tranquil universe. What was it about him that caused such a response? His eyes? Yes, he had amazing eyes – eyes that

205

could penetrate flesh and burrow deep into the soul (or so, at least, some of his sycophants thought). But no one saw those eyes when he walked into the Domino Room that day. His face? It could have been seen as a face of a biblical prophet -or that of a madman (one in the same said the cynics). But others saw it as the face of a dealer in snake oils. His stance? He carried himself as one sure of his ground, unlikely to give way to anything less than the hurricane winds of a force nine gale. Did he strike terror into the heart of his fellow man? It depended on who you were and what you thought. He was a person who treated others with deep respect and set a tone of high moral standards (said some), a fanatical head-thumper (said others) or a sinister newspaperman capable of anything that would further his ambitions (said the rest) but not one to make people quake in their boots, if boots they wore, or shiver in their socks if their toes weren't bare. (Though, if boots they had none and toes, indeed, they had bare, he probably would have written an editorial on the dire poverty that denied people the right to boots and socks in the blistering frosts of winter – even though it was summer – and then would sell some clothier on the idea of putting an advert in the very same issue advising people of their stylish and quite reasonably priced footwear.)

In truth, he was a complex man. Adored by some, vilified by others, Stead was the editor of the Pall Mall Gazette, a rather quiet weekly he had taken charge of some years before and had turned into a bullhorn for his various causes and enterprises. In his charge the Gazette had been transformed from a stolid, mid-Victorian journal read by people as unimaginative as its print to an entertaining, lively and audacious periodical that gloried in crusades, gossip and scandal and rejoiced in shouting about it from the rooftops. Like the 'New Humorist' rubric inflicted on Jerome, the movement Stead had come to represent was that of 'New Journalism'. (Reinforcing the notion that this was indeed a novel age by plugging in the required fresh and shiny adjective before any noun that seemed to have grown tired and worn in Victoria's reign of the first fifty years.)

Like most people, Z had mixed feelings about Stead and the Gazette. As a writer he appreciated that Stead seemed to give his journalists their head. As a Londoner, he approved of Stead's populist campaigns. However, as a Jew, he found Stead's romance with Russia and its xenophobic Tsar a little hard to stomach. Ever since 1881 and the assassination of Alexander II, who was looked upon, perhaps mistakenly, as a beacon to the anxious few in that troubled land who craved to become part of a European resurgence, all hope of stemming the endless nights of bloody knives wielded by the newly liberated peasantry, the uprooting of entire Jewish populations from villages they had inhabited for hundreds of years – all that seemed to become futile when the new Tsar, Alexander III ascended to the throne.

After making his formal introduction, the gentleman from Society Magazine accepted the envelope Z had handed him and opened it, carefully, so as to inspect the goods. It had seemed a fair trade to him, an introduction for an autograph which would be used on the cover of his next issue underneath a drawing of Lipski dressed in fashionable clothing, looking like a young roué, a man-about-town, a celebrity pin-up, perhaps to be posted on a bedroom wall with a caption reading 'the man who had a date with destiny.'

Displaying his prize to Stead, the gentleman from Society Magazine smiled the smile of the contented entrepreneur, for he knew the sales of his little journal would skyrocket the following week due simply to this autograph from the condemned man that he had just received. He assumed a man like Stead would appreciate this minor coup in the progressive yellowing of journalism, but Stead seemed strangely put out. Was it that Stead, for all his cunning tricks at boosting circulation, still had something of a moral code forbidding him to mock the dead – or those who would soon be? Or perhaps it was that he thought the ploy a bit too cheap even for the Gazette and more appropriate for a penny gaff on Whitechapel Street.

The gentleman from Society Magazine thought Stead's frown was simply sour grapes because he wished that grotesque scrawl for his own. And with that delightful belief percolating in his belly like a recently swallowed canary, he pocketed his bizarre artefact, made his excuses and left while Z, who seemed very uncomfortable at being part of this ridiculous ruse, looked at Stead with dolefully apologetic eyes.

However Stead, though he might have been beyond accepting autographs from soon-to-be executed convicts, needed no apologies for doing whatever was necessary to set up an important interview. Indeed, he would have expected it from any of his reporters – he may have even demanded it of them. But even more, he actually wanted a chance to speak with Z himself.

CHAPTER 25

STEAD, THE GREAT crusading editor, was interested in the Lipski case for reasons of his own. He had come up against the brute force of government before: several years back he had used the Gazette to launch a searing campaign to expose the shadowy trade in young children that was rife in the dark heart of London and he still had the scars to show for it.

In what came to be known as 'The Maiden Tribute of Modern Babylon', Stead had lead a secret team of investigators into back street bordellos to prove how easy it was on any given night to procure a child for less money than it would cost to purchase a pair of riding boots. The series of reports which resulted was brutally honest, shocking and direct. It laid bare the gruesome truth of the link between poverty, pandering and the trafficking in young children which was so rampantly ignored by the Victorian moralists.

Pressures from reformers had earlier pushed forward a Criminal Law Amendment Bill, but the threat of abandonment due to the government's belief that the public at large wasn't really interested in the subject, had given Stead the powder to fire his cannons up.

On July 4, 1885, readers of the Pall Mall Gazette had been issued with 'A Frank Warning' which announced that if Ministers were prepared to allow the bill to drop because the public was not keenly aware of its importance, then it was up to the Gazette to publish the findings of his Special and Secret Commission of Inquiry which he had set up to investigate the issue of child prostitution.

Promising an actual journey into a Dantean sexual underworld was not the act of someone who cares nothing for increasing his newspaper's readership. Indeed, it could have been argued by the many cynics who watched Stead's virtuosity with green-eyed amazement that voyeurism was still voyeuristic even when given the mantle of crusade, no matter how noble.

In the end, the series was reprinted in pamphlet form, selling well over a million copies in the course of a year. Translations sold equally well in Germany, France, and Sweden where people queued up at newspaper kiosks to get their dose of British smut.

It was, in all, a brilliantly effective journalistic enterprise that managed to balance bare-knuckle investigative reporting on the thin edge of salaciousness. Whether it toppled over into prurience may have been in the mind of the beholder, but Stead's accusations went further than sexual titillation. For those he charged with purchasing the wives and daughters of the poor to satisfy their lust were the rich and powerful – the business magnates, politicians and, worst of all, the judges. 'I heard of much the same people in the house of ill-fame as those of whom you hear in caucuses, in law courts and on the "Change,"' he wrote. And, for some, that was a sentence too far.

Just six months after the Criminal Law Amendment Bill was finally passed, due in no small part to the dust kicked up by the Maiden Tribute series, Stead and several of his colleagues were charged with criminal acts relating to one of the more dramatic incidents cooked up to expose the ease with which the trade in young girls was accomplished. In order to prove how simple the business was, Stead purchased a young girl named Eliza Armstrong from her mother, through a woman intermediary, herself a reformed prostitute now working for the Salvation Army. Eliza, who was only thirteen, was taken to a midwife – a known abortionist – who attested to the child's virginity. She then was taken to a room in a hotel.

Here the story gets a bit murky. Unbeknownst to young Eliza, the hotel was actually a brothel. Somehow, for reasons unclear, she was given a whiff of chloroform provided by the abortionist who had certified to the girl's virginity. The chloroform was supposedly to make the seduction easier – but, according to Stead, could be explained as simply part of the reality theatre which was taken step by step until... Until what?

Stead entered the child's room. She was groggy but still awake. Looking over at the bearded man staring at her with his dark, intense eyes, she became frightened and screamed. Her terror frightened Stead, himself. He fled. It wasn't till the next morning that someone from the Salvation Army came to take the child away, sending her to a secret location in France.

What sort of theatre was that? What was Stead up to? What kind of game was he playing? How far did he have to go to prove what everyone knew would happen next anyway?

The case of Eliza Armstrong could have easily destroyed a weaker man, but not Stead. The trial was his pillory but also his vindication. To be martyred on the alter of the Maiden Tribute Story was proof, if proof be needed, of his danger and effectiveness.

He was given six months in prison – even though the jury who convicted him found he was misled by intermediaries but that his actions were animated by only the highest motives. They pleaded for leniency. But the judge gave him six months in prison anyway.

And who was the prosecuting attorney that led the fight for Stead's conviction? Someone quite familiar to us, for it was none other than Harry Poland, the very same Harry Poland whose cold-blooded vehemence had now condemned

Israel Lipski to the gallows.

Needless to say, there was no love lost between Stead and Poland. And one might be forgiven for thinking that perhaps there was a trace of empathy Stead felt for the poor Jew caught in the jaws of the same machine that had tried to swallow him up.

Z, as we know, was already a qualified admirer of Stead's vociferous brand of journalism. He had been fascinated with the freedom of language Stead had encouraged, and the passions it aroused. The staid and boring pages of the Times paled in comparison. There was no question about it - the newspaper which was paving the way into the 20th century was undoubtedly the Pall Mall Gazette.

But Z was also aware that truth was often a victim of clatter. The beating of drums and the blaring of trumpets might be good for a march but sometimes drowned out the harsh whispers of reasoned discourse.

However – and this was an 'however' that was bold, capitalized and underlined in red - Z also understood there was no other paper in England, no other editor than Stead who would have the daring, the temerity, the reckless disregard for institutional and personal safety and well-being, who could throw caution to demonic gales and take on a story of a friendless, foreign immigrant most people – most of the establishment, anyway – desperately wanted, for some mysterious reason, to see swinging from a rope and then to be forever, erased from history as the removal of some unsightly stain on the mythological robe of the metaphorical Queen Victoria.

CHAPTER 26

HAYWARD HAD WRITTEN a letter which Z duly passed on to Stead that afternoon at the Café Royal. It read: 'Sir, - The poor fellow Lipski has this day been found guilty. I spent a considerable time with him in prison. I tested a statement made by him most severely and his plain, straightforward demeanour and his excellent character fully convinced me that he was not guilty of the charge brought against him. There are one or two points that are especially noteworthy. First, that his landlady, who pushed open the door, is not at all sure that the door was locked. Secondly, that the one ounce of nitric acid stated to have been purchased by the prisoner was, according to the doctor's evidence, all consumed in poisoning the woman, and it must have taken at least another ounce to have destroyed the coat. Also that the man's elbows had the skin rubbed off them and the skirt of the coat was burnt in such a way as to indicate that the man must have been lying on his back at the time. I do hope that these things may be considered and that some efforts may be made to spare the man's life.'

Stead read the letter and then looked at Z with his amazing eyes that bore into flesh like red-hot sunlight through a prism and asked if Z himself thought Lipski to be innocent. Whereupon Z replied that he felt the case against Lipski hadn't been proven and therefore he could not conclude that he was guilty.

It was an unsafe verdict, Stead agreed, and to send a man to the gallows on such a basis would itself be a criminal act. Therefore he was willing to put the powers of his newspaper at Lipski's service on one condition…

There was a moment of hesitation. Z looked out beyond their table and, for an instant, became aware of the myriad of conversations taking place at the very same time in the Domino Room. At each table was a different world, a different universe. Stories were being told, ideas were being debated, lies expounded, reputations sullied, challenges accepted, passions aroused. And here at their table Stead was telling him that he would defend Lipski on one condition. What condition was that he wondered?

Stead lit up a finely wrapped cigar that had been on a voyage of adventure poets could only dream about and allowed the musky fumes to envelope his head, disappearing momentarily behind a veil of smoke. His condition, the disembodied voice now said, was the Gazette would get first notification of any information that would be relevant to the appeal. Could Z promise that?

Of course Z couldn't promise anything of the sort, though he certainly thought that Hayward and the rest of the Committee of Defence would have little problem with that idea. As for himself, he was simply the messenger, a toothless intermediary who felt drawn to help in the defence of a man who was a victim of injustice.

But such things occur all the time in London, Stead reminded him. He could give him twenty stories of injustices happening that very day, each one would make him weep and wring his hands in bitter shame. Why was he so motivated to help in this particular situation?

What was he to say? That he identified with this sad, benighted lad as an immigrant Jew from Poland who had somehow lost his footing and slipped through the fissure that ran like an invisible seismic crack through London's East End, falling into a spiritual chasm where one could drop eternally downward into the hell of inner horror? Would the

214

collective plight of the Eastern European refugee make sense to a man who was toying around with the ideas of Madame Novikoff and her romance with the transcendent Tsar and the manifest destiny of Mother Russia?

It was best to turn the question around and ask what Lipski meant to Stead. Which is what Z did. And Stead responded without hesitation that Lipski, himself, meant nothing to him – though he was impressed with the young man's reported dignity and self-possession. What attracted him to this case was the blatant disregard for the basic rules of natural justice without which no civilisation worthy of the name could long survive. This above all was what drove him to unsheathe his powerful sword. For it wasn't the strong and mighty who deserved protection but the meek and humble – which is why God had given puny David the means to vanquish the philistine Goliath.

But was he not troubled to be seen protecting the unctuous immigrants, the beggarly Jews – the very people he had accused of bringing famine and disease to the native sons of England? Didn't he see the dangers in stirring up a hornet's nest of latent hatreds?

And, even more, didn't Stead know who Z was? Looking into his face, into his eyes, didn't he see that Z had 'Jew' written all over him? Didn't he suspect that Z was Lipski in another guise? Didn't he think that a Jew is a Jew is a Jew - some might be wealthy, some might be poor but they all have something peculiar about them, something of the night? Certainly Stead thought this, didn't he? Isn't that what he would have said if he could – sitting there with Z that day in the Domino Room at the Café Royal?

Perhaps. Perhaps not. What Stead thought was many things, some in blatant contradiction to some others. But aren't we all an undulating mass of conflicting compulsions?

215

Z, himself, was a Jew but an Anglicised Jew who sometimes fancied himself a Christian. England was his home, Victoria was his Queen. But he was also the son of a Yiddish speaking immigrant who left his family to live a monastic life in Jerusalem. So who was Z? Who was Z, really? Who was Stead? Who was anyone sitting in the Domino Room that day of our Lord in 1887?

The fact of the matter was that Stead saw Justice as more than an abstract idea, but as a visceral manifestation of everything good and holy and, like a latter-day St. George, it was up to him to slay the Dragon of Foul Play. And if in the process he could sell a few papers, well, who could blame him?

CHAPTER 27

AT THE SAME time Z was meeting with Stead at the Café Royal, Maggie was on a mission of her own. However, unlike Z, who was acting chiefly as an intermediary, Maggie's undertaking was a more risky venture.

What Myers had suggested, what he said was necessary, was somehow to gain insight into the judge's mind. For if a respite was to be agreed, it would have to be with Fitzjames Stephen's acquiescence. And for that to happen, for them to finesse this, so to speak, it would need a strategy that was seasoned with the proper information. Had the judge some second thoughts about the case now he had a moment to reflect? If so, what part of his cranial lobes required massaging to help along the process of re-evaluation? And if he were firm in his resolve – as Myers suspected he was – then what did he see as the political vulnerabilities that the verdict had laid open? For, like everyone in service to the Queen, there was not only moral rectitude, but career to think about. And when all was said and done, he suspected that career came before rectitude for each of them.

But how was she to find this out? How was she to discover the intimate thoughts of a reclusive judge in such short order?

Power, Myers had noted, was always concentrated in the hands of a very small coterie. Smaller still was the power elite in London. Maggie had the advantage of entry into that rarefied world about which people like Myers could only wonder. It's true that Maggie was somewhere on the outer fringes, but, unlike him, it was possible for her to find her way inside. And didn't she say that her cousin was friendly with the family of the judge's brother?

Unfortunately, Maggie had been growing apart from her well-connected cousin over the years they had been living in London. A relationship that had once been very close had started to drift as youthful intimacies often do when transferred to the more rugged terrain of adulthood. Cracks had always been there, Maggie supposed, but she hadn't noticed how splintered they were, like a finely lacquered vase that over the course of years had begun to show a spider web of lines foreshadowing its eventual destruction.

Theirs was still a relationship of need, however, if not always one of trust. Two young women alone in the heart of London were, for all their courage and daring, still two young women alone. Except Beatrice was never actually alone, not really. Not like Maggie who had increasingly cut herself off to focus on her writing and her art. Beatrice couldn't understand. She couldn't understand the fearful process of alienation that sometimes comes hand in glove with the quest for the muse who still remains elusive. For Beatrice was a creature of the intellect who had learned well the technique of sublimating passion. And yet the act of sublimation itself is an enigma. It takes you to curious places and leaves a bit of you dangling like an uncertain acrobat walking a tightrope wire that suddenly disappears into the darkness of the endless firmament.

And there was something more, something that went back to their early days of dreamy youth when certain inequalities were fantasised away. The daughter of a country prelate never doubted she was an equal match for the daughter of a wealthy businessman; the tossing of life's odious dice is not something easily accepted by those who see themselves through internal spectacles that transform the boring monochrome into a multitude of brilliant colours. Two young

218

girls in the euphoria of Spring could share their dreams and profess undying love to the ethereal breeze that will waft them soon away come the blistering gales of Autumn.

Both of them had compassion; both in different ways. Where Maggie was struck by the plight of the unfortunate, she wanted to understand and nurture them. For Beatrice, the dilemma was far more abstract. It was humanity she cared about, not people. Beatrice would change the world. Maggie would despair of it.

When they first meet up again in London, Maggie was a nurse and Beatrice was a self-taught economist working with a group of social statisticians collecting every bit and detail as they codified the poverty of East End London, methodically raking each layer and stratum like archaeologists exploring the ruins of some re-discovered world. After Maggie chucked in her medical career to write, throwing caution to the winds, Beatrice began to feel a secret resentment, for the structure and discipline she had imposed upon herself was painful and stultifying and part of her ached for the freedom to express the yearnings of her counter-mind, that other self which she had so carefully entrapped within a rigid mental corset. But watching Maggie's descent into the ghetto's dark obscurity frightened her. For Beatrice wished simply to observe – though only from a distance. And protected by her father's bursary, she had no real understanding of what it meant to live on the perilous edge of hunger. She knew it in abstract, but she didn't know it in her gut – try as she might to imagine it.

Maggie knew what hunger meant and she embraced it – not because she wished herself harm, but simply because she felt that Christ could only know the suffering of his people because he suffered with them: if they went without bread, he shared their fast; if they walked without shoes, he trod the

219

rocky earth with feet sore with bruises.

'Poor Maggie,' Beatrice would write in her journal, 'with her lonely tortuous life and envious temper. And yet for those in trouble she had plenty of warm sympathy – true *mitgefuhl* – for the failures of society. If only she had religion, that haven of rest and peace for the lonesome worker, the one anchor in this life of strange dreams and feverish feelings…'

Envy, like the other deadly sins, is often in the mind of the beholder, perhaps even more than greed and lust. For Maggie was Beatrice's alternative self, the one she so desired when in the quiet of her room she opened up her secret diary to once again explore the roots of her anguish. And because Beatrice could hardly allow herself to understand that she yearned so very much to escape her world of glittering numbers and elegant facts into the visceral grottiness of real existence, she created another Maggie in her mind – one that was so pitiful and poor, someone to be patronised.

Beatrice said nothing to her, of course – nothing specific, that is. But communication works in many forms – a glance, a gesture, an aura picked up like radio waves, instead of sound, broadcasting emotions. And most telling of all was the stillness – those moments of silence that punctuate the air with emptiness. Nothing speaks volumes. Silence echoes with the power of negation, for, like a vacuum, nature abhors it.

And yet, despite it all, they were still friends. They still had the loyalty of youth ingrained like an ethereal inner core which nurtured their forgiveness and allowed them to continue on as if they were yet who they were back then, back in the giggly days of girlish folly and deception.

So coming to Beatrice for help wasn't easy. But come to Beatrice she did. For Beatrice knew the people who Maggie needed in order to complete her mission.

Of course it was through Beatrice that Maggie had

attended the garden party some time back at the home of Leslie Stephen, Fitzjames Stephen's brother. But that was before the judge had meant anything to her. And now she needed to know more.

What she told Beatrice wasn't much. Maggie could, to her cousin's annoyance, be quite circumspect. But like any spy, she intuitively accepted the dictum that one only said what others needed to hear. And Beatrice needed to know very little from Maggie's perspective (though from Beatrice's own point of view, she needed to know everything – or at least a lot more than Maggie was prepared to tell her).

It was Beatrice's relationship with the Stephen family that Maggie wanted to exploit. What she was able to find out was that James Fitzjames Stephen, the Lipski trial judge, had gone off to Devon right after the case to stay with a man named Froude, the noted historian and student of the tendentious Scotsman, Thomas Carlyle, laterally known as the 'Sage of Chelsea'.

There was another side to Stephen, Beatrice told her. He wasn't a fool, nor was he a vacuous mandarin. He had a clever mind, she said, and he knew how to use it. What's more, she said, the Stephen family – and here she was thinking of Leslie Stephen in particular – were part of what she saw as the progressive elite who, some day, would help to complete the great shift in cultural and moral values which had been initiated some decades before by those like Huxley, the charismatic apostles of the magnificent Darwin.

That was not the side of Fitzjames Stephen Maggie had seen at the Lipski trial (nor in the little summer house set back in Virginia's garden). If anything, her image of the man was quite the reverse – a torpid, lethargic, moralistic bigot who, when putting on his grotesque black hat to announce that Lipski would hang, looked as untroubled as a boy who sets fire to the tail of a mongrel cur because he likes the smell of burning whiskers.

Perhaps he was tired, Beatrice explained. She knew for a fact that his wife had been worried about him. He worked so hard, she had told her. And his enormous case load was becoming a burdensome strain. There were times he would have chucked it all in to do what he wished – namely to write like his friend Froude, perhaps a history of British law – something that would firmly establish his reputation as a juror of substance.

And did they have a close relation, he and his wife? Maggie wanted to know. Beatrice told her that it was, as far as she could tell, as close as you could get without merging into one. And, curiously, when she said that, somewhere in Beatrice's mind a little memory of the future was triggered whereupon she saw an image of herself with a man, not particularly handsome (he had feet like a duck), but as brilliant as she, who would merge himself into her life both physically and intellectually - something which would empower her to become half of a Dynamic Duo that was famously adored and internationally feted.

Maggie, as we know, had already merged herself with a man, but hers was more controllable since his corporal body didn't actually exist and thus he wasn't the sort she had to clean up after. The idea of merging oneself with a real man intrigued as well as horrified her. However, if it were true that Stephen and his wife were close as all that – perhaps she could find out what she needed from the womanly half and not bother with the gruesome chore of searching up the far less fragrant other.

Mary Cunningham was her name before that day in 1855 when she and her husband, James Fitzjames were legally united. It was, according to her spouse, a marriage truly made in heaven. And even three decades on he could still say, without a modicum of facetiousness, 'We have lived in a state of such uninterrupted and continually increasing happiness as I should hardly have believed could exist in this world had I not myself felt it.'

For Fitzjames (or Fitzy as he was known to his friends) was nothing if not a romantic. He loved his children and he loved his wife. He loved the Queen. And, most of all, he loved England. And when he said, 'Adherence to rules of conduct founded on the principle of promoting the greatest happiness of the greatest number is the best pocket definition of justice yet propounded,' he probably meant it. And, yes, he was rather proud that his country, his great nation, could have abolished slavery even though it came at the enormous price of twenty million pounds sterling in lost revenue (not including all the vanished earnings from cheap sugar production in the West Indies).

But could one really quantify a moral debt like a transaction being analysed by a cost accountant? Fitzy could, because, in the end, the obligation of civilization was to manage, and any manager knows full well that without a proper cost accounting anarchy is just around the bend. Which is why he could write so scathingly about the spectre of European social upheaval and his feelings of 'fierce, unqualified hatred for the revolution and revolutionists.' For whatever their various defects or harshness, he felt it his duty to support all established institutions and, when they were attacked, to summon up the feelings of a scandalised policeman towards a mob. So it is also understandable that he could have written about the workers' rising across the Channel a generation before, 'I should have liked first to fire grapeshot down every street in Paris, till the place ran with blood, and next to try

223

Louis Philippe and those who advised him not to fight by court martial, and to have hanged them all as traitors and cowards.'

Yet life for him was good and often serene – especially those glorious months of delightful tranquillity he spent each summer in Ireland at his eighty acre estate in County Louth, not far from Drogheda, the site of Cromwell's most infamous massacre. He loved Ireland and his friendly Irish neighbours, but the idea of Home Rule filled him with a deep, abiding horror. For it was his nightmare that a reign of terror would thereby be launched that would make the French Revolution look like a winsome fairy tale. This vision of the future he saw through a demonic lens filling his head with dreadful images and sounds of hyena laughs and witch's cackles as a tidal wave of blood swept malignantly into India and the rest of the Empire unleashing the devilish banshees of chaos which would finally sink their poisonous claws into the nation he so loved, ripping it apart forever.

It was, he believed, only the firm hand of British Law and Order that would stop this nightmare from occurring. Power, therefore, must always be kept in control of the wise and responsible. Democracy for working men or agricultural labourers, in contrast, he said, was 'the last and worst creation of the devil.' Though, he added, as a quiet aside, 'if you went into public life you had to pretend to love it.'

Fitzy wasn't alone in believing there was a fear that stalked the land and that fear was of The Rising. Where it would occur or when it would happen was debatable. But you only had to open your ears, you had only to look around to see that evil was encroaching – day by day, hour by hour. In Ireland, India and England itself, it was coming closer and closer. Wasn't it Hobbs who said it? And he most definitely agreed: it was only the constant fear of punishment that

224

made men just. Terror was the Great Defender.

'We have gone too far in laying aside the punishment of death and it ought to be inflicted in many cases not at present Capital,' he had said in 1883 when asked to address the Parliamentary committee discussing possible restrictions of the Last and Final Judgement. But wasn't that a bit harsh, some on the committee had asked? 'If society could make up its mind to the destruction of really bad offenders, they might, in a very few years be made as rare as wolves,' he replied, as one might have done when addressing children who failed to comprehend a straightforward lesson in ethics.

The fools! Couldn't they see that the real danger England faced came from the uneducated masses? Without a firm and guiding hand, anarchy, blood and tears could only follow. And a thousand years of civilisation would collapse. It was so blindingly obvious!

But, as Beatrice had said, that was only part of the man. Like all brilliant jurists, he was complex. And did Maggie know that just two years before he had suffered a stroke? It was disabling and severe and questions had been raised whether he would ever work again. Yet there he was, two short years later, sitting once more on the bench, presiding over complicated trials. One certainly had to admire the man's commitment and endurance. Wasn't that something to respect?

Maggie, though, was thinking of the former Mary Cunningham and the curious link Beatrice had so casually dropped as a defining feature that had no further consequence. Mary Cunningham Stephen, she said, was the daughter of a clergyman. Just like Maggie, herself.

CHAPTER 28

Z LEFT THE Café Royal feeling that Stead would carry on a strong campaign to keep the Lipski case open and before the fickle eye of the public while investigations proceeded, helping to build pressure to force an appeal. He also felt that Stead's hidden agenda, his desire to use this story to weaken the government and to redress personal grievances - getting back at those arrogant functionaries who had injured him - could be counterproductive. But there were always hidden agendas, weren't there? Perhaps he even had one himself. Besides, the support of Stead and his newspaper was bound to make the case into a cause célèbre in certain quarters where people had the time, wealth and the untrammelled idealism necessary to celebrate causes (or anything else).

He strolled through Soho, making his way south, toward the Strand and then eastward toward Aldgate, that cruel entry point to another world, dividing east and west as starkly as a sentry post within a granite wall, partitioning the glitter of affluence from the decay of deprivation.

Those who passed through that portal could not but be impressed by the symbolic nature of the open abattoir, separated from the pedestrian by just a flimsy fence so they could hardly ignore the pitiful screams of the animals being butchered just a few feet away nor fail to take note of the blood which seeped under the rotting wooden slats they were forced to walk upon.

Once through that fiendish gate all was transformed. Z could have easily been in another country and perhaps he was. The dress, the smells, the language, the looks, the quality of sounds, the air, the feel, the mood, the tastes – everything was different. Everything. And Z? He was transfigured, too, once he passed through that sphinxian entrance.

Was it the musical rhythms of the speech or the way people moved – their gesticulations, their physical presence, their need to feel, to touch, to hold, to fondle? Was it that? Or was it the faces, the multitude of expressions, the coarser hair, the higher cheekbones, the darker complexions? There was something comfortable, something comforting, being around these people, he felt. Even though, if truth be told, even though they sometimes embarrassed him by their gawkiness, their crudeness, their inelegance, their superstitious minds, their humble prayers, their demeaning stance, their ridiculous determination to be who they were in spite of not being where they had been any longer.

Sometimes after being in the ghetto for a while, he felt the need to make a mad dash to the other side of Aldgate simply to breathe again. Sometimes it worked the other way around. Where was home? Where did he feel he belonged? Here or there? If he had believed in God, he would have prayed. And sometimes he prayed even though he didn't believe anyone was there to hear his hapless lamentations. He prayed for his people and he prayed for himself. Would it do any good? Only God knew. And if there was no God? Then it didn't matter, did it?

And yet there was another side to all of this. There was always another side. Like a hardened piece of dung that turns out to be a diamond in the rough with infinite potential facets, there was always the obverse view making a mockery of all preconceived notions. For he knew within the harshest deserts were springs of life that nourished the barren earth to bloom so amazing things would grow there. And he also knew these special oases could only be seen by those who

227

believed and that others would dismiss them with insults, calling them mirages.

He was headed for the office of the Record to see Mordecai and to explain why his article had been delayed – an article Mordecai both wanted and feared and so, having mixed feelings, would probably just as well accept a delay since neither option (to publish or not to publish) would bring anything but misery for him as his dependence on Jewish merchants for his meagre advertising revenue balanced against a readership anxious for stories about this most gruesome case which had finally put them on the London map, meant he would have to tread a political tightrope no matter what was said on the Lipski subject.

But Z had already left the Record, in his head if not in deed. He had remained there simply to keep his hand limber and his words in print while he put his ideas into form. For Z was coming within the height of his powers; it was that wonderful time of life when nothing was beyond him. He had energy, talent and that great passion of youth which allows one to soar into the eternal blue without considering the consequence of flying too close to the blazing sun.

Even though he was headed for the Record, it was not where his feet were taking him. He realised this only after he had made a certain turn off Commercial Road which brought him to a small impoverished thoroughfare named Berner Street that seemed to lead into an abyss called nowhere. But it wasn't nowhere he was headed, but, rather, somewhere. And that particular somewhere turned out to be an old two storey wooden building on that dark and dingy road which radiated a curious light, setting it apart from the other hovels that surrounded it.

The building had a sign identifying it as the International Workingmen's Educational Association. He had been here before – several times, actually. Only last month he had come to hear the great William Morris and watch the mesmerised crowd of Poles, Russians, French, Germans, Italians, Greeks and native born English as they clung, like one of the artist's intricately crafted patterns, on the façade of his poetry which punctuated the otherwise torpid ghetto air with the passion, hope and genuine belief of a better day to come if only the labouring classes would unite – even though few of them could understand most of his finely sculpted idiom.

This remarkable place was a superb example of the triumph of content over form, Z had thought. On the outside it was just another shabby house. On the inside it was much the same - bare, worm-wooded and austere. But the fires emblazoned here on most nights, overcoming the chill and the damp, the hunger and depression, with the heat exploding from the cauldron of passionate ideas, made it inconsequential that the place reeked of dry-rot, the walls were cracked and the paint was peeling from stem to stern. For in the heart of the ghetto not only were frocks for the wealthy being stitched in a multitude of sweatshops but words and ideas were being fabricated in the blistering coals of the melting-pot which would someday revolutionise the world and de-frock those who blindly ignored the brutal lives the frock makers endured. At least that is what those who came to this seemingly innocuous house on that non-descript street in one of the poorest ghettos of the European world truly felt. And that passion and heart-felt belief penetrated into the very cracks of the peeling walls, infusing them with the energy and powerful vibrations which Z felt envelop him as he made his way to the door of that electrically charged building, resonating with the cries of those who would have done with the gross indignities of human servitude and break the chains of endless toil.

229

Z had come there to see Krantz, the editor of the Yiddish weekly, Arbeter Fraint, whom he had met briefly at the defence committee meeting. Before he had left Hayward's office, Krantz had taken him aside, suggesting that they should meet privately and talk – indicating by the way he phrased his words and the expression on his face that there were certain things he would like to have said but Hayward's office wasn't the place to have said them.

That evening – the evening Z arrived - there had been a performance of a new play by the Russian émigré, Nikolai Vasilyevich Chaykovsky, a passionate utopian socialist who had left St. Petersburg to set out on a curious journey that would lead him to the American state of Kansas (at the very time Frank Lyman Baum, the little newsman from Chittenango, New York, was dreaming up his Wizard of Oz fantasy which he would locate in the same wind-swept grasslands where Chaykovsky had set up his anachist commune) and, eventually (though even a fantasist like Baum could never have dreamt it) back to revolutionary Russia where he would end up leading the anti-Bolshevik government at Archangel under the auspices of the Allied expeditionary forces.

Of course no one in the audience that night of two hundred socialist revolutionaries who had come to applaud their hero's work could have known that Chaykovsky, the one who touched their spirit and their soul, would end up on the side of those he railed out against. But strange things happen in the course of life if one lives long enough and Krantz, as well, when he looked back to 1887 from the distance of a hazy mountain top would hardly recognise himself. Nor would Z. Nor would anyone. For who we were and who we are is nothing if not relative to the particular star we are being observed from. As the world revolved around Chaykovsky, so too Chaykovsky revolved around the world. And if there

230

were infinite worlds for Chaykovsky to revolve around, then there were infinite Chaykovskys, as well. (Which is only to say that the Chaykovsky applauded by the revolutionary socialists at the International Workers' Educational Club that evening in 1887 was not the same Chaykovsky who joined the expeditionary forces at Archangel – even though he inhabited what was left of the body of the man who stood on stage that night and gratefully accepted the plaudits of those he would come to despise.)

Krantz appeared as a different man here in these surroundings. The other day at Hayward's office, he had seemed, if not quiet, somewhat restrained – reluctant to snap at De Souza's crude bait (offered up, Z suspected, more to humiliate than to threaten) and launch into a stormy altercation that would have proved nothing except to show he could fight back. It made him seem, perhaps, fainthearted but that would have been a misconception of the man who had travelled in many worlds and knew when the time was right to listen and when the time was right to roar.

But here in the International Workingmen's Club - here he was in his domain. Here his body was lithe and his eyes were nimble. Here people respected and admired him as their collective voice, empowering him to articulate those deeply held passions and desires they found such difficulty in expressing. For it was only in the Yiddish press that they could truly speak, debate and argue on a level footing. It was their language; it was their tongue. It gave them the tool they needed to verbalise, to put flesh on their raw grievances, their fears, their desires and make them tangible and real – something they could never do in English, a language that would always be their master's whip to bind them to the hierarchy of Empire at the very lowest rung. In Yiddish they

231

were free; in English they were bound in servitude.

Still a young man, not yet thirty years of age, Krantz had left his boyhood shtetl in Russified Poland only six short years before. But his sojourn in Paris as a student, tempered in the white hot dialectics of Hegel, Lassalle, Proudhon and the strange metaphysical stew of Yiddish anarchism, had given him both the intellectual credentials and the political savy to win the notice of those tired revolutionaries in London looking for new blood. Krantz was their man. In the simmering cauldron of East End politics, he made himself felt along with his comrades from the old Poilishe Yidl, the forerunner of the Arbeter Fraint, lending a powerful voice to the independent Jewish labour movement.

By 1887, out of nowhere, Krantz and his cohorts who banded around their weekly masthead of revolutionary Jewish socialism, now ensconced in the International Workingmen's Club, had suddenly become a force to be reckoned with. And just as suddenly it had become a threat to the Jewish Board of Guardians who, up till then, had encountered little organised opposition within the Jewish community to their draconian assimilationist policy of shaping up or shipping out.

Even though Z admired the forthright energy of these Jewish militants and, in the main, supported their cause, he found them lacking somewhat in their approach – particularly their insistence that the Jewish workers sever their ties to the religious and cultural institutions so central to their life as exiles in England. To Z, this denial of their roots, their heritage, whether based on mysticism or convoluted memoirs, was rending a people from their spiritual home which went far beyond the notion of God or religion. For what did it leave them with? A vague connection with an international proletariat who may or may not rise up sometime in the great and distant future? And, if they did, what would stop this same proletariat who had risen up from turning on the Jews just like the peasantry in Russia?

On the other hand, Z sometimes hated the Guardians almost as much as the anarchists did. In his mind, he still preserved an image of the despised Lord Rothschild presenting the awards at his school for poor immigrants, not deigning to touch their little hands lest he contract some putrid disease from their scum. His patronising words, which in essence demanded their life-long fealty for tuppence, still rang in his ears. For Z was one of those children forced to stand stiffly hour upon hour, dry of mouth and swollen of bladder, waiting for the Great Man to appear. And when he did, Z could see in his eyes, that this Highly Respected Lord of the Realm truly detested them, little urchins as they were. Yet it was so much in the Jewish tradition to offer service to the poor that he came and did his duty and then, Z thought, most likely, went home and had his servants scrub him down in the bath tub for an hour with the strongest disinfectant they could find in the Good Lord's pharmacopoeia. (This, by the way, was the same Lord Rothschild who was, much later, to generously assist Z in one of his more Quixotic ventures – but that's another story from another life and part of the multiple ironies and contradictions that make history so convolutedly adorable.)

The performance was over by the time Z had arrived, and the ragged collection of derelicts, penniless intellectuals and tired sweat-shop workers relieving thoughts of drudgery before the coming of the dawn, were filing out the multipurpose room that was theatre, lecture hall and work space, all in one.

Krantz had gone back to his office, a little attic room at the top of the stairs, and Z, having enquired to his whereabouts, had been directed there. Climbing the rickety steps and glancing at the dingy walls, fragrant with mould and mildew, Z wondered at the man who confined himself to a life of poverty, secluded at the top of this strange house which throbbed with unrealised dreams of Elysian fields in the aftermath of some ill defined Worker's Revolution.

The door to the tiny room was open. Krantz was sitting at his desk, underneath the eaves, focused on his writing. Z stood there for a moment looking at the man working feverishly under the flickering light of a burning candle and thought he saw himself. It was a strange sensation. Z could almost feel the pen in his hand, he could sense the words as if they were broadcast through some sort of mental telegraphy.

Krantz suddenly glanced up and the spell was broken. There was a look of confusion on his face – a momentary disorientation as he re-connected to the world of life from the world of pen. Then a smile of recognition and standing, he held out his hand, saying that he hadn't expected Z so soon but was hoping he would come.

There was a bottle of Russian vodka sitting on the shelf, a gift, Krantz said, from a young student named Vladimir Ilich Ulyanov (later known simply as 'Lenin') in appreciation for an article Krantz had written in defence of his brother who had recently been hanged for plotting to assassinate Tsar Alexander III.

Two glasses were wiped clean, the vodka was poured and Krantz proposed a toast to the liberation from the yoke of tyranny and the triumph of the spirit, which certainly was vague enough for Z to celebrate wholeheartedly and, in response, he drained his glass with the same alacrity as Krantz and then allowed him, without objection, to pour a refill.

Looking at the clear, corrosive liquid in his tumbler,

Z wondered aloud whether this was the spirit Krantz had toasted and, further, if this gift of appreciation hadn't a curious connection to the dreaded event which had brought them together. Though this man, Vladimir Ilich's brother, was hanged for a plot, what was Lipski about to be hanged for? A murder he may or may not have committed?

If Lipski is hanged, Krantz replied, the connection would be contrary. Vladimir Ilich's brother was hanged to frighten the masses. And Lipski would be hung to placate them. But both would have been hung to get their respective governments out of a mess. And saying that, he followed Z in bolting down this second glass of liquid heat and vigour.

There was, in fact, a more substantial reason for wanting to see Z, Krantz told him, wiping away the residual fiery droplets from his chin. Referring back to the meeting in Hayward's office, he wanted Z to know that there was a spy in attendance who was not at all interested in truth or justice but only in maintaining the status quo. And if that meant sending an innocent man to the gallows – so be it.

Of course Z understood that Krantz was referring to De Souza and though he was not about to defend someone whose links to the Guardians was well established, he was loath to go as far as Krantz in his accusation. Could Krantz, he asked, amplify on this?

Did Z know, asked Krantz, that the Arbeter Fraint had been forced to cease publication since May? It ceased, not because they lacked the funds or the staff, but because certain leaders of the Anglo-Jewish Board of Guardians, who viewed the paper as a danger to the community, had set out to destroy it. They had first attempted to bribe their printer and failing that, they bribed the compositor with a one way ticket to New York. The printer was then threatened once again. If he persisted in continuing his contract with them, his other work would be withdrawn. Sadly, even this brave man finally gave way to the odious forces of repression.

But this wasn't all. This they could contend with. Funds were being raised as far afield as America to provide them with a press of their own so they could control their means of production and thus defy that hideous censorship, so devious and underhanded. All this could be expected in the heat of brutal class hostilities. But what was obscene, what Z probably didn't know, was the diabolical depths these forces were prepared to go in order to protect their power and their privilege.

Then Krantz looked at him searchingly and after a moment of silence, his gaze shifted up to the skylight window, out into the starlit night beyond the cosmos of the Milky Way. And he asked if Z recalled that terrible episode at the Yiddish theatre in Princess Street last January.

CHAPTER 29

BACK IN HIS chamber, Z searches through his file of clippings till he finds the one he wants. It's an article from the Jewish Chronicle, dated January 21, 1887:

Even though it's only six months old, the clipping is already showing signs of age with the paper darkening around the edges. But in his mind's eye, the events are still sharp and clear, as if time has refused to relegate these memories to the storeroom of the past, locked and forgotten.

> *A shocking disaster is reported by us this week. Seventeen poor people were trampled to death in a panic on Tuesday at the Hebrew Dramatic Club, Princes Street, Spitalfields...'*

He mulls over the words – *'A shocking disaster'* – and thinks it such an inadequate way to describe that dreadful night when the world seemed to stop in its orbit and everyone blinked in disbelief until the reality had finally hit home to them. The ghetto had imploded, suddenly shrinking in size, for everyone knew someone who had been there.

> *'A larger audience than usual was assembled for a benefit night when the alarm of fire was raised. Someone turned off the gas lights; and in the darkness there ensued a terrible scene. The first impulse of the crowd was to rush out, but some of those near the entrance, after obeying the instructive desire for the open air, recoiled and turned their faces to the hall again in the vain endeavour to help their relations.'*

He had been among those who went to the West Ham cemetery to witness the internment of some of the victims, for he had known one, a sweet young girl of sixteen. A shy child, a bit lame and slightly cross-eyed, she had intrigued him by always managing a smile even though everyone knew that hers would be a difficult match in the ruthless matrimonial bartering game. She had so little. Her clothes were threadbare, hanging limply on her narrow frame like a sack to dump potatoes in. And yet she had her love. Not a boy, not a man but the theatre – her theatre, the Yiddish theatre. And she looked forward to those wonderful evenings of visceral delight, holding on to those precious moments and jealously coveting them like a cache of exotic treats, to be secretly dipped into during her long and tedious hours sewing miles upon miles of cotton garments she would never possess for someone she never knew and never saw but who paid her father tuppence out of which she received a miniscule allowance to save up for her next secret foray into the surreal world of the ghetto playhouse.

Z knew her as one of the characters he had studied for his stories of the Jewish East End. There was something about her silly, cross-eyed look, masking a quiet sense of naïve rapture, that fascinated him. Now her body lay cold in her cheap coffin of rough wood – the best her impoverished father could afford. And Z couldn't help but wonder why an all-knowing God would forsake such a special girl as her instead of one of the miseries whose outward beauty disguised a soul that was dry and moribund.

> 'Whole families had gone to the play together and many a distracted mother turned bewildered to gather her flock. That return, that looking back meant death. The irresistible surge from the rear of the hall pushed on and passed over the prostrate bodies of these hesitating women. Of the seventeen dead, many were no more than youths...'

What had happened on that terrible midwinter night in those frigid months before the blistering heat of Jubilee summer? What had happened really? Krantz had stared into his eyes, searchingly, as if trying to discover something in Z that may or may not have been there – something that Krantz had sensed in him, a seed, a spore, a bionic crumb which may not yet have germinated.

There was no fire in the theatre that night. There was no smoke. There was nothing at all to indicate a danger. Yet someone raised the alarm. Someone shouted that fearful word. Someone doused the gas lights. Someone caused the panic to occur. Why did it happen? What purpose did it serve?

Z looks down at the clipping and studies the terrible headline again:

'Shocking Disaster! Seventeen Trampled in Panic at Hebrew Dramatic Club!'

It was the Yiddish theatre, not the Hebrew Dramatic Club. Why couldn't they bring themselves to use the word? It was the Yiddish theatre - that heart and soul of the immigrant community, adored by those who still looked at the Russian pale as their spiritual home. It was their theatre, the theatre of the Ghetto. It was the theatre that mixed the esoteric and mystical with the spontaneity of life - the shouts, the laughter, the sighs, the raw exaggerations of joy, pity, remorse, compassion, unbridled love and unrepentant passion – that showcase of the peasant soul, rooted in centuries of wanderings of a landless people. All this was expressed on the stage of the Yiddish theatre to the eternal embarrassment of the Guardians of Anglo-Jewry.

And the best of the best of the Yiddish theatre was the troupe of Jacob Adler ensconced in the heart of the ghetto in a recently converted building through the largesse of a Dorset Street butcher in January, just one year earlier.

The story Krantz had told him differed somewhat from the articles Z took from his file of clippings. A rumour, Krantz said, had been circulating for some time that the Guardians once offered Adler and his troupe money to emigrate to the States. Adler had, of course, refused, saying that they were needed more in London's East End. Later more money was offered, along with veiled threats. Adler refused again.

Then came the fatal evening in question. On the 18th of January a special benefit performance was being given and the audience had swelled to five hundred, crammed into the tiny playhouse space. At the height of the drama being depicted on stage, someone in the building cried 'Fire!' and suddenly the gas lights went out. Panic stricken, the audience stampeded toward the exit.

Seventeen people were crushed to death. But there was no fire. And several weeks later, Adler and his troupe left for New York, leaving behind the charred remains of their distress.

In the same file, Z finds another clipping dated February 18. This one reads:

> 'Now that the verdict has been given at the inquest held upon the Spitalfields disaster the silence imposed upon us by the reasonable requirements of journalistic etiquette is relaxed and we are at liberty to point out the moral of the sad tale – we plainly tell our foreign brethren that one of the most direct causes of the recent disaster has been the persistent isolation in which they have kept themselves from their fellow Jewish workmen – in all social amenities of life. When they want aid in sickness or distress they are willing to claim their privileges as Jews living in England, but in all their social relations they keep themselves aloof from us and thus forgo the advantages of such an institution as the Jewish Working Men's Club where every practicable precaution has been taken to avoid such a calamity as the late panic. The recent event ought to be a lesson to avoid such performances of strolling minstrels acting in the jargon of the foreign contingent. In making

these remarks we are urged by a consideration of the best interests of those brethren of ours whose chance of livelihood is largely diminished by their not helping to hasten the process of 'Anglicising'. We have felt at liberty to give this piece of advice as we have fortunately been the means of alleviating much of the distress which has been caused by the accident that gave rise to our remarks...'

Such arrogance, such ignorance, such lack of understanding brings out in him not anger, but a feeling of deep remorse. Why remorse? To use that word, is there not implied a sense of guilt? And why should he feel even a modicum of culpability? Could it be that such corrosive thoughts spring from the poisonous well of loyalties that are somehow conflicted?

But, he thinks, why should there be conflict at all? Aren't the Guardians and the poor Jews of the Ghetto a single people – one and the same? And then he thinks, perhaps not. They profess the same Biblical ancestors, but what does that mean? Certainly they claim a similar heritage of historical suffering, but suffering is a universal human malady to which Christ, Buddha or Mohammed could relate. In truth, they call themselves a 'People' only when it suits their purposes, he finally decides.

So where does that leave him, he wonders? His heart is firmly in the Ghetto, but his mind has been truly Anglicised. And so he feels that tinge of guilt, part of sorrow and remorse, that comes from a sense of betrayal, no matter how small, no matter how miniscule, no matter how seemingly insignificant.

He picks up another clipping and reads again:

'The disaster itself illustrates in a most striking manner the responsibility of all London Jews to one another. Whether English or foreign the Jews are a collective whole in the eyes

241

of the world at large and whatever befalls one section is held to apply to the whole community ... if there is any tendency to repudiate the solidarity among us, this shocking disaster would be sure to show the impossibility of doing so. The reputation of the London Jews is bound up inexorably with that of the Russian Jews of the East End...'

Z underlines this last sentence with his pencil. Here we get to the crux of the matter, he thinks to himself. It's a question of reputation, isn't it? The reputation of the London Jews has somehow become bound with the Jews of the East End. There it is in black and white. The Anglicised Jew was embarrassed by the foreign Jew's lack of Englishness.

So what was he saying, Z had asked Krantz? Who was it he was accusing? Was this really a cabal? Could this suspected action have been a cynically motivated, diabolically evil response by the Board of Guardians to the nuisance of a rag-tag theatre? This is something Z finds impossibly ridiculous.

And while Krantz had savoured the irony of someone like Z minimising the power of theatre that reaches deep into the community's spirit, into its soul, he patiently (or patronisingly) explained that extirpating poisonous ideas from the minds of the peasantry was something at which feudal overlords were quite adept. In the case of the Arbiter Fraint, there was no question that people from the Guardians would stoop to any means necessary to shut them down. Their actions, in that case, had been short of cold-blooded murder. But in the case of Jacob Adler's Yiddish Theatre, they – or someone at their behest – had shown what vile lengths they were prepared to go in cleansing the thoughts of those they claimed to be their brethren.

Z shakes his head. As much as he questioned the motives of the Guardians, he cannot bring himself to contemplate the terrible idea that these men, however foolish or misguided,

242

might have actually done what Krantz's addled mind had brought him to suggest. For all their vain stupidity, Z feels he still has them to thank for his hearth and home, with good friends and a blossoming career, safely ensconced in the bosom of empire, here in the greatest city in the world, London, England.

CHAPTER 30

IT IS MORNING. Z is in Hayward's office. A space has been cleared amongst the clutter, giving him a small area to work in. He is helping to prepare a six page pamphlet which is to be distributed in an attempt to build support for Lipski's reprieve.

But how are they to begin? How are they to make these several pages of print do the job that's required? For that to happen, Z argues, the pamphlet must be clear, powerfully incisive and compelling. He suggests that perhaps they might open with an admission that the judge's final instructions had taken the defence by surprise and there was no opportunity for them to comment on it to the jury, thereby implying that the trial had ended unfairly without accusing Fitzjames Stephen directly of an unwarranted intrusion, even though, of course, it was.

Hayward and Myers then outline the most contentious issues that would force any right-minded observer to rethink the safety of the verdict and Z, taking notes, quickly formulates a series of crucial questions, to be set out in bold, followed by a short response: (1) Why did Rosenbloom not hear anything considering the fact that he was in the room above and the partition dividing the Angels' room from the staircase leading to Lipski's room was only a quarter inch thick? (2) Why did Schmuss leave after a few minutes when there were plenty of raw sticks lying about and he was a man apparently in abject need? (3) Can one have confidence in the identification of Lipski in the hospital as the person who purchased the acid when according to the statement of the hospital nurse he was taken straight up to the bed where

244

the prisoner lay and on which a detective was sitting? (4) Where did all the acid come from that caused the damage? (Certainly not from the single vial!) (5) How could Lipski have covered up his own coat with Mr Angel's coat and then crawled under the bed, dragging an eggbox after him? (6) Were not the abrasions on Lipski's elbows because of his struggle while on his back? (7) How is it that Mrs. Angel's bedding was marked with acid mixed with blood, but acid mixed with blood was not found on Lipski or his coat? (8) Was the door to the Angels' room, in fact, locked? And, even if it was, couldn't anyone, as the experts had stated, easily have turned the key from the outside – especially someone like Schmuss who was trained as a locksmith?

Words. Z steers away from turgid sentences while thinking to himself that words can simply be words or they can magically transmute into something more, something resonant, something beyond the syllables, the vowels or consonants, like the pigments used to make a painting or the symbols used to formulate a musical composition. And it's that touch of alchemy Z tries for. But can magic be imposed? Or must it simply happen? He is trying to be workmanlike and the result sounds to him so wooden and pedantic. Yet if these words are to do their job they must be cultivated, they must be nurtured, they must be honed and winnowed.

Still, he must constrain himself. He doesn't take easily to tendentious argument; but there is a life at stake, he keeps reminding himself. And to save a life, anything is justified. It is, after all, in the Jewish tradition that life is sacred and even Biblical pronouncements must consider this as uppermost. Words, therefore, must find a balance between the sacred and profane, even if it is an uneasy one. But words are important to him and, therefore, he treats them with respect. And, even more, he feels responsible for them – which, though

245

honourable, can also be dangerous.

There is a fine, old grandfather clock standing in the far corner of Hayward's office. Its rich walnut case is in need of polish and the brass fittings are tarnished but the glass door behind which the pendulum resides has been kept clean, unlike the clock face itself, which leads Z to think that someone was more interested in seeing the swing of the pendulum than the actual minute.

For a moment he finds himself hypnotised by the rhythm of the suspended weight, a silvery disk like a metallic sun in a flattened orbit swinging side to side instead of round and round, and he realises that the progress of time is different than the passage of the hour. The circular motion of the dial, the face of time, defines a moment and freezes it for an instant till another instant in the future can be comprehended. But the eternal rhythm of the pendulum, swinging back and forth and back again, forever and forever, conveys an idea of timelessness.

Time, however, is something in short supply as far as Lipski was concerned. Eternity would come soon enough. And Z forces himself to look away from this grand reminder of mortality cast in faded wood and tarnished brass and concentrates, once more, on his task at hand.

With a flourish, he completes his final phrase and hands it on to Myers to inspect. Myers makes a few notations and then passes it to Hayward who reads it over and nods his head in satisfaction. Hayward appreciates Z's style and feels not the slightest tinge of envy or resentment even though words are his trade too – though in a different sense. For Hayward they're semantic tools, precise and formalistic, practical and tedious, with meanings archaically defined in dusty tomes dating back to the Henries and the Richards.

But this pamphlet is neither writ nor brief. It is a clarion call to arms. It must touch that inner self wherein the conscience slumbers and passions may be roused.

So corrections made, off it shoots. There is a sense of urgency. No time to waste. (A notion further emphasised by Hayward's throbbing metronome.) First, hand carried by a runny-nosed messenger boy to the copyist and then to the publisher, already primed and waiting, where the type is set. A printer, cloth cap pulled jauntily over his forelock, his brow liberally smudged with lampblack, holds a page proof up to the bright electric light, thinks fleeting about that poor, unlucky Jew who's the subject of his endeavour, before signalling his OK, the press can roll. And then, in a fog of acrid ink, the pamphlet pages start to fly, one by one, from the great clattering cylinders of the Koenig-Bauer High-Speed Litho Machine, the pride of this busy workshop set away in the backstreets near Cheapside – just one of hundreds of small, independent printing enterprises churning away in the heart of London.

The old mahogany clock hasn't long to wait before a delivery wagon pulls up in front of Hayward's law office and two strong men, one painfully thin, the other the colour of ruby red ale, trundle up the stairs with bales of printed matter tied up with coarse hemp and still having that redolent odour of something fresh off the press.

On receipt, Myers takes out his penknife and rips open one of the packages. He pulls out several of the newly printed pamphlets and passes them around. There is a slight frisson in the room, an electrical tingle, as their little manifesto is passed from hand to hand. It has created a large dent in their meagre defence budget, but if it does its job well they all feel it certainly would have been worth it.

They quickly set to work addressing envelopes and stuffing pamphlets within. A number are immediately hand

247

delivered to the editorial offices of the daily newspapers that huddle greedily together in the vicinity of New Grub Street. A few are sent further afield to the Jewish weeklies. Cunninghame Graham has arranged for a copy to be sent to the Home Secretary with a supporting letter written by an elderly, Liberal MP, not directly associated with the 'trouble makers'.

The pamphlet is also to be shown that evening to an old acquaintance of Hayward's, Sir Edward Clarke, an attorney who the year previous had been responsible for saving Adelaide Bartlett from the hangman's noose with such adeptness at countering the monumental evidence against his pretty client that even though she was happily acquitted of poisoning her husband, nobody really believed she was innocent (bringing a famous surgeon to remark, 'Now that it is all over, she should tell us in the interests of science how she did it').

Sir Edward, as Hayward would later tell them, read the pamphlet, looked up, furrowed his brow and said that a copy should be sent immediately to the trial judge. Hayward, of course, reminded him that this sort of direct communication by the solicitor was without precedent. And Sir Edward had told him to damn precedent and just do what needs to be done. Sir Edward, of course, as he had become Solicitor General, could have passed it on to the judge himself, but that would have also been unprecedented. And Sir Edward, as helpful as he was, wasn't going to put his own reputation on the line for an impoverished East End Jewish Immigrant (as he would some years later for the likes of Oscar Wilde) but time was of the essence and, if it was a respite they were after, then Hayward would just have to bloody well send it.

Hayward that very evening took a deep breath and did what he was advised. With the pamphlet, he enclosed a personal letter to Justice Stephen, excusing himself for this most unusual action by saying that he had been encouraged by the judge's well-known reputation for fair-play and as there were only days to spare, he felt that the judge would understand the urgency of placing this new information before him, which, for various reasons, hadn't come out during the trial.

Myers read the letter after it was written. So did Z. Both of them thought it good and encouraged Hayward to send it.

It was duly sealed and sprinkled, and given to the delivery boy (whose nose continued to drip, but, thankfully, not on the package) and sent off with good wishes and a blessing of eternal hope, however tenuous.

CHAPTER 31

THE BUSTLE OF Cheapside faded away as night fell and buildings emptied of their masters – the accountants, the brokers, the lawyers, the scribes – who made their way by cab back to their cloistered homes or, in the case of those harried staff on the lower rungs of God's immutable hierarchy, by train to some dreary outlying suburb. Then the streets of that fanciful square mile, the heart of the far flung British Empire where an endless flood of paper was processed each and every day affecting, in some mysterious manner, the lives of a tea picker in Darjeeling, a sheep-sheerer from the Australian outback, a Shanghai opium trader, an African diamond miner and a coolie laying railway track to take fatted cattle from the Argentinean Pampas to a dirty slaughterhouse in Buenos Aires - those narrow streets so filled with monied energy, those offices flowing with oceans of inky blood, emptied, each and every one. And then all was quiet. All was serene. Even a stray dog caught in a focused beam of moonlight was left alone as it lifted its hind leg to pee against a sculptured plinth supporting the heroic representation of some Conquering Lord of the Realm on Horseback.

Cheapside was now at peace with itself, with God and with Mammon. Quiet and Darkness ruled; shadows wandered in the stillness of the night, spirits of the plague and long forgotten Romans. Everywhere but one: deep into the night, while all surrounding was asleep, the office of John Hayward, Solicitor, 27 King Street, Cheapside EC, second floor, had its gaslights still burning.

People were coming and going at all hours. Food was brought in – bread, butter, pickles, mustard, onions, chicken,

250

ale. The air stank of strong cheese and stale tobacco. A kettle full of water atop a kerosene stove was always on the boil. Some people were sleeping at their desks in mangy clothes, competing with the cheese for supremacy of odour. The place was a mess. Rubbish - nutshells, butts of cigars and cigarettes, discarded wads of paper - littered the floor. But one could sense a feeling of heightened energy existed. This little office, once an ordinary solicitor's domain, with all the boring implications, now was alive, vital, empowered, buzzing with vigour and crackling with fire.

Hayward's office had become Lipski Defence Central. Over the days since the end of the trial, something remarkable had happened. Instead of the letdown and lethargy that comes from defeat, a new determination had arisen coupled with a shifting mood on the streets of the East End. During the trial, the focus had been on the event itself and the grisly details of the murder. But after the verdict was in, after the swift and brutal ending when the curtain was drawn, the props were packed up, the stage lights were doused and all that was left was an emptiness in the chamber, at the dock - where once the judge and jury sat, there now was just a hollowness that already had begun to rot and a residue with its sour, lingering smell had begun to trail out the door and down the streets and alleyways and back into the ghetto. And back inside the ghetto, people's nostrils had begun to burn and their eyes began to water from the acrid stink that had become ever stronger as each day passed and the clocks ticked off the seconds till the man they once had all abhorred would be hung in the cold morning light for a murder he may or may not have committed.

This realisation had hit the ghetto like a thunderbolt. Suddenly, overnight, petitions with scrawled signatures supporting a reprieve began to pour into Hayward's cramped

251

chambers. And so came the volunteers – workers, traders, teachers, do-gooders – people from all walks of life who asked how they could help to stop this young, immigrant Jew swinging from the gallows.

Not everyone was convinced, of course. But there were enough to send out crews of canvassers, to the markets, to the shops, to the bath houses, to the synagogues, the shules. And everywhere little knots of people gathered, like clumps of flotsam, to argue and debate about that luckless young man and whether some vile injustice was being enacted upon him.

Even the Jewish weeklies that had kept their silence earlier on because they were loath to stir things up in an atmosphere where foreign Jews were being vilified as the reason native Englishmen went jobless – even these cringing vehicles of the cowering middle classes had begun to have second thoughts. Some now came out in support of a reprieve because 'it is no great honour for the Jews when one of them is hanged.' But still a gnawing fear that some demonic box had now been opened and, once that the lid was off, who knew what would start crawling out of it. 'When an ordinary person kills a person everything is quiet,' wrote the editor of Die Tsukunft, a popular Yiddish weekly, 'it will not occur to anyone to call another person by the name of the murderer. But when Lipski is sentenced to death, the ordinary people taunted other Jews by shouting "Lipski!" at them. Two weeks ago, Saturday, it happened in Brick Lane. Last Saturday in Church Lane there was a great fight between Jews and locals and all because of him...'

Sides had been firmly drawn. On one, the crowds bayed, 'Hang the Jew!' and jeered at all the other 'Lipskis' whose features seemed to define them as his brethren. On the other, there were those horrified that one more Israelite would be nailed to the cross, without a benevolent God to save him (not that God seemed to be in the habit of saving Jews from crucifixions).

The shadowy East End streets, normally perilous enough, were now doubly rife with danger. Mothers kept their children inside claustrophobic houses. Men walked quickly to their work, avoiding certain roads and nervously glancing over their shoulder to see who, if anyone, was following them. Women stayed away from pubs. People seemed to roam the streets in groups and few went anywhere without a friend escorting them.

But in the city at large, the case had yet to take hold. People still ate their breakfasts at leisure and read the morning press with more interest given to the latest stock offering for a new fangled device to mass produce boots using a patented automatic riveter then to a story buried deep in the pages of the Times about some Jew found guilty of a capital offence who would be punished accordingly as justice had dictated.

Back in Hayward's office, the morning had arrived and faint rays of blemished sun filtered through the grubby windowpanes. The sounds of early horses clip-clopping down Kings Street were heard, along with the shouts of newspaper vendors and the tramping of the first battalions, the lowly paid army of cleaners, scullery maids, runners, handymen – all those needed to start the Cheapside day.

As the morning dawned, there was a quickening of pace. The rum was passed around from hand to hand and the coffee brewed, allowing them to shake off the long night's aches and stiffness. And then, back to work. They were going through the schedule of the day when a rapping sounded at Hayward's office door, the handle turned, and a little messenger boy, not more than twelve, with a too big cap flopping over his face, came in to deliver an official-looking packet to John Hayward, Esq and, having been given a farthing for his trouble, the little messenger boy, with a toothsome grin, tipped his cap and bounced out again.

All eyes were on Hayward as he carefully opened the envelope with the glistening sword-like implement handed him by Myers, took the letter out, unfolded it, perused it quickly, refolded it and slipped it back inside its enclosure.

All eyes were on him as he pursed his lips. All was silence. The only thing they were certain of, those others in the room, was what had been delivered by the messenger lad was very important. And finally when Hayward spoke, what he said brightened the room with a smile from his cracked lips instead of his usual gently formed frown. For he announced that Justice Stephen had requested a meeting. (Cheers!) And that the meeting would be held at the Law Courts , right after adjournment, on the 8th of August, Monday afternoon.

CHAPTER 32

HOPE, THAT JOYOUS spring of all endeavours, had come in the form of a scribbled letter from the judge. That he had requested a meeting, gave heart to Lipski's rag-tag committee of defenders. The pamphlet had clearly done its job and now that the gnawing questions that lingered on after the trial were in the public domain, the issue of respite had been given wings to fly above the tawdry world of legalisms (though awkwardly, perhaps – something like a rooster who wishes to soar but hasn't yet found the proper aerodynamic know-how).

Still, this would likely be their only chance to speak with the judge whose agreement they would need if the appeal were to commence. Therefore it was absolutely crucial to get their facts and strategy correct. But what points should they stress? What more could they add to what the judge had already read?

At their first planning session after Justice Stephen's letter had been received, Z argued that more intelligence was required; information that would give them a feeling for the judge's state of mind and what particular questions he might ask. They already had some notion of the man – he was, according to Hayward, someone who saw himself a master of the law - firm but (in his own eyes, at least) right-minded and fair. He also had a reputation to uphold and it would be hard for him to agree to an appeal based on his foolish summation at the end of the trial, as that would be admitting fallibility verging on incompetence. There would have to be something else, something new that hadn't been brought out in court. If they were to agree that Judge Stephen was an honourable man (and there was no real evidence he wasn't, argued Hayward) then they could also assume he must, by now, have doubts. Their task, therefore, should be to strengthen those misgivings to the point where a respite was the only reasonable outcome.

Krantz, as always, is concerned that they are being too innocent about the political realities of this appellate game. There are other forces at work and unless those were understood and the pressure points located then there would be only tears to follow.

But where would that information come from? Where would they derive it?

When Myers has the opportunity to speak with Z alone he tells him that they indeed have their sources and they have been able to acquire information about the judge's state of mind. This informant must be kept secret, but Myers allows Z to see his notes written from the material he had surreptitiously acquired.

These notes bring Z to believe that the Judge does have reservations, however, he still clings to the idea that Lipski has been safely convicted. He seems to have looked at the relative probability of the two competing scenarios – Lipski's version of events versus that of Rosenbloom and Schmuss – and concluded that Lipksi is still the most likely culprit.

After studying these observations for a while, Z concludes there is a basic problem that will be hard to overcome. For they are working on the assumption that an appeal will be successful if they can provide enough nagging doubts about the safety of Lipski's conviction, whereas, the judge seemed to be saying that someone would have to hang for Angel's murder, and if not Lipski then Rosenbloom and Schmuss. And, if that were indeed the case, then they would have to show evidence pointing to the culpability of these other two impoverished workers – also refugees, also Jews. Simply showing Lipski probably didn't do it wasn't enough; they had to show that it was definitely Rosenbloom and Schmuss.

And yet they hadn't the people, the organisation nor the skills to launch their own investigation into alternative theories of the crime. Besides, the various worlds of the itinerant immigrant were dark and mysterious. The clannish divisions were strong and personal loyalties solid as granite. To get inside any of those worlds would take time and patience. Patience they had; time they had not. The real truth was probably beyond their grasp. All they could hope to gain would be a runny custard of rumour and intimation.

So, thinks Z, their only option is to continue chipping away at the shaky edifice that had been constructed around Lipski's conviction. One question that had been troubling him was the nature of Lipski's injuries. These had been sloughed off as insignificant by the prosecution and not actively pursued by the defence.

Z had taken it upon himself to revisit London Hospital and to interview the resident staff. Dr. Calvert, the house surgeon, had given evidence at the trial relating to an examination he had performed shortly after Lipski had been brought to him by the police, still dazed and partially insensible.

At their meeting, Calvert seemed dismayed that his testimony had been twisted by the prosecution to suit their purposes. He told Z that he had expected the counsel for the defence to follow up and query him about the manner of Lipski's injuries, but for some curious reason they hadn't bothered and the impression had been left in the minds of the jurors that there was no significant marks of violence on Lipski's person. But the abrasions on his elbows were severe, Calvert told him, and these could well have been from rubbing over a rough, wooden surface. Even more, the

257

struggles of a man on his back in shirtsleeves could likely have been the cause of such injuries.

Z asked Calvert to sign a statement to that effect, which Calvert did quite willingly. He also included a comment concerning the question of the acid, reiterating that, in his opinion, it would have taken more than the contents of the vial exhibited in court to have produced the damage and stains to Lipski's jacket and his person when coupled with the amount forced down the throat of the murdered woman.

Back in the office, Z shows Calvert's declaration to Myers. And Myers, in turn, shows Z a report that had been commissioned from a doctor located through the Lunacy commission (though who had done the commissioning wasn't exactly clear to him), which stated that the cause of the unconscious condition in which Lipski was found was probably due to sudden fear or shock acting in conjunction with physical violence. The statement was signed by a mysterious Dr. Grover, who ended his report with the words, 'No other explanation appears to me to be reasonable.'

Z's initial elation at reading this communiqué from the realm of the madhouse keepers, modified by Myers who takes this missive with due caution, telling Z that for every authority they can gain, the Home Office can find three to counter. It is a question of resources, of which the Government has much and they have little. Besides which, opinions rather than facts count for almost nothing – unless, of course, the opinion comes from experts hired by the prosecution.

CHAPTER 33

Z HAD LEFT the heated atmosphere of Hayward's office to attend a meeting with his friends, the Young Turks of the new London literary scene who gathered each fortnight to exchange pleasantries, chat and discuss the issues of the day – all of which camouflaged their real purpose which was to see who was doing what and whether there was anything in it for them. This kind of self-selecting grouplet which served as a network for eager minds and willing flesh, were cropping up in small cafés throughout London. It was the sort of time when people sensed that change was in the air and if you were young, smart and not averse to struggle there was opportunity galore (though, of course, this freedom of opportunity could ultimately lead to the workhouse).

In fact this was another aspect of the new age erupting in the zenith of Jubilee Summer. And what made these Young Turks different from the Young Turks of the past had more to do with class and background than genius or disposition. For these Young Turks were penniless except for the income they might accrue from the sweat of their brow or the nib of their pen. And when Z had looked around at those who shared his table at that small Italian café near the beacon of the reading room at the British Museum, he saw not pampered gentry but uncommon men from diverse backgrounds – like Barrie, who came from the Scottish Highlands and whose father had tried to earn his living as an artisan weaver; or Shaw, the self-proclaimed 'social downstart' and itinerant Irishman; or Jerome who had grown up on the streets of Cockney London; or like himself, the offspring of immigrant Jews who thought matzo balls were the traditional food of

England. These Young Turks with different views and from different linguistic circumstances were starting to reshape Britain and the class-ridden language that had tried to tether their thoughts and passions. These were the men who had liberated themselves from Sheridan and Shakespeare and formulated their own art in their own manner (as Shakespeare once had done himself).

They had listened with fascination to Z's stories that night of the man all London was coming to know as the Jew who was bound for the gallows. And though they sympathised with the anger he expressed at the bluntness and cruelty of British justice, they cautioned him as a friend and as an artist, to keep his head and not lose it along with Lipski's, no matter how passionate he felt. For art, as Jerome reminded him later, as they walked together past the glittering lights of Shaftsbury, had its own obligations. The world could be bleak if one allowed it; life, indeed, could be brutal. He, himself, had come to that realisation one terrible night, not so many years ago, when his childhood had suddenly ended, full stop, and he found himself alone, without parents, without money, without anyone or anything to count on. And how did he respond to that dreadful awareness? First, or course, by tears, but then, curiously, by laughter at the ridiculous state he found himself in. Ever since that moment he had come to see the only antidote to a world of terror and fear was humour and, if Z could excuse him for being a bit maudlin, friendship and good cheer.

So, he continued, why didn't Z consider taking a break with him? He was organising an excursion down the Thames. There were two of them already, not to mention his dog, and wouldn't it be dandy if Z could make it three? They'd meander down the river, stopping here and there, pack in some food, some wine. Perhaps they'd meet some ladies on the route, perhaps not. But certainly there'd be a story in it. Maybe even two. So why didn't Z give himself some time off from his noble quest and come along?

Now back in his room, Z relives the evening in his head and finds himself both angry and distressed. He has never felt so distant from his erstwhile friends as now. For they have failed to understand the depth and urgency of his commitment. Part of him is shocked at his own reaction for possibly he hasn't realised his feelings till now – he had neither the time nor the inclination to search his soul for reasons why he had suddenly become so consumed by the plight of someone he had never met and, for all he knew, might actually have committed the most brutal of murders.

But, perhaps that was the point. Perhaps he had come to the place where Myers and Hayward had been all along. For without having the evidence which would stand up without question in a court of law, they truly believed Lipski to be innocent. And, even though Z wouldn't have articulated this, he had come to that point himself, reaching that moment of belief, when faith and trust merge into one, and reason is overcome by knowledge that is received by other means which have little substance in a world structured by the precision of Aristotelian logic.

He knew he was being pulled somewhere by a very powerful force; but he was somewhat loath to analyse the whys and wherefores. It was too soon and he was still torn between the different parts of himself, the different elements of his being, to consider the nature of his compulsion and what it meant beyond the need to save a man-child whose face transformed in the dark of night, as he lay restless in bed, half asleep, half awake, into his own or sometimes that of his father's.

These kind of meandering thoughts were also unsuited

to the task at hand. He needed every ounce of strength and concentration to maintain his frantic race against the clock that stubbornly waited for no one. This clock, which had so recently become more powerful and demanding as factory life took over from the workshops, as towns and villages were forced to comply with the nature of conformity brought to them by the Masters of the Railroads, now ruled life as never before. It had come to rule Lipski's existence and now it had come to rule his. The idea of a day which contacted and expanded according to the nature of the seasons, the planetary movements and the biological rhythms of life, was superseded by a mechanical notion of society more suited to an economy that saw people as products and time as wealth.

For Z, time had always been more complex. Perhaps it had something to do with the special history of his people who, for survival, needed several notions of time – one physical and the other spiritual. The physical one was necessary to establish social relations and to maintain their contiguity with the world outside. The spiritual one was needed to preserve their faith and hope and trust. It was only in this multiplicity of worlds that their inner self could flourish even when their flesh was being maligned.

Time, therefore, was not one thing. Indeed, there were many clocks, some of them interconnected and some of them running in a universe of their own design. They told time in cycles of short duration and cycles that were long. To take one clock into account while ignoring the others, gave only part of a picture that was painted in many perspectives. Truth, therefore, if there be such a creature, lay in a realm that subtly changed its nature depending on which clock you were connected to at any given moment.

Simple, it was not.

CHAPTER 34

HIS MEETING WITH Fitzjames Steven was quite positive, Hayward told those who gathered round the small conference table that evening when he returned, tired but hopeful. The judge had listened to him with interest and seemed to think that the points he raised were deserving of the most careful attention.

Did that mean he would be supporting the call for appeal? Or, at the very least, asking for a respite?

These questions Hayward couldn't answer. He was careful, he said, to maintain a proper decorum, conscious he was walking on perilous grounds and that any false movement could have sunk them into an unforgiving quagmire. The judge, he felt, needed to be nudged along, inch by inch, without being put in a position where he reacted out of defensiveness rather than reason and compassion. True, he had come away with nothing but a feeling that progress had been made. But Justice Steven had indicated that he would like to meet with him again, quite soon, to go over the issues they had discussed – after he had some time to consider them.

Krantz, in annoyance, had asked whether this new meeting would take place before or after Lipski was hung. And Hayward, quite calmly, responded that nothing would be gained by exploding the situation when without the judge's cooperation Lipski surely would die. For, if Fitzjames Steven had questions in his mind, Matthews, the Home Secretary, had none and, in fact, was anxious to get the poor lad hung and buried and out of the front pages as this case was causing him no end of embarrassment. At least this is what he was told by friends in the Solicitor General's office who seemed to know what was going on within that inner sanctum.

Greenburg, on his part, congratulated Hayward on a job well done. Things, he felt, were falling into place. The petition drive had been more successful than he had hoped. Instead of hundreds of names, they had collected thousands. And, through the efforts of Cunningham Graham, they now had a long list of MPs willing to support a statement from the House calling on the Home Secretary to grant a respite. What's more, the Lipski case was being used as an example of why judicial reform was so desperately needed. Two changes, in fact, were being proposed by the opposition – the right of the accused to be a witness on his own behalf, and, more importantly, the setting up of a court of criminal appeal which would act independent of the trial judge and the Home Secretary.

That was all well and good, Krantz pointed out, if Lipski was to be a martyr to liberalising an arcane, and, in his eyes, a rotten system of justice. But if it was Lipski, himself, they were trying to save then he wasn't sure these side issues of judicial reform were helping his case or giving the government just one more reason to get him quickly out of their hair.

Z also felt the importance of not getting side-tracked. The focus needed to be on Lipski and him alone. The days were quickly passing and something would have to happen fast or else they would still be begging, hat in hand, while the noose was being fix around Lipski's collar. Hayward may be right in finessing the judge, he felt. What else could he do? Justice Stephen might even be sympathetic, but in the end the decision wasn't up to him, not really. If they wanted to stop the execution, they would have to reach the powers above.

Perhaps he would like to write a letter to the Queen, Krantz suggested in a tone that matched the gently derisive shape of his features.

Perhaps that wasn't a bad idea, Z replied. But it wouldn't be them who could write it. And looking around for De Souza, he noticed he was missing.

Later Myers told him that he hadn't seen De Souza for a while. He was a busy man; not easy to contact. But he was someone important to have on their side. After all, he worked for the Rothschilds, didn't he?

So De Souza was a merchant banker, Z thought to himself. Of course people in De Souza's position had enormous leverage and power. If it came to that, Z supposed, it was a route they would have to make use of.

Even though he didn't like contemplating the idea of bowing down to the aristocracy, Z was a pragmatist. There were roads he would rather not travel, but sometimes the choice wasn't his. So if he needed to go down that road after all, he just took a deep breath, held his nose, and did it. Not always, of course. Pragmatism, after all, did have its limits. But the idea of certain problems being of exceptional nature and therefore allowing for exceptional solutions was something that was well ingrained in him. Even the most orthodox of his people lived by that concept.

If a devout man, for example, was faced with a situation where he need either eat a certain food prohibited by his dietary laws or die, there was no question that the food would be consumed. For eating the forbidden food might be a sin, but a greater sin would be to cause such a stupid ending to his life because he was too proud to eat something theoretically taboo to save himself. Even his God would have thought him an idiot.

This, in essence, was the nature of pragmatism as passed down through the generations to Z. One did what was needed to be done when the situation called for it. It was the safety valve built into a culture which allowed its people to survive in an alien world with their moral values intact.

Even Krantz wouldn't have had a problem with this idea of pragmatism due to special circumstance. Nor would Myers. Nor would Hayward. But Hayward coming from a Christian background was steeped in the notion of repentance – or, in other words, paying dearly for ones sins. The image of Christ suffering on his cross retained, in a metaphorical sense at least, a certain terrible beauty of martyrdom. Whereas for the Jews, the cross was nothing to be gloried in as, all too often, it was reserved for people just like them. They didn't feel the blessed pains of soulful suffering, just the hurt of rusty nails pounded with heavy hammers through their flesh. And the blood that seeped from their ragged wounds was hardly transcendent; it was hot and sticky and stank of existential misery and torment.

However, the better side of Christ which touched on the ideas of peace, forbearance, justice and forgiveness, and that empowered men like Hayward and women like Maggie to devote themselves to selfless acts of human salvation (as much as anything as grand as salvation can ever be selfless) – this sense of Christian mercy had a certain purity about it which Z much admired. His people, he realised, were impelled out of a sense of misbegotten guilt. Where did it come from? All he was certain of was that it had always there – in the darkness of his closet, in his shaving mug, in his cereal bowl, in the pocket of his trousers. It was there when he felt bad and it was there when he felt good.

Then where did it come from? Certainly not from the Great Accusation; he didn't buy into that at all. Those dark shadows imposed by centuries of blame were only taken seriously by the accusers themselves projecting onto the Jews their own torment at somehow having missed their opportunity to meet the Son of God before he had been swept back into the Miasma of the Universe. But what if Christ had stayed? What then? What if he had gone to Rome? Would he have been welcomed there or thrown bodily to the wolves? What if he had met an ancestor of the Pope? Would that Papal predecessor have given him bread and washed his swollen feet in fragrant oils or set his hungry dogs on him?

And, even more intriguing, what if he had been accepted as the Lord of Lords? Would he have had to set taxes in the Kingdom of Heaven on Earth? And what if those taxes were set too high? Who would his people have rebelled against? No, Christ only made sense as a universal martyr who died for the sins of everyone. So those who threw stones at the Jews might just as well have thrown stones at themselves. That wasn't the source of the guilt used so effectively by his people to keep their offspring in tandem.

So if it wasn't that, what was it?

What was it, indeed? Z knew, of course, as did everyone who came of age as a son or daughter of the Diaspora, of the Great Wandering. Perhaps they couldn't articulate it. But they knew. They knew it in their heart of hearts because it was a primal force that was rooted not in the intellect but in the blood. It was a force that said that they were meant for better things than simply to wander the earth like gypsies. And those better things could happen only when they returned to their home, back to where they had come from.

But where was that? Where had they come from those many years ago? Where had they left? Was it that little plot of land in the Levant, where their ancestors would turn each day as the sun rose slowly in the celestial heavens? Was it that fertile crescent somewhere to the east, where they had fructified? Was it the richness of Moorish Spain where they had gloried for bountiful centuries? Was it the Kingdom of the Khazars that had mysteriously vanished like a land-locked Atlantis, spewing their people far and wide over the fertile Caucasian heartlands? Was it the lands to the north where they lived in relative peace and happiness in small villages and farms? Was it that confined and nurturing Pale where Russia and Germany and Poland and Lithuania met in a cultural and linguistic montage of beauty, wailing, ugliness and splendour? Was it the world of the shtetl? Or was it the ghettoes of Venice, of Frankfurt, of Vienna, of Rome where the gates closed each and every night to keep out the terrors and create the illusion of safety and solitude?

Where was home? Was it a place on Earth? Or was it another country of a different universe?

CHAPTER 35

SONNENSCHEIN'S WAS A local café in the heart of the ghetto. It was small, dirty and smelled of rancid chicken fat and chopped liver, but it also had a certain unique charm due to the exuberant presence of the owner who once had been a minor performer in the Yiddish theatre and now contented himself in serving his impoverished audience edible morsels from their Eastern European trough of remembrances and providing a space, small as it was, to act out their own miniature dramas that had more to do with the land of beet borsht than the one of beluga caviar.

Z stopped by here occasionally to have tea served Russian style in a glass with a wedge of lemon and a cube of raw sugar, which custom dictated was clamped between teeth, upper and lower, to be sipped loudly (the noisier the better) while picking up on the neighbourhood gossip, traces of which, like the indelible stains from tannic dregs, would eventually find their way into his ghetto tales.

The characters who came here at all times of day were well known to him by sight if not by name. But everyone here knew everyone else and even if they didn't actually *know* them they knew someone like them which, as far as they were concerned, was just the same. It was, therefore, somewhere they felt comfortable and, small and insalubrious as it was, sheltered from the buffets of the alien outside world. What's more, it provided them, the clientele, with a moveable feast of information, which flowed from table to table as conversations ebbed and swelled. It was not unusual at all to find a person entering into a debate that was being held three tables away from him, giving the appearance of a chaotic meeting hall.

Who needed newspapers there? Even though newspapers – especially the Yiddish press – were strewn communally around, they were mainly used to wrap up the precious leftovers to take back home and add to meagre dinners. For here news was being made on the hoof, filtered through the practiced anecdotes of these natural story-tellers who could turn a simple, one-line incident of a man who lost his hat into a never-ending saga of love, grief, jealousy and betrayal – all with an obliquely Ashkenazi twist to it, like a gigantic overly salted pretzel.

This motley circus of the dispossessed, a collection of everything the water-taxis had brought in from refugee ships that arrived day after day at the ports of Tilbury and Southampton, had found a joyous home at Sonnenschein's – a place where they could be themselves and re-create their former life in food and banter.

The bulk of the café work, of course, was done by Mrs. Sonnenschein, a portly woman of indeterminate age who wore her flaming red hair rolled and knotted at the back of her head (though, what began as a neatly coiffed chignon, ended up, after a day of cooking, cleaning and excitable discussion as a ragged puff ball of the sort that cats, for no particular reason, might tangle themselves up in).

Mr. Sonnenschein was more comfortable playing the role of petulant host, part-time friend and, to Mrs. Sonnenschein eternal displeasure, frequent money lender to a multitude of *gonifs* (in her words) or writers, artists and businessmen (in his) who were just a farthing short of some magnificent venture which would resound in glory throughout the universe (or at least the back streets of Whitechapel).

This particular day that Z came in, Mrs. Sonnenschein was to be seen engaged in a heated debate with a sour faced, bedraggled man who once, it was said, many years ago, had been rich and happy (though nobody knew exactly when), about the nature of The Kugel and whether it was best made with noodles or potatoes. Mr. Sonnenschein was at a table of appreciative *shnorreres* (appreciative because in order to get them to listen he topped up their glasses with a carefully measured drop of exceptionally cheap schnapps, a case of which had been given to him by a wandering merchant in exchange for several nights' food and lodging which turned into a week and then a month) bellowing forth the lines of his favourite passage from the Rag Picker of London (which had been adapted from an earlier play entitled The Rag Picker of Odessa – which, itself, had been adapted from an even earlier one called The Rag Picker of Paris, first performed to laughter and tears at the time of the Paris Commune in 1871).

Already a star in this cloistered firmament, Z was greeted by Mrs. Sonnenschein who was thankful to have any excuse to break off her Kugel Dialogues with a man whose brain, she had decided, was no bigger than an a grain of uncooked kasha, by an effusive mixture of welcome (how good it was to see him) and complaint - Where had been so long? Didn't he like them anymore? And then barraging him with questions – Why did he look so thin? Wasn't he taking care of himself? Why hadn't he yet found a wife? And, by the way, did he want to meet her niece? A very fine and intelligent young woman; she didn't know how to make blintzes, but that's what was happening to young girls these days – they would rather read than learn to cook for their husbands. And he needed a good woman to fatten him up. Wouldn't he like a nice piece of strudel? Of course he would!

And then Mr. Sonnenschein, not to be outdone by his woman, waving his arms effusively and shouting out – Why?

What had they done to him that he should have stayed away so long? Had he found another place to eat his strudel? Could he really find strudel somewhere better than that made by Mrs. Shoeneson? Of course not! So what was the reason? Was he near to death? Did his money run out? If so (in sotto voice, pretending not to be overheard by his wife, who, of course heard every word as she was meant to) Z need only ask and he would lend him enough for a month, a week or the rest of his life, if necessary, at a small but reasonable rate of interest, of course (followed by a wink to Z and an innocent smile to his wife who glared back at him).

So why had Z come that evening? True, it was a bit of home where he could let a part of him relax and be itself (the rest of him was left outside in the damp, waiting, impatiently for that other part, the beet borsht self, to glutton-up on fatty food and folksy non-sequiturs, where meaning came not from straight lined logic but through convoluted twists and turns in a giddy, sometimes brash and sometimes gentle, roller-coaster irony that reminded him where he came from and not to take that part of him he left outside too seriously even though it was cold and wet and hungry).

But why had he really come? Why had he been drawn there now after so many months of absence? He used to come on a regular basis, writing up notes on the people and jotting down their stories, laughing with them, crying with them, dreaming with them. But then it stopped. Had it something to do with Jerome and his quiet asides as they walked down the fashionably Bohemian streets of Bloomsbury after a day at the reading room in the British Museum? What a marvellous writer he could be if only he could leave the ghetto. The bright lights beckoned and the brilliance of his pen could be applauded by more than just a bunch of hopeless refugees without money, influence or power. There was more to life than chicken fat. For here they were, in the heat of Jubilee Summer, with the red stain of Empire covering half the map, and here they were in the centre of it all, with voices that could span the millennium. Who could ask for anything more than that?

CHAPTER 36

THERE WAS ANOTHEr reason he had come to Sonnenschein's that day. It was to garner information that could be procured no other way. For the ghetto was a complex organism with its own eyes to see, ears to hear and lungs to breathe. Sonnenschein's could be its ears – one of the thousands that were connected to this strange amalgam of spittle and slime, hopes and mystery. It could also be its eyes: eyes that were everywhere, for nowhere in the ghetto did one find that very English notion of personal space or the pleasures of obscurity. There were too many eyes and too many ears for that. Physical privacy was unknown; the only sense of seclusion existed within the world of the mind, that single realm where one could be alone. For some this mental space expanded into a miraculous universe that winged them far from the dirty streets of Whitechapel. For others it contracted into a tight, vascular ball, compressing all the miseries of fear and deprivation.

Z, in fact, had come to Sonnenschein's on a mission. Up till now, few strands of evidence had been gathered which could be used to cast enough serious doubt as to the safety of the verdict that would influence a bull-headed Home Secretary like Matthews and certainly nothing that would have sweaty editors rushing to stop the printing of their latest edition while new headlines were composed that shouted 'Lipski Proved Innocent!'. And with only one investigator, very young and inexperienced, trawling the labyrinthine streets of the East End for clues, using the part-time services of Greenberg for translation, while the precious sands of the legal hourglass emptied granule by granule like drops of vitrified blood draining from Lipski's veins, there was a growing feeling of inertia. For the sense of buoyancy that was felt in Hayward's office had more to do with the blind hope of belief than the harsh reality Z sensed when he was off on his own, disconnected from the tight group that formed the nucleus of Lipski's defenders.

True, on the political front at least, progress had been made. Cunningham Graham was preparing his question to put to Matthews, the Home Secretary, in the Commons and sixty MPs had already signed a petition asking for reprieve with more to come. But the government was beginning to see this case shift from minor irritant to major annoyance which detracted from important issues on their agenda, like the dreadful Irish question, which had left them as a wounded beast, angry and defensive. For this case had opened up a rag bag of other issues, casting a searchlight on the sinister poverty of Whitechapel and the unrelenting surge of immigrants swelling into the slums of the East End, stirring up base fears and resentments among the even more impoverished native born citizens. (This, of course, had the benefit of shifting blame for joblessness from government policies to alien refugees who, supposedly, were grabbing all the work. But that, the government understood from witnessing the anarchy unleashed in other parts of Europe, required a lid kept on the simmering pot, with the fire turned down, lest the bitter stew of toil and trouble boil over, scalding everyone). So if there were pressures for respite, there were even more pressures to get this case over and done in order that the dirty linen of London's dispossessed be stuffed safely back into the dark closet of ignorance once again.

But if Sonnenschein's was anything to go by, there was another front to the Whitechapel murder case that was emerging. That day when Z came in, the talk was of nothing but Lipski (with the exception, of course, of the Kugel Dialogues and the recitation of bits from the Rag Picker of London). A petition lay prominently on the counter for people to sign (several pages had already been filled with scrawled signatures – some in Hebrew lettering, some in Cyrillic) and a poster, with the boyish face of the prisoner wearing a disarming smile advertising a meeting of Jewish anarchists to save Lipski from the clutches of International Capitalism (conveniently side-stepping the fact that he was a nascent sweat-shop owner).

Arguments, debates and monologues flowed freely from table to table concerning the latest rumours and innuendos springing to life without rhyme or reason, like some strange, hermaphroditic organisms. Sipping his tea, eating his strudel while doing his best to listen in, Z found himself awash in outlandish theories of collusions, conspiracies and cabals. Some thought it was a plot cooked up by the Russian Tsar to push his pogroms into England. Others swore they saw the wicked hand of the church, secretly promoting the Blood Libel and quietly lending its authority to rumours that the murdered woman was actually a Christian whose blood Lipski had used to make his matzos. (An argument then ensued as to whether using blood to make matzos would actually cause the flour to rise, defeating the idea of unleavened bread and therefore one could no longer, in truth, call the finished product 'matzos' as the name, itself, meant 'bread that doesn't rise').

As these crazy ideas spun through the grizzled air like little whirlwinds that washed over the greasy tables until they petered out only to be replaced by another squall just as ridiculous, Z realised the difficulty of being a spy in a community of disconnected refugees where the line between fantasy, fact and fiction is so dreadfully thin. On the other side of Aldgate there were fictions too that posed as fact, but those fictions were generally unquestioned. Here everyone had their own fictions, it seemed. And they all offered them up into the great morass of confusion which only others of their sort could filter through and hear. For humour, irony, innuendo and drama were all part of their language which helped them find solace in pain and cope with the meaningless tragedies of life which had given them little, if anything, to cheer.

But what, Z wondered, was reality anyway except an agreement by certain groups to observe things in a similar manner? England had cobbled together a set of social and political realities that had been enforced by language and custom. Here in Sonnenschein's, much to the dismay of the Anglo-Jewish Guardians, the language of English and customs dictated by propriety and deference, were banished and replaced by the loud and boisterous energy of irrepressible spirits that, like shipwrecked sailors, had found themselves marooned on an island where the natives were as strange and curious to them as the Hottentots were to the crews swept by savage seas onto the coast of Southern Africa.

He, of course, was between two worlds, so sometimes things at Sonnenschein's made sense to him and sometimes they didn't. He liked the food and he liked the humour. He liked the feel of a community where no one inspected his nose nor asked him where he came from as it was simply assumed he came from the same place as they did. But where were they going? They might be eating now, but tomorrow they'd surely be hungry again. So what was to become of them? And what was to become of their children?

Perhaps that's what the Guardians might have said as well. Should they stay or should they go? If they go, then God be with them. But if they stay, they had better become

Englishmen.

Z was thinking about all this for the umpteenth time when he was approached by a young man with bright eyes, intensified and made larger by the potent lenses of his wire-rimmed spectacles perched comfortably on a calm, unthreatening face that must have charmed both men and women. This young man, whose name was Rabinovitch, sat down at Z's table and began to chat with him – something that would never have happened in an English café without the necessary preliminaries of introductions and queries as to whether intruding on one's personal space was warranted. But, as mentioned, there was no personal space here anyway. And, therefore, there was no question as to whether this young man had a right to sit down at Z's table and start a conversation. Nor would it have seemed strange if several other people sat down as well, entered into whatever dialogue was established, and then, just as things were getting interesting, left to engage in another debate somewhere else. For, if Sonnenschein's was like a pond, each table there was like a lily pad for the customers to hop upon, croak a bit, eat a few flies and then move on.

Rabinovitch, as it turned out, was a sometime journalist for the Yiddish press, a poet, a playwright, a novelist, who earned his meagre living as a scribe or letter writer for the multitude of Jews who wanted to correspond with some official agency but hadn't the language skills to accomplish it. Rabinovitch, of course, knew Z by sight and reputation and had read his stories and columns avidly over the several years he had been in London. So, even though they had never actually met, Rabinovitch felt he knew Z well enough to consider him a comrade because as well as having read his writings, he knew people who knew him, which was enough to establish a connection. And even if that weren't the case,

278

this was Sonnenschein's and, therefore, Rabinovitch knew it was quite all right to sit down and talk because the people who came here were without much affectation. Poverty was a great equaliser. Paper hierarchies are quickly dispensed with when people are poor, for basic needs quickly overcome pretence.

Besides, there was something Rabinovitch wanted to say. He knew that Z was involved in the Lipski case and, in his own manner, he was as well. But he had been picking up on some curious stories and he wanted to pass them on because he felt that they were being lost or ignored in the tempest of the moment. It had to do with the events at Batty Street right after the bodies were found and the crowds had begun to gather. The prosecution had selected certain witnesses, he said, who supported their case and they had ignored others. These others, who were ignored, had a different story to tell. Perhaps Z would be interested in hearing about them?

CHAPTER 37

OFF STAGE, OUT of the range of the footlights, there was another performance that had been enacted and another audience that had witnessed it. This was the shadow world of an audience without the price of admission and performers who would never be allowed on stage. For the trial of Israel Lipski was choreographed around a sequence of incidents that were deemed to be true and therefore, in re-enacting them before invited guests, the eyewitness accounts were carefully vetted to conform to a pre-constructed vision. Anything that detracted from this scenario was deemed simply incorrect or even mischievous.

In the hubbub and confusion after the body of Miriam Angel was discovered, there was an ebb and flow of people on the stairs of the Batty Street house, pushing upwards and then down again, passing information, like vital crumbs of nourishment, to the hungry crowd below which was quickly accumulating outside on the road. This was before the police had been able to set up a cordon to limit the number of people on the scene. But even afterwards, there were some who had got through the ragged and poorly contained police line - friends of the family, friends of friends, or those who just appeared to be members of the household.

These people, like phantoms, soon disappeared into the night. No one was bothered about them. They had an invisible presence because they were held to have no substance or value. But they were the face of the ghetto, a monster with a thousand eyes that saw things back and forth and sideways, filtered through several millennia of history and processed by a neurological network that contained infinite notions of the past, the future and the present.

But now, some many weeks afterward, stimulated by the verdict of the trial and Lipski's imminent demise, stories had started drifting out, emerging slowly, oozing like sap from wounded trees in a dense and tangled forest. At first they seeped into the rumour mill like thinned molasses with hardly enough substance to butter a pancake. However boiled in a heated cauldron of innuendo and gossip, these threadbare anecdotes grew more viscous and heavier.

What, for instance, was one to make of the man who had stood by the doorway of Angel's room at the Batty Street house when the search was being enacted and saw someone remove a vial, similar in appearance to the one exhibited at the trial and said to have contained the murderous nitric acid, quietly from his pocket? What was one to make of that? Or the whispers heard by another, which, translated from the Yiddish, meant 'Don't worry, I'll take care of it.' Hushed remarks that indicated nothing at the time but later seemed quite ominous. Or the man who had come to the house earlier, unreported in the trial events, who claimed to have seen two strange men rushing out of the door just as he arrived.

In the confusion, in the emotional tempest which swept over them, in the excitement generated by the crowd, the heightened drama and the horrible nature of the crime, who actually had the presence to piece anything together then? It was only afterward, after many days had passed, and the visions of the day were re-run again and again in not-so-addled minds that they suddenly became aware of things that had been eating at them which made no sense in the crisp and clean version of events that Lipski's prosecutors so blithely conjured.

CHAPTER 38

IT IS LATE in the afternoon. Z is back in his room, sitting at his desk with his pen, freshly dipped in its brass ink well, poised above a virgin sheet of paper. A tiny drop of ink rolls off the nib and splatters onto the emptiness. No matter, it is only a tiny blotch and Z is not such a slave to neatness. Take a look at his room – clothes scattered on the floor, dirty dishes piled precariously on a counter, masses of books and papers stacked helter-skelter everywhere. So what of a tiny blotch of ink falling on the cleanness of a brand new page? It saves him the trouble of decrying the first mark – that initial foray into transcribing the subconscious that cannot but sully the sublime nothingness that contains the potential of perfection in its yet-to-be state before the author tampers with it.

But what Z sets out to write is not what he wants, for he is too obsessed with Lipski and the events that have rushed past like a tempest inundating everything in a wind-swept gust. So instead of writing what he wants – which is still unknown to him and will not be known until he writes it – he makes an entry in his journal: 'Saturday, the 13th of August, 1887.'

Then he puts down his pen. Where to start? So much has happened in such a short time. The emotional rollercoaster went unabated reaching new highs and lows which if charted on a graph would have looked like the madness of the stock exchange or the beating of a frantic heart.

So he closes his eyes. And what he sees is himself walking down Aldgate and then along Leadenhall till it becomes Cornhill; then past Bank and down Cheapside, finally reaching King Street where Hayward's office is located. He sees himself walking swiftly, taking long strides, his angular body driven forward, his head thrust out in a determined manner pushing forth against the Easterly breeze that carries the stench of industrial waste back toward the ghetto that had nurtured him. From his jacket pocket, a copy of yesterday's Pall Mall Gazette protrudes noticeably and he clenches it firmly in place with the long, tapered fingers of his writing hand.

Entering Hayward's office he sees Greenberg and Myers seated at the meeting table. They look up as he comes in. Z takes the Gazette from his pocket and waves it above his head. Greenberg grabs his own issue from the table and waves it as well. Myers grins. Z had never seen Myers grin before. Not a true grin of unabashed pleasure. But his smile soon faded.

Opening his eyes again, he notices the very same paper sitting on his desk. He reaches out and brings it closer to him. Then, unfolding it, he smoothes the creases and looks it over once more.

It was Stead and the Pall Mall Gazette that had taken up the case for reprieve with a crusading spirit that went far beyond the plight of the beleaguered young man. Z had known that more than saving an innocent life from the gallows, Stead wanted a story that would launch another frontal assault on 'Modern Babylon'. For even though Stead despised injustice, he hated the Tory Home Secretary, Matthews (the 'Papist anti-Christ') even more; he hated Poland, the prosecutor who had banged him up in prison for his ill-fated Maiden Tribute exposé; but most of all he hated Justice Stephen who epitomised to him everything wicked about class-ridden England where blithering, bumbling, sexually obsessed hypocrites wielded power with brick bats given to them by Her Majesty, the Queen, and thus, in proxy, by God.

Not that Stead had much time for Jews, especially the

283

waves of hapless immigrants littering up the shining shores of New Britannia, taking jobs from real English workers and dishonouring Mother Russia, as the Tsarina's friend, Mme Novikov, had convinced him. But even a Jew, in Stead's zealous mind, deserved the promise of True British Justice.

Z knows this about Stead and yet the Pall Mall Gazette, the newspaper Stead captained and wielded like a mighty sword of truth and vengeance, was feared, loathed and admired in equal parts. What Z understands, and what could not be denied, is that the Pall Mall Gazette was read by the high and the mighty as well as those who wished to bring the high and mighty down. The Gazette was capable of moving mountains whereas sometimes Z feels (in his darker moments) that Hayward's motley crew could hardly shift a grain of sand.

After all, where were they now? Three short days remained before Lipski's execution. Certainly Hayward's meeting with the judge had led him to feel there was a shred of hope – if only they could find the trick of loosening the Gordian knot that bound the hesitant Justice Stephen from asking Matthews to declare a reprieve. And if what they needed was a clarion call to wake the native urge for righteousness in the liberal middle-classes (or, at least, give it a nudge), Z had to admit that the Gazette could be the trumpet with which to do it.

Even then Z had a lingering and abiding premonition, like a visitation from future's ghost. There was a certain bravado about the Gazette that smacked of the foolhardy. As the canons from Stead's galleon blazed, it often set fire to the fringes rather than the target, itself. But, Z thought, at least the canons blazed. And perhaps that's really what was needed. For the newspaper that had been flapping in his jacket pocket as he walked swiftly toward Hayward's office the other day, was indeed a clarion call. And this issue of the Pall

Mall Gazette of August 11, 1887, as a forceful summation of the case, the lingering doubts and the unanswered questions, would lead anyone with head or heart to conclude that, at the very least, the charge against Israel Lipski remained unproven.

Z pages through the issue once again, casting a writer's eye over the length and breadth of this scorching discourse that often seemed to hover perilously close to tirade and invective. Yet it captured the mind as well as the emotions. It was, Z thought, a work of journalistic daring-do. And simply from a sense of professional curiosity, he tried to analyse how Stead had done it.

Thunder was first hurled at the readers, themselves – something Z felt was strategically both brilliant and dangerous. He remembered reading it with a reaction of shock and then admiration for such a mad and ingenious bit of bravado: 'As the Home Office has been allowed to drift into a blunder,' it began, 'the public, which might have prevented such blundering, must share the responsibility.' That was enough to make them prick up their ears, Z thought. And it continued: 'What we now ask the public to do is to hear the prisoner's case restated before they become, in however slight a degree, parties to what, if that case be worth anything, would be a judicial murder ...'

What followed was a very reasoned and painstakingly thorough discussion of the case against Israel Lipski, the admitted facts, the theory of the prosecution to account for them and Lipski's explanation in his defence. Then, one by one, the questions that lingered: What happened to the fatal vial of acid? Was the door to Angel's room really locked? What was the motive? What happened to the sovereign Lipski had in his possession the night before the murder? How did the skin get to be rubbed off both Lipski's elbows?

How did Lipski become insensible? Why did no one hear a single scream or sound of scuffle? And, most importantly Z felt, if Lipski did murder the poor woman, how did he succeed in doing it? In the words of the Gazette, 'First there came the struggle with the murdered woman, in the course of which this slightly built young man with a feeble fist must have dealt her four or five blows, enough to stun her. Then he must have given her the acid, and himself the acid; have sprinkled his coat therewith in the peculiar manner above described; have taken his coat off; have covered it up with the other coat which was found above it. Having done that he must have crawled under the bed, insensible... All this surely makes a large demand on one's credulity. If there were other conclusively damning pieces of evidence, one might be content to accept such things, hard to believe though they be. But remembering what had been adduced above, can one honestly say that those difficulties now pointed out should be lightly put aside – especially as every one of such difficulties at once disappears if the prisoner's own story be accepted?'

And finally, the inevitable conclusion – the *coup de grace*: 'What we have thus adduced is what Mr Hayward put before Mr. Justice Stephen, and what caused the most acute and most unbending of judges to have the gravest possible doubts as to the propriety of carrying out his own sentence. The responsibility now rests on the Home Secretary. But it is for the public, to whom the Home Secretary is in the long run responsible, to insist on it that he shall not make them parties to the terrible risk of committing under form of law a crime hardly less heinous than that which did Miriam Angel to death.'

So when Z had walked into Hayward's office waving that magnificent copy over his head, how could he have known, how could anyone have known, that the very next day their hopes would be dashed.

Hayward wasn't there, he remembers. Myers told him he was having his second meeting with the judge and then … And then? Then he was meeting Stead. Why Stead? Because that was the agreement.

Myers, it seems, had told Hayward to be careful. Hayward, he said, was honest, honourable and trusting – marvellous qualities for a saint but dangerous for a lawyer. He was a good man, Myers said, and thus he feared for him. (As one does for all good men, Z thinks to himself, recalling the conversation.)

But the second meeting had gone splendidly. Indeed, Hayward was quite euphoric when he had returned later that afternoon of August 11th. Poland was there as well, Hayward had told them, to provide the prosecution's response to his questions. But Justice Stephen was disquieted and not at all pleased with Poland's replies. And afterwards, when Hayward was chatting with the judge's clerk on his way out, he was left with the distinct impression that Stephen was troubled by this case – more troubled than the clerk had ever known and he had been with the judge for over fifteen years!

Myers had asked Hayward: So your conversation with Stead, when you went to the offices of the Pall Mall Gazette – how did that go?

Oh, very well! Very well! Stead is definitely with us!

And what did you say to Stead? Myers asked him, his eyes slightly narrowed. Did you tell him everything? Including the little chat with the judge's clerk?

Hayward shrugs. That was significant, wasn't it? It provides us with evidence of the state of Stephen's mind.

And you told Stead that? Myers asked him.

Of course I insisted that everything the judge told me

287

must remain confidential, Hayward had said. He won't attribute anything to me. Of that he promised.

And Z recalls the look that Myers gave him – a painful expression of sadness and of sorrow.

CHAPTER 39

Z'S PEN IS now flying. He is writing about events as he witnessed them – though, as a writer, he is bound to embellish what he experienced - for his pen quite often has a mind of its own.

He is thinking about Lipski, pleased that the drums were being banged for his release – or, at the very least, a delay of execution – but concerned that it might now be out of control and that a political game was being played behind the scenes to which he was not a party. Mulling all this over, he realises the pressures of last week had been extraordinarily strenuous taking up an enormous *tranche* of his time - though, certainly, he feels his own work could hardly come before the life of that unfortunate young man. ('I do not complain,' he writes. 'There is much to be learned from this trial!')

Suddenly he hears a rapping at his door. He has been so deep in thought there is a moment's delay before he answers it - and is surprised to find no one there when finally he does,. Later, he discovers a note had been slipped underneath. The message was marked: 'Urgent!' And it requested that he return to Hayward's office at once.

'It was not a joyous scene when I arrived,' Z writes. 'Myers was alone in the office, looking as glum as I have every seen him. He's not the most ebullient of men at the best of times, but this, I thought, was different. His eyes contained the misery of nations and his shoulders, usually solid and erect, slumped under the weight of something ponderous.

'"Have you seen it?" he asked, looking at me as if certainly I knew what he meant – which, of course, I didn't.

'He pointed to the table whereon there was a pile of

journals and newspapers. "'Today's Gazette, he said. Have you seen it?"

"'Yes, of course. It's very good, though I might have written it differently."

"'Have you read the 5th edition?"

"'I'm not certain what edition it was that I read", I admitted.

'He handed it to me, carefully folded so that I could see the offending passage. I copy it here in full, as much to remind me how fine a line there is between odiousness and honour, as to have a record of betrayal (even one for a cause that is just).

When Mr. Hayward left, the editor of this journal was placed in one of those difficult positions in which all the commonplaces of ethics seem to point one way and paramount and imperious duty in another. To save Lipski – to prevent a judicial murder of the most aggravated kind, one way lay open, and only one way. Publish the fact that Mr Justice Stephen is, to say the least, haunted by a terrible doubt as to whether Lipski is not as innocent as the poor woman for whose murder he is to be hanged, and his execution becomes morally impossible.

But then the conversation was private, the interview confidential. We were in precise terms interdicted from using it. If we published it, Mr Justice Stephen might be very angry. Mr Hayward would fall into disgrace and we should have to face the odium of a breach of confidence. 'You have no right to use a private conversation.' 'If you don't, an innocent man will be hanged.' 'But save Mr Hayward's client.' 'And no one will trust you any more.' 'Well, when a life is at stake they had better not tell me anything that would save that life and expect me to keep it secret.'

And so, after many arguments pro and con, we decided

that our first instinctive conclusion was the true one, and we publish the above statement just as we received it...'

'I looked up at Myers, who had been following my eyes as I read. He bade me turn the page and continue:'

When going to press a boy brought up a letter from Mr Hayward, couched as follows:

Dear Sir – I do most sincerely trust you will not report my private conversation with the judge; it would ruin my professional standing and, what is more consequence, it would be adverse to the interest of my poor client. – Yours very truly, John Hayward.'

CHAPTER 40

HE MET HER at the coffee stall on Garrick Street just outside Covent Garden. They sat at a rickety table the stall keeper had placed there for the convenience of his customers who shifted as the wayward sun from the earliest costermongers still rubbing their sleepy eyes, to businessmen staving off the boredom of their jobs, to shoppers come to fetch their daily fare, to tired workers wanting liquid vigour, to ladies of the night who might share a penny's worth of cocoa whilst dreaming of their princes.

'The judge was furious,' Maggie said. 'He wrote his wife to say it was a wicked lie from end to end.'

'How do you know?' Z asked.

'I have my sources which I shall protect better than that awful man who dares call himself a journalist.'

Z looked at her and thought what a remarkable woman she was. It's not that he hadn't felt that way before, it was simply as time went by this subliminal realisation had transformed itself into conscious admiration.

Certainly the judge was furious and the consequences were not as Stead had predicted – the people did not rise up demanding action; Justice Stephen simply reverted back to his native intransigence. Yet there was still hope, he thought, if only a glimmer - like the tiny flame that flickers from a dying candle.

And there were things happening that ratcheted up the pressure for Matthews to relent and offer a stay of execution. A petition with over two thousand signatures had been forwarded to the Home Office. And that very day on the floor of the House, a question was to be put to Matthews by

Cunningham Graham.

'What more can be done?' Maggie asked, as much to the rising moon as to the man who set opposite. 'It's so late in the day.' Then fixing Z once more in her gaze she said, 'Certainly there must be someone of importance who can intercede...'

What she didn't say, what she couldn't say – at least not to him – was that surely there were people, his people, who were powerful enough to come to Lipski's aid. What about the Rothschilds? Or the Mocattas? They wielded enormous power. Surely people like that could force insignificant creatures like Matthews and Stephen to listen.

But she didn't say that to him because part of her knew it was wrong. She knew deep down that issues like poverty and injustice had to do with one's position in the world and those who controlled the wealth of nations owed allegiance to power itself regardless of race or religion.

Another side of her, however, truly thought that Jews tended to be – well, there was no other word for it - conspiratorial. Where this feeling came from she didn't know nor did she ever try to analyse it. Mostly she was able to quell what she regarded as her baser instincts. But sometimes, like now, they surfaced despite herself.

'Greenberg has spoken with Baron de Worms,' Z told her.

'The MP?" she said.

He nodded. 'Parliamentary Secretary to the Board of Trade. Baron de Worms, it seems, knows Matthews quite well. Their families were both involved in Ceylon...'

'Doing what?'

'Helping set up plantations for the coffee trade – till the blight started killing coffee off. Then they switched over to tea.'

'Fellow Empire builders,' she muttered.

'At least it's a connection,' said Z. He didn't say that Baron de Worms was also a Jew, because he understood what she had left unsaid – she didn't need to say it aloud for him to comprehend her feelings because he assumed that deep down all Christians felt like that. And he knew that the Baron was as far removed from the penniless Ashkenazi hoards as Maggie was from her own Saxon forebears. "Greenberg is trying to convince him to set up a meeting between Hayward and Matthews. Hayward has also written to the Queen. A final plea before the hangman comes.'

Maggie found herself staring into his eyes and thinking they were eyes unlike any she had seen in a man. Gentle and strong: an appealing combination. But there was also vulnerability and something else; not exactly sadness, rather a sense of the French *tristesse* – a kind of sorrow that comes not so much from the head but from deep inside the heart. A sadness that is, perhaps, ancestral.

Z, on the other hand, was looking past Maggie at the coffee stall itself. Like hundreds of others that had sprung up around the city, it provided a cosy café atmosphere without walls and often without tables and chairs (though sometimes, like here, a rickety one or two). Coffee was brewed in large, five gallon tins set over a charcoal brazier keeping the essence – well mixed with burnt carrot and chicory – piping hot throughout the day and evening. A display shelf held an assortment of cakes and buttered bread. Another held the coffee mugs and saucers.

He had recently done an article on the coffee trade and had found it a fascinating business. So the link that had been forged between Matthews, the Home Secretary, and de Worms, Parliamentary Secretary to the Board of Trade, being coffee related set off a chain of strange ideas in his head. Why, for instance, had Lipski's landlady been out the morning of the murder? To fetch him a fresh pot of coffee, of course. Coffee that he didn't drink, as the landlady had testified. When she had later felt the pot, it had already cooled. Just as the leads in this convoluted case had grown cold and distant.

But Maggie was thinking how calming it was to be sitting with him there, out in the open, by the wonderful market of Covent Garden that she so loved. At this time of the evening there was still a residual buzz even though the market itself had ceased for the day because, in truth, the market never ended. The finish of one day simply coincided with the beginning of the next in a lovely continuity of movement like stars dancing in the firmament. And, if truth be told, Maggie felt more comfortable here than in the great and grubby markets of the East End. It was more – how could one say it without being rude? – more English, wasn't it? (There is nothing shameful, she thought, in feeling more comfortable with one's own – even if one sometimes didn't really know who one's own actually were.)

And where else could they be sitting if they wanted to drink a cup of coffee as well as talk? The café at the British Museum was her first choice, but not at this hour. That's where she'd meet her fellow readers and chat about the ideas of the day with women like Eleanor Marx and that sweet young writer, Amy Levy, another Jew of course, who reminded her slightly of Z, himself.

Then there were the writers' cafes of Bloomsbury set around the Museum, as if huddled there for safety as well as companionship, and those even more bohemian ones in the muddy streets of Soho. But you could never be alone there; in fact, you'd be almost sure to meet authors touting their latest book, painters back from Paris, Russian Narodniks, travelling acrobats. So a coffee stall by Covent Market wasn't a bad place to meet if you wanted to be alone, especially if the things you had to say needed to be said in private.

But they weren't engaged in idle banter. As the evening was swallowed into night, the mood shifted and their tone became more sombre. Death, up till now, had been held at bay by faith and by the ticking of the clock which still had many hours. But now the hours were few and fewer and faith was starting to flounder. For in three short days the young man Lipski would die, strangled at the end of a hangman's rope. And British Justice, they felt (for different reasons), would possibly die with him.

CHAPTER 41

A WEEK'S REPRIEVE! The papers would have shouted it out except they weren't printed on Sunday. Z learned about it from Myers who had sent a note by special courier.

'I wanted you to know, Hayward received a copy of the telegram sent by Matthews to the governor of Newgate – it reads as follows: "In communicating the enclosed Respite to Israel Lipski, be good enough to inform him distinctly that it is granted not from any doubt existing in my mind as to the verdict or sentence, but merely to enable his solicitor to make certain enquiries which he has asked to be allowed to make. The convict must clearly understand that unless these enquiries put a new aspect upon the case the sentence will be carried into effect. I am, Sir, your obedient servant, Henry Matthews."

The Committee for the Defence of Israel Lipski gathered at Hayward's office that afternoon to celebrate. Hayward's wife had baked a beautiful cake to mark the occasion – but nobody could figure out if it was kosher. So it sat forlornly on the conference table looking moist and luscious while everyone there – Hayward, Myers, Greenberg, Krantz, Z and Maggie – gazed at it with eyes burning with lustful hunger.

'What would be in a lovely cake like that to make it not suitable under Jewish law?' Maggie whispered to Z.

'Lard,' he whispered back. 'Hayward doesn't know whether his wife used lard or butter – or both.'

It was Krantz who finally took up the knife and began slicing off pieces and handing them around.

'God will forgive us,' he said.

And everyone gratefully accepted their slice, except Greenberg who, patting his ample tummy, said he was restricted by his very severe diet demanded of him by his heartless doctor.

But everyone, including Greenberg, accepted a glass of champagne from a magnum which had mysteriously appeared – though no one claimed to have brought it.

They toasted Lipski with fervent wishes that this short respite might lead to his freedom. They toasted Hayward for his single-minded determination to defend an innocent man regardless of personal cost. And they toasted Myers, who was the anchor that kept the good ship Defender from floating off aimlessly into the endless miasma – though he, himself, pooh-poohed the idea.

It was only then they saw the note which had been affixed to the magnum in such a way as to have been easily mistaken for a label.

Greenberg read it out: 'From W.T. Stead, Editor of the Pall Mall Gazette. Three resounding cheers to Mr. Hayward and his staff!'

At once the room fell silent. And it remained so until Greenberg raised his glass and offered up another toast:

'To Stead and the Pall Mall Gazette!'

The room remained embarrassingly quiet.

Then a strange thing happened. Hayward raised his glass: 'To Stead and the Pall Mall Gazette!' he said.

And they all drank to Hayward's toast. All, that is, except Myers.

CHAPTER 42

Z HAD BEEN furiously writing articles for the Jewish press, trying to build the momentum for commutation as well as cast a net into the community that he felt held the key to solving this maddening case, once and for all. For he suspected that a person or persons unknown had information that could help gain the missing piece still absent from this grotesque jigsaw. And these persons unknown could only be found by trawling the depths of the ghetto – not through the English press but by means of the media that could leap the linguistic divide into that hidden world journals like the Pall Mall Gazette or even the Jewish Chronicle could never penetrate.

Besides, the established Jewish press shied away from publishing anything that seemed to be championing Lipski. Even Mordecai at the Jewish Record told him, 'This case has gone on far too long,' as he handed back Z's proffered article. 'If one Jew didn't do it, then it was two. And that would double our trouble, wouldn't it? Did you read what happened in Kishinev the other day? Another pogrom! You think it can't happen here? Ask my friend from Prague or my other friend from Vienna!'

The most he could get out of Mordecai was a quiet plea for respite, simply asking for British fair play, if not full-blown justice. To Z it was a cap-in-hand, thank-you-sir, if-you-would-be-so-kind, sort of pleading that he would have nothing to do with.

So it was left to the anarchist Yiddish press printed by ancient machine or copied by hand on single sheets of foolscap and distributed in places like Sonnenschein's Strudel House or plastered on dirty brick walls throughout the East End.

But who were they, really, this ghostly audience? These were people fighting back starvation and, if lucky enough to work, spending sixteen hours a day cooped up in dark, squalid, sweaty hovels. Lipski was an immigrant Jew and people in the East End of London might sympathise with his plight, but they had seen death in many forms, each one brutal and grotesque. They had seen children malnourished and girls forced into prostitution so their families could have a crust of bread. What was justice to them when the mortuary wagon was just around the bend?

It was Jerome who told him what Z probably knew but couldn't admit to himself. 'This Lipski case is a quagmire. Once you step in it's hard to extricate yourself. But you don't want to sink so deep that you suffocate alongside him.'

'It's gone far beyond the guilt or innocence of a single man,' Z told him, realising, of course, that Jerome wouldn't understand.

It was true. Jerome didn't understand what Z was actually trying to say. But he did understand something else. 'Have you read that new book by Louis? It's already sold thousands of copies here. And it's all the rage in America. It's called, *Strange Case of Dr Something-or-other…*'

Z shook his head.

'I saw Henry the other day – Henry James. He thinks it's a work of genius. It's about a man who always treads the straight and narrow, kind and charming – you know the type. But he has a secret desire to explore the moral hinterland. So he invents a potion that releases him from his propriety – except it all goes wrong…'

Of course, Dostoyevsky played around with this idea some years before. Z had read him in French as his work hadn't been translated into English yet. (And when it was finally translated, it was done by an English schoolmarm who censored the passion and Eastern European angst with a flick of her pen.)

That wasn't the point, he told Jerome. There are demons in anyone that could emerge under certain circumstances. But sometimes these demons are invented by those in power who find it necessary, for reasons of their own, to burn a few witches.

CHAPTER 43

Z AND MAGGIE are walking together back to the East End from Hayward's office. Maggie has taken a folded sheet of paper from her bag and hands it to Z as they stroll.

Unfolding the paper, he sees that it is written in child-like script.

'It's a copy of a letter from Judge Stephen to his wife,' Maggie tells him. 'I showed it to Myers but I didn't want to show it to the others.'

Z reads through the text. He is quite adept at reading as he walks. Indeed, he has completed entire books while strolling through Hampstead Gardens. And this is what the copy of the letter said:

'I have decided to return tomorrow after thinking over and over Lipski's case. I decided at last, this morning, to telegraph Matthews to respite the man for a week, to satisfy the public and avoid the appearance of haste. I do not doubt the man's guilt, but I thought the execution was to follow too quickly on the consideration of the case and I felt also that when we held our final conversation on Thursday night, I had been rather tired and hurried, and I wished to make assurance doubly sure. I shall therefore go back to town tomorrow, thoroughly restudy the whole case, from first to last, and probably come back to my first opinion, for I do not see how anything new can come out. I am dreadfully vexed about the whole matter, as you can imagine, and the worst of it is that everyone will say I was bullied into it by that blackguard Stead. In fact his disgusting interferences tempted me violently to hold off from all interference at all, but that would have been a vile motive to act upon. I have tried to do right, but it has been a most trying time, and I shall not forget it for a long time...'

Finished reading, Z re-folds the paper and hands it back to Maggie. 'How did it come into your possession?' he asks.

'I was given it by a friend,' she says.

'Your friend needs to practice her penmanship,' he replies.

She purses her lips. 'It tells us what we're up against, doesn't it?'

'We were under no illusions,' he says. But saying that, he realises they probably were. Those who knew Justice Stephen told them he was a stubborn man with fixed ideas. However, some thought he was malleable. His elder brother, Leslie, was a friend of artists and was well known in bohemian circles. Justice Stephen didn't live in a bubble.

But reading the letter the judge wrote to his wife, does reinforce Z's initial instinct that if they were depending on Justice Stephen to free Lipski based on a reconsideration of the trial, they might as well call in the hangman.

CHAPTER 44

BACK IN HIS room, Z mulls over the events of the day. There had been, at first, a flurry of excitement in Hayward's office. Once the starter's pistol had been fired, and the hourglass was again turned on its end, they could see the minutes fall away with the dripping of the sand.

But, unlike the first week, when they had been caught unawares, they had their tasks. The question was – where to focus? There were the two men – Rosenbloom and Schmuss. Investigations went forward noting their movements both after the murder and now. There was also the vial of acid labelled 'Camphorated oil'. Could they trace the origin? And could they challenge Moore, the shopkeeper who claimed he sold nitric acid to Lipski, making him into an unreliable witness.

'You already have,' Krantz reminded them. 'You have the statement from the ward nurse that Moore was brought straight to Lipski's bed where a detective was standing guard. How could anyone consider that a proper identification? What more could you ask? You achieved what you wanted and it didn't get you anywhere.'

Then he went on: 'You also had two locksmiths attest how easy it would be to lock a door from the outside when the key is protruding from within. You found an expert who said it would have taken at least two ounces of acid to damage Lipski's coat and to go down the throats of both him and the woman. So what happened to the other vial? They simply found another expert who said you'd only need one. What good did it do you? They just find someone from their side to contradict any testimony you bring forth. Like Dr. Calvert at the hospital who said that Lipski's abrasions on his elbows could only have come from a trauma similar to the one Lipski said happened to him. What does the prosecution do? They either ignore it or else find someone who says no, it didn't happen like that – it happened like this. It's our experts against their experts. How can you possibly win?'

'Then what do you suggest?' asked Myers.

'Forget playing fact against fact or speculation against speculation. It's not about that anyway. They don't care if Lipski is actually guilty or innocent. They just need someone to pay for a crime they'd rather not bother about anyway. If every Jew killed another Jew, they'd be quite content. But this is messy for the Tory government and they want it cleaned up straight away. So the only chance you can win is by showing them it's more worth their while to set him free than hang him.

'And how do you suggest we do that?' asked Greenberg, who found himself losing patience with Krantz – as he quite often did.

'Either by making Lipski a cause célèbre – so much so that the Liberals take up his case as a way of bringing the government down or by handing them Schmuss and Rosenbloom with confessions from one or the other – preferably both of them.'

'That's the two Jews for one game,' said Greenberg. 'I don't like it.'

Krantz shrugged. 'Then you're pinning your hopes on the Pall Mall Gazette, aren't you, Mr Greenberg?'

After Krantz and Greenberg left, Z was alone with Myers.

'I don't like that man very much,' said Myers of Krantz, 'but I must admit he has a point.'

'You wouldn't give up?' Z said, without believing that he

would.

'No, of course not. But both Hayward and I believe that the Pall Mall Gazette is our best hope. I can't forgive that man Stead for what he did, but we need him.'

So the strategy was laid. The investigation would continue and new information would, of course, be forwarded to the Home Office, but Stead would have access to all the material as further ammunition for his scattergun.

CHAPTER 45

DESPITE Z'S UNEASE about where the investigation was going and which direction it should go in order to gather the most compelling arguments that might possibly influence the Home Office or the judge, things began to percolate on their own. The Lipski case had catapulted itself into the heart of the ghetto like a meteor crashing into the primal waters of the East End, throwing up bits and pieces of flotsam in its wake. And Hayward's office had become the mission central where all these bits and pieces were sent to be sifted, sorted and classified into categories of crazy, plausible or potentially important.

A motley queue of people wandered into Hayward's office, night and day. Among others, the rabbi of the Hambro Synagogue came forward to tell of his conversation with the man Harris Dywein who had testified at Lipski's trial that he had found the vial containing the murderous acid under the dead woman's bed. Dywein, the rabbi said, later told him that he had actually found the empty poison bottle on the table and as he was afraid the blame might be attached to the husband of the murdered woman, he placed it in his pocket and then, when Lipski was discovered, he took the bottle from his pocket and placed it underneath the bed.

The Pall Mall Gazette ran the story with great fanfare: '...it is indisputable that this fresh evidence also gives a new aspect to one of the crucial points of the case!' Though they didn't indicate what inferences its readership should actually have made from this new information, the message was clear – questions abound! Can the government truly say that Lipski's guilt is beyond all reasonable doubt?

But, just as Krantz had predicted, the Home Office threw each and every testimony, statement or unearthed piece of evidence back, claiming that upon investigation they were either implausible, unverified, or unfounded.

Z tries to attend the daily meetings at Hayward's office – one in the morning, one in the late afternoon – as often as he can. Hayward, himself, is commuting back and forth from the south coast where his family is on holiday. Myers is always there - sometimes Greenberg, sometimes Krantz, sometimes Maggie. Depending on the current news – which can shift ten times an hour - there is always something going on, a frisson of excitement or a deathly pall. But there is also renewed energy and Z suspects that he and the others are feeding off that electricity which sparks and crackles like one of those new fangled generating plants which will soon be lighting up the world.

Once he asks Greenberg, 'Would it have been different if Schmuss and Rosenbloom weren't Jews?'

'It would have been different but it would have been even more complicated,' Greenberg replies. 'Think about what would have been the response if the Jewish community had been seen to be protecting a guilty Jew by implicating two innocent Christians!'

But to Z it makes no sense at all. If Lipski is innocent and his story is true, it follows that Rosenbloom and Schmuss are guilty. And it didn't matter whether they were Jewish, Christian or Hindu.

That evening he goes over the casebook he was keeping. Nothing incriminating had been found about Rosenbloom. His landlord claimed that Rosenbloom had been a quiet, sober and inoffensive tenant over the ten months he lived there. Even Sarah Katz, the sister of Lipski's fiancée, whose husband had hired both Lipski and Rosenbloom almost a year before and had taught them both the stick making business – even she had given Rosenbloom a sterling reference, saying that she and her husband had taken him back into their employ just a week after the murder.

Then how curious, Z thinks, that Mark Katz, her husband, had stated publicly he thought Lipski to be innocent and would certainly give him his job back again if he ever saw freedom. Z rubs his chin and tries to consider the implications. The wife says she'd hire one, the husband says the other. Would they have them both work side by side having accused each other of murder? He wonders if Sarah Katz was perhaps trying to protect her sister, Kate Lyons, who had been engaged to Lipski for some months prior. Hayward told him that Kate Lyons had visited Lipski once in prison but no more was seen of her since then. What had been their relationship, he wonders? Z, of course, had seen it many times before – the marriage of convenience set up between a likely greener and an eligible woman who might not have been that eligible to the native born.

Yes, he thinks, Sarah Katz most likely was trying to protect her sister by severing whatever links, however tenuous, still remained between the two. And he makes a mental note to use this unhappy character – this downmarket bride who is left in matrimonial limbo when her intended is no longer a family asset – in one of his stories about the ghetto.

But Schmuss, he thinks, is a pickle from a different barrel altogether. There were those who came to testify that Schmuss was in desperate need of money. So why did he leave Lipski's workshop after only ten or fifteen minutes when there was obviously work to be had? And how did he get the money to go to Birmingham just a week after the murder?

Others had contacted Hayward to inform him that one

of the four Russian locksmiths who were supposed to have met Schmuss the morning of the murder – a man called Totakoski - had been heard to say, 'If I had stated the truth at the police court two people would be locked up and Lipski would get off free.'

Another of the Russian locksmiths – Emil Barsook – who had just been released from prison where he had served a short sentence for petty theft, claimed that Schmuss had told him on the morning of the murder he had a woman and when Barsook asked him what sort of woman she was, Schmuss replied, 'You don't want to know all about that, she is gone.' Barsook told Hayward, 'When I heard that Lipski said two greeners had killed the woman, I believed Schmuss and Simon had done it.'

In the end, Z closes the casebook and throws up his hands. So much of this information was based on rumour and innuendo and one thing always seems to cancel out another. So where is the boundary between truth and lies? And what can one make of evidence that comes from people who have hidden loyalties or simply want to protect what little they have in their meagre lives?

Of course, the Pall Mall Gazette used each of these new revelations to full effect – working them into a daily story that lent yet more doubt to the safety of Lipski's conviction. But, Z thinks, it is one thing to cast doubt and quite another to prove the negative – that Lipski wasn't a murderer.

There was one piece of evidence Z feels could possibly be the key to a successful appeal. If they found a witness ready to swear that Lipski wasn't at the Batty Street house during the time of the murder, it would go a long way toward proving his innocence. Lipski, himself, had stated he was at the Portobello Market that fateful morning to purchase a sponge for varnishing his sticks. Could they track down the sponge seller?

Sponges – Z knew all about them from stories he wrote; they were precious as diamonds or mean as dirt. Shipped up from the great mart of Smyrna, they could cost, wholesale, as little as 6d a pound or as much as 21 shillings, depending on the quality. The good stuff went to the finest homes, the rough and gritty sponges were cut up into pieces that grew small and smaller as the chain of resellers grew long. In the end there were the greeners – the foreign Jews just off the boat looking for something cheap to buy and light to transport. They buy a piece of sponge for a penny and then cut it into four or maybe eight or, if they think they can sell them, maybe even sixteen, to be used by someone like Lipski who couldn't afford more than a farthing's worth and just needed something to brush a quick coat of lacquer onto a wooden stick.

They came and they went these itinerant Jews with baskets strapped around their necks. They all looked old and bearded even if they weren't. And on any given day there were tens if not hundreds of them plying their trade. Here today and tomorrow, who knew? Today they sold sponges, tomorrow oranges, the next day wooden clothes pegs. They sold what they could buy, when they could buy it, as long as it was going for a song and light enough to carry.

So looking for a bearded Jew who sold a sponge to Lipski eight weeks prior, who would also remember him out of the hundred fresh-faced, boyish men who wanted a piece of a sponge to wipe the nib of their pen or to clean the smudge from their spectacles was not the easiest of tasks. And even if they found this protean man, who probably spoke not a word of English, would he be brave enough to come forward and challenge the authorities who wanted nothing better than to

311

see him back in Tsarist Russia?

Z spends a precious day trying to track down the mysterious sponge seller to no avail. But that night the demons once again emerge as Z is tossing in his bed. He is somewhere strange and yet familiar. At first he recognises nothing and is fearful he is lost. But the sounds and smells and tastes that linger on his tongue, all his senses tell him that he knows this place well and he is in the midst of Portobello Road searching for the mysterious seller of sponges.

In his dream, the street is filled with great bearded men in long black coats and wide brimmed hats who all wear baskets strapped around their neck that dangle and dance as if keeping time to a dirge. As he pushes his way through the densely packed crowd, he hears the street cry, 'Sponges! Sponges! Here are sponges!' But each bearded man in a long black coat who turns round to face him has something different in his basket – fruit or seashells or lumps of coal. Yet he continues to hear the cry in the distance – 'Sponges! Sponges! Here are sponges!' Frantically he pushes his way forward. The bearded men now are like crazy Russian dolls and as he turns each one around, they glare at him with wild eyes and grimace and shout at him in Yiddish. Desperately fighting his way through this scrum of maniacal demons (for this is how he sees them), he hears the call of 'Sponges! Sponges!' getting closer and closer till finally there is only one bearded, black coated man before him. And putting his hand on the man's shoulder he turns him round, ever so slowly, and sees a basket full of beautiful, beautiful sponges strapped over his shoulder. And looking up into the sponge seller's eyes he sees something very peaceful, very calm. And the man who sells sponges looks at him and smiles the way only a father can smile and says, in Yiddish, 'Israel, my son,

312

at last I've found you!'

And then Z wakes up, gets out of bed, goes to the basin, fills up a bowl and splashes his face repeatedly with brackish water.

CHAPTER 46

HAYWARD HAD JUST returned from one of his visits to see Lipski at Newgate Prison and was giving his report to an afternoon session of the rump committee for Lipski's defence.

'I told him the week was going very fast but that there were many who were now supporting his appeal. He appeared quite cheerful despite his condition and when I commented on his disposition, he told me that the Lord would not forsake him as he had done nothing wrong."

'Does he realise that commutation still might mean life imprisonment?' asked Myers.

'I've told him that, of course,' Hayward replied.

'How did he respond?' asked Krantz.

'When the good reverend translated my words to the poor fellow, he simply smiled and said he'd rather die.'

'Who was translating for you?' asked Z.

'The rabbi who ministers to Lipski now. A very important man in your community, I'm told. His name is Singer. Do you know him?'

Yes, Z knew him quite well. Master of Jews College, London; minister at one of the wealthiest congregations in the city, Singer was a pillar of the Anglo-Jewish community.

'I'm surprised it's fallen to him,' said Z.

'I'm not,' said Krantz, who was just getting up to leave.

'Reverend Singer takes his ministrations quite seriously,' said Hayward. 'He's been spending a good deal of time with Lipski reading over passages in the Old Testament, he tells me. I hadn't realised what a deeply religious man Lipski was …'

'Rabbi Singer isn't so bad,' Z said to Krantz a while later. 'He's taken a strong position on maintaining unlimited Jewish immigration unlike some of the Guardians who would rather see it curtailed.'

'There's an article Singer has recently published in the Chronicle,' Krantz replied. 'It might be worth your while reading it.'

Z stopped by the Jewish Record later that day to speak with Mordecai and, in passing, asked him about the article Krantz had mentioned. Mordecai, of course, had a copy which he happily lent to Z.

Then Z made arrangements to visit Simeon Singer.

CHAPTER 47

SIMEON SINGER WAS seated at his great oaken desk, half
hidden by a tower of books, his head bent myopically in
studious demeanour – a position Z knew well – squintingly
focused on a document he may have written himself (or
wished to have done). Around the periphery of the desk was
built a disordered wall of papers and tomes of various shapes
and ages, perhaps as protection or defence or simply an
outcropping of ceaseless rabbinical vigour. Behind him hung
a picture in a gilded frame of the Ruthenian Alps painted in
the romantic style of Casper Friedrich or Joseph Koch. The
walls on either side were lined with leather-bound volumes
and plaques and portraits of ancient sages – Maimonides,
Rashi, and Judah Halevy amongst others – along with a great
and glowering image of Queen Victoria.

Rev Singer wiped his eyes with a small piece of cloth he
pulled from his waistcoat pocket and replaced in a mechanical
gesture that appeared to be a product of endless habit. Then,
putting his spectacles back where they belonged, he looked
at Z (with clearer vision, perhaps) and said, 'How good it is to
see you again! Please, sit down! Sit down! We've known each
other far too long to go through tiresome formalities.'

Z took one of the plain wooden chairs at the side of the
desk, moved it so his gangly legs could hang free without
hindrance, and, before sitting down, thanked Rev Singer
in language both floral and contrite for seeing him on such
short notice – a ritual Z knew was required despite the rabbi's
insistence on dispensing with ceremony. (For as much as Z
hated –in fact, despised – pretence, he was well aware of the
small compromises necessary to lubricate social interaction in

a world that gloried in hierarchies.)

As he studied the face so near, yet so far – the eyes, both gentle and forbidding; the countenance, both kindly and severe; the beard, so grimly redolent of the biblical prophets yet disarmingly avuncular – Z thought there was something about the man he both feared and admired. Not that he saw Rev Singer as fearsome in himself. Rather it was something strange and unsettling that Singer brought out in Z; something Z couldn't determine and would have been loath to analyse even if he could.

Certainly there were similarities between the two men along with their differences. Though Z was in his early twenties while Singer was nearly twice his age and though one could trace his ancestry to the shtetls of the Russian Pale while the other was rooted in Germandom, both had suffered deprivation in their youth, both were products of Jewish Free School grants and, significantly, both saw their salvation (or escape from economic degradation) in books and learning.

But Rev Singer was the minister of the gigantic New West End Synagogue, built in1877 under the auspices of Baron de Rothschild, with its great red Gothic arches flanked by two square turrets rising a hundred feet high, between which was set a magnificent circular window that let in God's light with as much grandeur and drama as any Anglican cathedral could muster.

And Z was merely a writer and a journalist.

Still, Z admired Rev Singer because Singer spoke out where others stayed silent. He spoke out for tolerance, forbearance and sanctuary when many who saw themselves as guardians of Anglo-Jewry simply wanted to protect their status and hard-won privileges without having an army of Russified immigrants try to sup in their kitchen (even if some of them could read and write Hebrew along with their bastard Yiddish).

And yet - what was it? Could it have been Rev Singer's buoyant optimism which kept repeating itself in various forms and seemingly boiled down to a simple equation: that we live in glorious land at a glorious time so we must count our blessings and celebrate our good fortune. Thus we owe a duty to the nation that has nurtured and protected us – as well as a duty to our people. One without the other is neither satisfactory nor sufficient.

Their paths had crossed many times before. There was the Jewish Free School and Jews College, of course, but later there were all the events that Z had covered in his role as either journalist or participant-observer where Singer had raised his melodious voice, inspiring his audience to do God's work on behalf of God's people and Queen Victoria, whom he so loved and admired.

'You expressed some urgency in your note,' said Rev Singer. 'But you weren't explicit.'

'Time is running out,' Z told him.

'For what?' asked Rev Singer.

'For a man who is about to die,' said Z.

'We are all about to die,' replied Rev Singer. 'The real question is whether we will die in heaven's grace. But I suppose you're referring to that unfortunate young man, Lipski, who is presently in my pastoral care. You understand, of course, that my conversations with anyone who confides in me are sacrosanct.' A gentle smile crossed the Rabbi's face. 'And you, my friend, are a journalist ...'

Z said, 'I fear the young man has been unjustly convicted.'

Rev Singer said nothing but stroked his beard. ''The bible reminds us that none is without sin,' he said finally. 'There is the perceived guilt of a man and the perceived guilt of a people. We see things through multiple visions. But there was a trial and a man was found to be guilty by a jury of his peers.'

'There was a trial,' said Z. 'But there was no justice.'

'The process of law is cumbersome,' Rev Singer replied. 'It always was and most likely always will be. But in parts of the world, not so very far away, there is no process at all. I hardly need remind you of that.'

'And if the young man you now counsel is innocent?'

'If he is innocent, then two Jews are guilty – not one. And they claim the same rights both as Jews and as Englishmen.'

'Look at him and look at them,' said Z.

Rev Singer looked at Z instead. There was a note of compassion in his voice as he spoke. 'If we are to judge guilt or innocence on outward appearances then we are all in serious trouble, my dear friend ...'

That evening several newspapers reported yet another gang of youths attacking Jews while shouting 'England for the English!' and calling out Lipski's name as they pummelled them.

CHAPTER 48

MYERS, SOME DAYS before, had created a calendar of sorts – simply sheets of paper tacked together in descending order that announced the days remaining till Lipski's appointment with the hangman. The young messenger boy employed by Hayward to deliver important letters and documents at a moment's notice, was given the job of tearing off a page from this do-it-yourself device each morning – a task he accomplished with a combination of ceremonial decorum and childish zeal, fixing his gaze on each new page as it was exposed - 'Seven Days to Go', 'Six Days Remaining!', 'Five Days Left!' – as if he were God's own agent of the apocalypse.

Z had taken a liking to the young lad, who claimed to be twelve years old though he looked to be ten. He walked with a slight limp, which hardly impinged on his duties, and was so short that he had to stand on tiptoes in order to reach anything over five feet from the ground. But he was game for all that was given him, rarely complained, and had eyes that sometimes were solemn and sometimes could twinkle.

In order to keep their spirits high, if for nothing else, Myers had the boy hang multicoloured bunting from the cornices (which he accomplished by standing on a wobbly stool further heightened by a thick stack of directories) along with plastering the walls with headlines from the Pall Mall Gazette, so that anyone who entered could hardly miss the point of this makeshift operation:

'JUSTICE AND THE JUBILEE'
'A LEGAL MURDER!'
'HANGING OF AN INNOCENT MAN!'
'FATE OF LIPSKI!'

'LIPSKI'S REPRIEVE AND ITS MORAL'

'WILL LIPSKI OR THE HOME SECRETARY SURVIVE?'

'DARE WE HANG LIPSKI?'

'THE RACE FOR LIPSKI'S LIFE!'

'SPARE THE MAN!'

Today as Z enters the office he steps over past signs which have been torn from that somewhat morbid almanac (which no one has bothered to sweep up as there had been so many other things to do) and notices only one page is left hanging limply from its mooring. But he hardly gives it a second glance as it has already lost the meaning Myers had intended when he first constructed this catalogue of descending days. For time now has a different flow – rapidly compressing itself into a tight continuum with no beginning and no end – even though the fight for commutation has reached its final hours in the world of clocks and calendars.

Just yesterday Cunningham Graham informed them there were over a hundred MPs who had signed a petition demanding a stay of execution which was to be presented to this amazingly long session of Parliament even though many MPs had already left for their holiday.

What's more – except for the dyed-in-wool Tory press – most newspapers have taken up Lipski's case and have published endless editorials stating that the time has come for Matthews to seriously review his position. Even the mainstream Jewish newspapers are now pleading for commutation. And the Pall Mall Gazette has thundered on in Lipski's defence, like an unstoppable juggernaut.

Only the government and the government's cronies are still baying for Lipski's head. But the momentum, they know, has shifted. Lipski's defenders are now riding a tidal wave of support and the government, hard pressed to respond,

321

is under relentless pressure to give in and, at the very least, commute the sentence of death and disemploy the hangman.

And now came word that Hayward's advert in the press asking for members of the jury to contact him has paid off. Two of Lipski's jurors have sent telegrams to the Queen asking for mercy and Hayward is about to forward a third one.

Suddenly Z knows – deep down wherein resides the certainty of knowledge – that they have truly won and, within hours if not minutes, a message will be received from the Queen sparing Lipski's life. As for the rest of this valiant committee of defence, no one feels this might be Lipski's last day on earth, a notion their sense of conviction refuses to allow – as if by force of will alone they have constructed a sweet reality where natural justice (as they see it) could not but prevail.

CHAPTER 49

WHEN Z LEAVES Hayward's office that fateful day of Sunday, the 21st of August, he is feeling a pleasant hum of contentment. The sky outside is bright; the sun is beaming down, the birds are gaily twittering and the people he passes on the street, smile at him instead of frown. It's good to be alive, thinks Z, this year of Victoria's Jubilee. It's good to feel that calm of certainty, knowing things are right and that despite the machinations of Imperial Mandarins, justice – true British Justice – will be done.

Perhaps it was the latent cynicism, inherent in all Jews, that made him always question, always suspect, always fear the loss of his critical sensibilities. Perhaps he clung to scepticism as a lifeline lest that intuitive mechanism of survival – Jewish survival honed over thousands of years - be somehow imperilled. But just for today, perhaps he could let it go. In a dozen years, he thinks to himself, it will be the 20th century. A new world was being born. Even in his short life so much has come to pass. People from all classes, all races, all religions were learning to walk free. Jews like him had gained nearly the same privileges as Christians. And people's voices were being heard in ways never before dreamt. Certainly it must be true – there was a new age dawning and he was part of it. The old world was being transformed by the unleashed energy of millions. You could sense it in the air, couldn't you? You could hear it in the crackle of the light bulbs blazing incandescent signs that pointed in one direction and one alone – toward the evolution of humanity. The trains, the telegraph, the typewriter, photography had changed the way we thought; all manner of life was in a happy state of transcendence. The ancient regimes were collapsing and in their wake, poverty, superstition and injustice would also crumble.

And feeling his spirits soar, he looked up into the sky, into the vastness of the cosmos and saw a cloud passing overhead. How perfect, he thought, how agreeable! Floating there so sweetly in the blue, it proffered hope – a magic carpet that would someday fly him higher than the moon. But as he watched the cloud, which at first was nothing more than wispy lace, he saw it start to grow dark and darker.

Then from behind he heard a voice he recognised: 'Sir! Please Sir!'

He turned around and met the eyes of Hayward's little messenger. And he knew at once that something had happened.

CHAPTER 50

THE SUN WAS fading from the sky. Z wanders aimlessly through the thickening London fog. In the winter, coal fires burning in thousands of homes and hovels spewed out toxic geysers of soot and tar. Combined with factory effluents and the noxious dampness rising from dank and narrow alleyways, a lethal mixture was created of sulphurated smoke and carbonated dust that hovered over London like a blanket of gloom. But now the cooling waters of the estuary were sucked in by the August heat producing a more benign and graceful sea mist that swirled like a hazy veil and painted grey the setting sun.

He loves walking in the fog when the air is breathable. It serves as a shroud that makes everything less obvious and thus allows him to keep his writer's anonymity, to observe without being observed, and to think without being interrupted by any visual stimulus.

It seems to him like hours since he started his directionless march, but it could well have been just twenty minutes. He has no way of telling nor does he wish to know. But when he arrives at where he ends up, he thinks that even though he hadn't consciously planned to be there, it's probably where he wanted to go.

St. Katherine Docks. He had come some weeks before when he had first met Maggie and given her a tour of that peculiar entry point into the heart of Empire. Today he stood alone and gazed out into the choppy waters of the Thames, into the miasma.

He waited and watched. And soon he saw them, emerging from the mist: one, then two, then three, then four – the small landing craft rowing immigrants to shore. He heard the sloshing of the waters, he felt the spray, and then he saw the bodies – women, men, children, young and old, coupled and alone, entire families, some holding firm, some fearful, knuckles white, faces pale, but eyes all fixed on the nearing landfall of the place they'll soon call home.

The boatmen, tough and weathered, land their swaying vessels by the river shore where the immigrants are to disembark, demanding sixpence for the short ride from the nearby steamer anchored just a hundred feet from the embankment. And then, one by one, two by two, they grab their meagre belongings and trek the narrow, muddy path to the Irongate Stairs which leads them finally to the quayside. Thin, bewildered, hungry, still terrified and exhausted by the endless journey from eastern homelands, their first sight of London is a dark, forbidding archway crowded not with passengers – as they are the first ashore - but with salivating agents and touts, licking their chops like wolves might do at the thought of meeting a flock of wayward mutton.

Z watches, transfixed, the scene that has been played out so many times before and for so many years. What goes through his mind, yet again, is that he is seeing the end of that gigantic funnel stretching from the Eastern hinterlands sucking the dispossessed of Polish Russia, like a monstrous vacuum pump, and spewing them out here, at St. Katherine Dock, right before him. These people are destitute – not like the ones who will continue on to America. Many are the poorest of the poor. They all appear to him thin and famished: gaunt faces, hollow eyes, shivering from the water's chill or simply from extreme exhaustion. They swarm ashore like tired ants. Their luggage is a battered box or just a soiled piece of cloth in which to tie a few possessions. There is no joy in their faces for reality has struck. The promised streets

326

of a London paved with gold have turned out to be a muddy path that leads to stinking smoke and sooty dust.

There are some lucky ones, of course. They will be met by family or friends or landsmen who have promised to take them on. Life will be hard but they will survive and some of them will prosper. But for many, he knows that they will just be grist for an unrelenting mill that will grind them down to grizzle. They will share a mattress in a filthy room that reeks of dread and putrid water. They will subsist on hellish soup, stale crusts of bread, maggoty cheese and rotting vegetables. If they are lucky enough to be given sweated labour, they will work from dawn till midnight in a room nine feet long by nine feet wide with fourteen others. And for six days of ceaseless toil they will earn, at the most, six shillings – half of which they will send back to the Pale in order to bring their families to join them. But before that eagerly awaited day, some will hang themselves in desperation – as happened last week and the week prior – in order to escape the unending horror.

Z watches, invisible, shrouded by the fog. He watches as a writer would watch, with compassionate detachment. But then he sees a face, the face of a young man – a young man alone, caught up in the gathering crowd. The young man gazes into the distance with hesitant eyes. He is unsure which way to turn, which way to go.

Nearby Z sees the sharks begin to circle. They have the young man's scent in their nostrils and the quickest one approaches and grabs for his bag. The young man looks confused. The shark, however, knows its prey and explains to him in Yiddish, Russian, German, English – whatever language the young man wishes – that he, the shark, is here to help the young man find a room, a job, a place to feel at home. The shark smiles and shows his teeth. He asks the

327

young man where he's from. Warsaw? But of course, that is where the shark is from too. They are landsmen. Brothers – almost. Come, says the shark. It is a dangerous city, this London. There are bad people, mischievous people out to take his money. The young man protests – he has no money. The shark winks – not even a little? Just a few coins, admits the young man, that are hidden in his shoe. Just enough to see him through till he can find a way to earn his living...

And here is where Z finally decides that he can be invisible no longer.

CHAPTER 51

Z APPROACHED THE young man and the rogue who was about to carry him off, introducing himself – in Yiddish, of course – as a representative of a Jewish welfare agency and, in doing so, took the young man's bag from the shark who spat and protested. But Z knew he wouldn't make too much a fuss as there were many fish beached on shore that evening and there were always police close at hand - not to help the immigrants but to stop any altercation that might disrupt the flow of humanity from here to dingy East End rooms or West End brothels (it didn't matter to them as long as they kept up the flow and cleared the quayside with a minimum of trouble).

Taking the young man aside, Z felt impelled to explain it all to this anonymous immigrant with the face of a child – to tell him of the pitfalls and the dangers in coming to this fantasy world called London where everything was divided into two - one harsh and grotesque, the other sublime and the beautiful but the one that was sublime and beautiful was always out of reach for those who were confined to the harsh and grotesque. (In saying this, of course, he completely ignored his own writings about the ghetto which created a world that was exactly the opposite.) He even considered suggesting that if the young man truly cared about his future and his family's happiness (he must have a mother and father who loved him and feared for his safety, didn't he?), then he should think seriously about getting back on the steamer that brought him here and returning home to Polish Russia. But, of course, he didn't because he also knew there probably was no home to which the young man could return, and, if there

329

were a home, it was most likely even more unsafe than here.

So, instead, Z took out his wallet and gave the young man ten shillings. Then, tearing out a piece of paper from his notebook, he wrote out the address of a boarding house and also a note to the woman who ran it – a sometimes writer with whom Z was acquainted – asking her to put the young man up for a week or so.

The young man, still dreadfully confused, could hardly express his gratitude but to Z that wasn't important. He simply wanted to see him safe for reasons of his own – reasons he had no inclination to explore at this particular moment. For Z was a man possessed and now incapable of understanding the forces within him.

But when the young man left, following Z's explicit directions (the boarding house, in fact, wasn't very far), Z saw the quayside had filled with masses of immigrants who were still disembarking, still trudging up the Irongate stairs, still being ferried in boat after boat from the offshore steamer. And as he looked around he saw them – one and another and another and another. All with boyish faces that looked exactly like Lipski – or as Z imagined Lipski had looked not so many months before when he had come ashore at this very harbour.

Z made his way home through the warren of narrow streets and back alleys which he navigated blindly. He rarely took a carriage or tram if he could at all avoid it. Walking helped him think, allowing him that sense of fluency wherein his mind could soar. Jerome called him a 'peripatetic writer' as if that were, itself, a genre – and perhaps it was. Partly it helped release the edgy nervousness, a product of his high speed metabolism that kept him buzzing half the night and needing to discharge that surfeit of energy crackling in his head, one way or another, lest he explode or go completely mad.

Certainly, he knew that the potential of madness lurked within, though he had learned to channel and redirect these primal forces. But what if an outlet had been denied him? What then?

We all tread a very thin line, he thought; at any moment we could slip, plunging into the darkest nowhere. Such is the danger of disconnection from the herd, of daring to live in isolation. A man alone can so easily lose his bearings. Indeed, where was he now? He hardly recognised the street he was walking on, though he had faith in his internal compass of physical direction. But what of his moral compass? Could that still be trusted?

And what of his people? Who were they, in fact? The endless waves of penniless immigrants swarming onto St Katherine Docks? His fellow writers like Jerome? The community of free men and women who marched behind the tricolour?

Then he thought, the young immigrant at the quayside, the one he gave ten shillings – what would have become of him? Did Z's imposition help? Or had he only delayed the inevitable?

CHAPTER 52

HE WASN'T EXPECTING to see her sitting on his stairs when he came home, but he wasn't surprised by it either. Though at other times he might have been disconcerted, today he found it right and, oddly, natural.

Unlocking the door to his room, he ushered her inside and offered her his easy chair as he went to pour some brandy. She glanced around his spacious quarters (spacious only compared to her own dank room) and noted the random piles of books and papers, the sharpened pencils instead of plants protruding from a flowerpot.

Gratefully accepting the glass of amber fluid he handed her, she took a sip and immediately felt the intoxicating flow of radiant warmth course through her body. That rawness from moments before, the prickly sensation on her skin, the aching hollowness inside her, the throbbing of her forehead gave way to a hesitant calm like the brief respite on open seas when a small glimmer of sun peaks through the eye of a raging tempest.

He sat across from her on the divan that doubled as his bed. Looking at this peculiar woman nestled in his easy chair, he found himself curiously thankful for her presence. Strangely, he could think of no one else with whom he would have rather shared this terrible moment. No one but her; a woman he scarcely knew and hardly understood.

She gazed back at him with moist, enquiring eyes, as if beseeching him to explain the unexplainable and he realised that she was already aware of the disquieting news he had recently been given.

When he finally found voice enough to speak, all he could do was simply ask if she had seen the actual statement. And all she could do was shake her head, confirming that she hadn't.

Reaching into his pocket, he pulled from there a crumpled piece of paper and then, smoothing it out, he handed it to her.

As he does, Z finds himself back in Hayward's office after the little messenger boy had tracked him down. Myers meets him at the door. By now Z realises something is desperately wrong. He can see it in Myers' face and thinks never in his life would he want to see a face like that again. And that image of utter despair lingers over him.

Maggie read the statement that Z had copied onto a scrap of vellum just a few hours before. She read it once and then a second time even though each word was like a knife that cut deep inside her. But she needed to read it twice in order to comprehend.

This is what she read:

> *I, Israel Lipski, before I appear before God in judgement, desire to speak the whole truth concerning the crime of which I am accused. I will not die with a lie on my lips, I will not let others suffer, even in suspicion, for my sin. I alone was guilty of the murder of Miriam Angel. I thought the woman had money in her room. So I entered, the door being unlocked and the woman asleep. I had no thought of violating her, and I swear I never approached her with that object, nor did I wrong her in this way. Miriam Angel awoke before I could search about for money and cried out, but very softly. Thereupon I struck her on the head, and seized her by the neck and closed her mouth with my hand, so that she should not arouse the attention of those who were about the house. I had long been tired of my life, and had bought a pennyworth of aqua fortis*

that morning for the purpose of putting an end to myself. Suddenly I thought of the bottle I had in my pocket, and drew it out, and poured some of the contents down her throat. She fainted, and recognising my desperate condition, I took the rest. The bottle was an old one which I had formerly used, and was the same as that which I had taken with me to the oil-shop. The quantity of aqua fortis I took had no effect on me. Hearing the voices of people coming up stairs, I crawled under the bed. The woman seemed already dead. There was only a very short time from the moment of my entering the room until I was taken away. In the agitation I also fainted. I do not know how it was that my arms became abraded. I did not feel it and was not aware of it. As to the door being locked from the inside, I myself did this immediately after I entered the room, wishing not to be interrupted. I solemnly declare that Rosenbloom and Schmuss knew nothing whatever of the crime of which I have been guilty, and I alone. I implore them to pardon me for having in my despair tried to cast the blame upon them. I also beseech the forgiveness of the bereaved husband.

I admit that I have had a fair trial and acknowledge the justice of the sentence that has been passed upon me. I desire to thank Mr Hayward for his efforts on my behalf, as well as all those who have interested themselves in me during this unhappy time.

This confession is made of my own free will and is written down by Mr Singer at my request.

May God comfort my loving father and mother, and may He accept my repentance and my death as an atonement for all my sins!

Sunday 21ˢᵗ August 1887

Israel Lipski

When she finished, Maggie neatly refolded the paper. He

could see her hand was trembling as she passed it back.

Neither of them spoke. Perhaps they couldn't find the words – or, more likely, it hurt too much to say them.

Maggie finally broke the silence, telling him that she had been with William Morris working on the latest issue of Commonweal when she had first heard about Lipski's confession.

Despite his sudden unconcern with the ways of the world and those who were given the privilege to define it, Z was intrigued. William Morris was someone he greatly admired, both as an artist and thinker, combining the elements of imagination, sagacity and reason that Z would cherish for his own. And he wondered aloud what the learned man had made of that lightning bolt which thundered from the sky that day, shocking them to their core and making them reconsider, consciously or not, the very essence of their being.

Morris hadn't been at all surprised, she said – though, at first, she had found his equanimity quite baffling. Those who had never believed in his guilt have no need to do so now, he told her. That the poor lad confessed, and admitted the justice of his sentence, was to be expected for it was absolutely essential to the stability of the government and to the system of capital punishment. So, according to Morris, why should anyone be surprised at the last minute appearance of such a neatly packaged document, written in perfect English, that ticked off each point of contention and exonerated everyone involved – the judge, the jury and the government?

Z let those thoughts, tendentious as they were, drift though his head. And then he asked whether she felt that way as well.

Did she? Well, perhaps, but mostly she felt confused. As the quiet certainty of yesterday had been savagely ripped from her breast by that odious statement, she needed to know whether Lipski was actually guilty of such a terrible crime, not in her mind but in her heart. And then she turned the question around. How about him? What did he feel?

What did he feel? Anger? Remorse? Bitterness? Betrayal? No, he felt none of those emotions. Perhaps it no longer mattered, he said.

It was clear from her expression that she didn't understand. It mattered to her, she told him. It mattered a great deal.

Of course , he said. And so it should, but it was Lipski, he meant – it no longer matters to him. And saying that, he went over to his desk and shuffled through some papers till he found what he was looking for.

Rabbi Singer, he told her, the reverend who was ministering to Lipski had written an article that Krantz suggested he consult. It was entitled 'The Glory of Martyrdom.' He had copied a brief passage. And, clearing his throat, he read it aloud to her:

'The spirit that gave an almost superhuman strength to our fathers ought not to have perished. There is abundant need for it still. It is the spirit of rectitude which knows the right and wills it. It is the spirit of the Fear of God, which banishes from the heart all other fear. It is the spirit of sacrifice, that purifies and hallows every life, as naught else can do...'

As he finished reciting the short passage, he re-directed his eyes from the article to her, wondering what she made of this very Orthodox notion that attempted to link the present crisis in the East to the mythic resistance of the ancient tribal heroes.

Of course she was familiar with martyrdom, she told him, as she had read the lives of the saints when she was a young girl. But how did this relate to Lipski? If he were a martyr, what was he a martyr for, and even more, what was he a martyr to?

How could he make her understand when he barely understood himself? He reminded her what Hayward said when he last saw Lipski in prison – that he would rather die than spend his life in gaol.

And she replied that anyone could say such things in the heat of the moment - that the idea of a lifetime of enforced misery is horrible but life, itself, is precious even if the conditions of life are vile. Besides, there are those on the outside who would have continued to struggle for his freedom.

There are also those on the outside who may have died for his continued existence – at least that's what Lipski came to feel, he said.

She looked at him questioningly and he wondered if any Christian could understand the idea of Jewish martyrdom. The 'spirit of sacrifice that purifies and hallows every life' was a far cry from salvation through mortification of the flesh the saints so gloried in. The historic Jew was bound to the sanctity of life and the avoidance of pain (that would be inflicted on them without mercy by others so why inflict it on themselves?) Self-harm to expiate one's sins made no sense at all in the metaphysics of Jewish existence, he told her. But there could be no greater good than to sacrifice oneself for one's people.

Perhaps Maggie couldn't understand the history of suffering and survival that was, Z sometimes thought, coded in the psyche of all Jews. But could he understand how important it was to her to honour justice, simple justice that established basic truth and right from wrong?

They were, at that moment, worlds apart and yet they desperately needed to be together.

337

Maggie looked over at the picture of Lipski that Z had cut from one of the journals and had pasted to the wall by his desk. It was the drawing of a handsome young man in stylish jacket and cravat with hair neatly trimmed and combed in a foppish swirl that fell in a charming manner gently over his forehead. The artist had captured something dreamy in his eyes, she thought – something dreamy and sentimental. She glanced down at the floor, at the tattered rug beneath her feet that appeared to be a thousand years old and had come on camel from the furthest regions of Mesopotamia. Then, looking back up at Z, she gazed deeply into his eyes. 'I don't think I can be alone tonight,' she whispered.

CHAPTER 53

ON MONDAY THE 22nd of August, 1887, at a quarter to eight in the morning, the bells of St. Sepulchre's Church opposite Newgate prison began to peal. Shortly before eight the hangman, the prison governor, and the Sheriff (Sir Henry Aaron Isaacs - a Jewish fruit merchant, recently knighted and recipient of a special Jubilee Medal for services to the Queen), went to the convict's cell all resplendent in their grand, official robes. Lipski awaited them dressed in the same suit he wore at his trial just eight weeks prior - with the simple addition of a dark blue yarmulka fixed atop his youthful skull. In a professional, business-like manner, his arms were bound by the executioner and then, as if this had been rehearsed a thousand times, with great pomp and ceremony, a precisely choreographed procession slowly marched from the convict's cell to the scaffold - a warder on either side, the executioner behind and Rabbi Singer in front, chanting with Lipski the ancient Hebrew prayer *Adon Olom*, which, since Babylonian times, was intoned by penitent Jews.

At the hour of his death, Z and Maggie were sitting side by side, hand in hand, on a bench in Victoria Park – the very bench where they had sat some days before – staring quietly across the pebble path at the flower garden that was still bathed in morning's dew. They huddled together - both they and the flowers - in anticipation of the moment: the flowers for the dawning of the sun; they for its extinguishment. And when that curiously synchronized moment came (which they knew by the chiming of the bell at Bow Street Church), at that precise instant, the mist lifted, the sun came out, the trap door of the hangman's platform sprung open, Lipski's body plunged into Eternal Darkness, and Z squeezed Maggie's hand with such dramatic force that the awful crunching of bones was heard to echo through the emptiness.

Looking over at Maggie, he saw the tears stream down her cheeks. Not from pain, he soon realised, but from something else.

'Do you see?' There was a sense of wonder in her voice, a sense of awe.

He followed her line of sight and saw it too. A bird – a magnificent bird had spread its wings and taken flight. Together they watched it soar high above their heads, circle once, then twice, then fly away in an eastwardly direction to parts unknown.

EPILOGUE

IN THE YEARS that followed, Z became a writer so famous that he was feted throughout the English-speaking world. But the events of those eight weeks in the summer of 1887 stayed with him like the London fog, sometimes appearing frilly and light (as in the springtime of his youth), sometimes dark and foreboding, partially occluding the successes that came from the nib of his ceaseless, ink-stained pen. For a long time he was plagued with lingering doubts: was that boy, Lipski, with his sweet face and limpid eyes, actually guilty – as his last-minute confession professed? Or had he been willingly sacrificed so that others, who swarmed then and swarmed still from their ancient homelands, might seek refuge in this island kingdom which had offered Z, and those he called 'his people', the promise of a future. But like all promises, this one came with a caveat. Hope, if hope there was, would be for the next generation or the one thereafter.

Back then, he had told Maggie that guilt or innocence exists on many levels and, perhaps, there was a greater meaning to those events played out in the summer of Victoria's Jubilee which thrust the life and death of a simple man into a wider perspective. Maggie, of course, was having none of that. Justice to her was visceral and had everything to do with the sanctity and inalienable rights of the individual. Whatever that man-child did or didn't, his trial and conviction in a court of law was nothing less than a travesty. And, to her, it represented a terrible object lesson in the unbridled power of the state and the hypocrisy of British justice.

For her own part, Maggie had become progressively embittered through countless struggles that started as bright sparks and ended as damp, deflated squibs. Being a woman who demanded absolute integrity both from herself and others, she began to question (and thus lose favour with) those she formerly looked upon as leaders in the struggle for a more equitable society. She was outraged at the erosion of rights (or historic myths which claimed those rights) in the land of her birth that had been populated by her ancestors for countless generations. Seeing the social democratic cause she espoused in her youth more and more exploited by vainglorious men who spouted popular slogans and then used their new-found power for personal gain, she began shifting her focus to the far-off lands where people had begun to rise up in resistance to what she saw as the brutality of overseas colonialism (which she compared to the internal colonialist policies she had witnessed in London's East End).

Z had tried to keep in touch with Maggie. He had felt a strong connection with her intellectually, though he hadn't been physically attracted until that night she had come to his room and asked to stay.

Maggie, however, wasn't the sort of woman who easily gave herself to a man. Certainly she was romantically inclined, even if life had already taught her some cruel lessons regarding the perils of romance. She was drawn to Z. She found him fascinating – exotically so. And she didn't fear the social and religious barriers that had been erected through eons of history. But she was her own woman and instinctively felt that any long-term commitment required more from her than she was able to give.

Before Maggie left England forever she met Z one last time. It was at the same outdoor café on the fringe of Covent Garden where they had met years before when both were young and the future was still whatever they could imagine.

Looking at her sitting sedately at the table across from him, Z thought this might very well have been then and that the distance between past and present was simply a blip in the continuum of earthly existence. But much had changed since they spent that extraordinary morning together on a rough wooden bench in Victoria Park, hand in hand, listening for the bells of Bow Street Church that announced the terrible act played out at Newgate prison in the early hours of 22 August 1887.

He wore better clothes now, as he could afford a tailor (even if his tailor was a bit of a schlemiel). Her clothes were still hand-me-downs from her cousin, Beatrice, or things she wore a decade before, mended and patched many times over. But beyond the clothes and a trace of greying hair, it could have been 1887 – at least for them.

She asked him about his books and his recent theatrical career. He told her of New York, of his amazing experiences there exploring the vast recreation of the Eastern European Yiddish culture in Manhattan, Bronx and Brooklyn and his fascinating meeting with President Theodore Roosevelt who much admired his play about the melting pot of peoples that gave America such a vibrant edge at the start of the new century and pointed the way toward a blissful new tomorrow.

She told him that she had continued to write stories about the dispossessed, about the crimes of injustice. And he detected in her a kind of melancholy he hadn't noticed back then, those many years ago.

And his marriage how was that? she had asked him.

He had married a wonderful woman; someone very supportive of his work. She read everything he wrote and had become his best friend and most ardent critic. He would be lost without her.

Was she of the same cultural background?

343

She was Christian but desired, as he did, to integrate the wisdom of the ancients with the knowledge of the moderns.

And was he content? It was an awkward question, perhaps, and one that surprised her as much as him, but she felt she had to ask it.

He replied but the question seemed to transport him to another part of himself, deep and secret. Instead of the personal response she had wanted, about his feelings and emotions, he spoke of something beyond the individual having to do with a greater hope and longing. And it was this longing she knew related to something missing in herself. What he said and what lingered in her mind afterward, was that he could never be content until his people had all found safe harbours.

For a while they were silent. They drank their coffee and she had waited till their eyes met, as if she were searching for confirmation of an ineffable sign that would allow her to continue.

Then, fixing him in her gaze, she asked if he could tell her who they really were – those he called 'his people'?

Maggie left a few days later on a steamer bound for Calcutta. Z heard no more from her but a few years later he noticed an article in the Times about a group of English women who had became active in the Indian National Congress. Along with the theosophist Annie Besant, Maggie was mentioned as one of those who had helped campaign for Indian home rule.

As Z carefully cut this article from the newspaper to add to his box of clippings, he was reminded of his final meeting with her and the question she had asked him which still lingered in the air.

That very question – 'his people': who were they and

where did they come from? – had obsessed Z throughout his adult life. He had come to believe they weren't actually the ancient Hebraic tribes that left biblical Israel many thousands of years ago. Those he referred to as 'his people' were both less and more. They were the many and diverse groups of nomads and wanderers, traders and farmers, poets and musicians who had somehow ended up populating the great expanse of Eastern Europe from the Baltic to the Crimea - whose hair and eyes, features and complexions, were a mixture of everything and everyone but who, to a greater or lesser extent saw themselves as 'Jewish' and spoke a common tongue.

It was with these masses of Eastern European Jews, once happily settled and then progressively impoverished over the last decades of Tsarist rule, that Z so strongly identified; for there is where his parents and his grandparents and countless generations before them had lived. There is where Lipski came from, too. And Z sometimes thought, for fleeting moments, if a few wrong doors had been opened or right ones shut, if certain opportunities had been lost, or if the prevailing wind had suddenly changed direction, he could have been Lipski himself. For wasn't his first name also 'Israel'?

ENDNOTE

THE TWO MAIN characters in this book, Maggie and Z, are based on real people – Margaret Harkness and Israel Zangwill – who lived and wrote during the period of this story. Some of my characters' observations allude to their actual writings. Z and Maggie, though, are fictional hybrids that, in my mind at least, developed a life of their own.

BRIEF BIBLIOGRAPHY

Englander, David. *A Documentary History of Jewish Immigrants in Britain 1840-1920*; Leicester University Press, 1994.

Harkness, Margaret. *In Darkest London*; Black Apollo Press, 2003.

Friedland, Martin L. *The Trials of Israel Lipski*; Macmillan, 1984.

Fishman, William J. *East End Jewish Radicals 1875-1914*; Duckworth, 1975.

Kriwaczek, Paul. Yiddish Civilisation: *The Rise and Fall of a Forgotten Nation*; Phoenix, 2006.

Udelson, Joseph H. *Dreamer of the Ghetto: The Life and Works of Israel Zangwill*; University of Alabama Press, 1990.

Vital, David. *A People Apart: A political History of the Jews in Europe;* Oxford, 1999.

Zangwill, Israel. *Children of the Ghetto*; Black Apollo Press, 2004.

Lightning Source UK Ltd.
Milton Keynes UK
UKOW04n2209061117
312304UK00002B/5/P